BROTHER JONATHAN:

OR,

THE NEW ENGLANDERS.

IN THREE VOLUMES.

VOL. I.

WILLIAM BLACKWOOD, EDINBURGH: AND
T. CADELL, STRAND, LONDON.
MDCCCXXV.

BROTHER JONATHAN.

CHAPTER I.

JONATHAN PETERS. — INDIVIDUAL YANKEES. —
CHARACTER.

ABOUT one year before the " Battle of Lexing-
ton ;" a sharp skirmish between the New England, or Yankee bush-fighters, and his majesty's
troops, who were sent over to keep the peace, in
the revolutionary war of North America, there
came to the household of a Yankee presbyterian
preacher, of Connecticut (one of the New England states) a stranger, of whom nobody knew
any thing, except what he chose to tell of himself; either when he came, or when he went
away. He was a peaceable, stern, proud man,

—friendless, they believed; poor, they were certain. He was unhappy, too; and so, were the country people about him; for they could find out neither his calling, name, nor business — nothing to confirm; nothing to contradict his own story of himself, which was given out, piecemeal; a word or two, at a time — a date here; a name there, — and amounted, after all, to little or nothing, as they understood it.

At last, having beset him with questions, at every turn, for nearly a month; way-laying him the while with certain of their chief guessers, chosen for the purpose, all of whom he baffled with surprising ease, they gave up the notion of discovering who he was, or what, for a bad job. They went home to their business, persuaded only of two things, — that he was one of themselves (a Yankee)— and a match for them; while he went rambling about, in the wood, up the mountains, over the burying-ground, — any where, and every where, in truth, but where other people went.

Nay; such was their self-denial, at last; or his unconquerable resolution, that he was permitted, every "Sabbath" afternoon, to pass through the crowd by the " meeting-house;" or to wander among the graves (near one of which, that of the preacher's wife, he was frequently seen standing, after night-fall) without being pestered, or plagued with a single " guesser."

He was a regular visiter at Mr. Harwood's (the presbyterian preacher); took his " pudding" there, three times a week; and supper, almost every night. The whole family were afraid of him; — that is, they stood in awe of him; felt uncomfortable, if he looked into their eyes; and started, if he spoke to them abruptly; and yet, no one of them; or, at any rate, not more than one, would have been willing to see him go away, for ever. They had come to look upon him, in truth, as one of their number; and most of them, in spite of his cold, positive, severe temper, to feel toward him, as if he had a right, beyond that of a stranger — a way-faring man — to their table and fire side.

It was very true, that no one of all the questioners, guessers, and spies, that beset his way,

for so long a time, had ever been able to find out
why he had come so among them, into their
savage country; or, wherefore he was, what all
agreed in believing him to be, — a miserable man.
But what of that? His language was powerful
and beautiful; his words, truth; and himself,
unhappy. It was also true, that, even the little,
which they were able to glean, of his own story
from his own lips — hasty and brief disclosures —
partly by accident, partly by design — was of a
nature, not very likely to prepossess them in his
favour. But what of that? It was the policy of
the man, perhaps, to appear worse than he was;
that he might grow upon their love and veneration, as they should come to know him better.

It was also true, that, of the whole neighbourhood, — that is, of all those, who lived within
a good hour's ride of one another, — no two
individuals had come to the same conclusion
respecting the man, himself; his temper, age,
or calling; and yet, every one, or almost every
one, had a fixed opinion of his own.

Thus; the preacher, for example, who had a
fine opportunity of studying him at all hours,

under a variety of aspects — *he* came to a settled belief, which he never failed, in some way or other, to express, after a time; particularly if he fell in the way of a stranger, — that Squire Peters had been, was, or would be, a " shining light" in his generation. — But, while the preacher said this, with an oracular shake of the head, in a sort of under voice, he never thought proper to say more; so that every one, of course, put such construction upon the speech as corresponded best with his own opinion. " His power of argument," said the preacher; " his knowledge of scripture; his learning in theology; his amazing eloquence, are quite enough to satisfy *me.*" But he said this after having been defeated at his own game — Divinity, — with his own weapons — the Saybrook platform, and Bible — before a part of his congregation; so manifestly, that he had no other way left — none — of keeping up his credit. Jonathan Peters had conquered him; " therefore," said Abraham Harwood, " he is an extraordinary man."

But a military personage, of " pootty considerable" authority, in the province of Connec-

ticut, one Mr. Brigadier Ephraim Johnson,
the boy of "old Nehemiah Johnson;" or, as they
called him to his face, in the fashion of the day,
one "Mr. Deacon Brigadier" Johnson — *he* came
to quite another result, which he, too, whispered
in the ears of all that would listen to him, as if it
were treason that he was muttering; namely,
that neighbour Jonathan, squire, or no squire,
was a military man, who had seen some hard-
fighting, " too," in his day.   This opinion
had no little weight; for, as every body knew,
it was not hastily given.   The brigadier, — so
called, by the way, because a relation of his, who
had served under Wolfe in the old French war,
had left him the military coat, which he wore
during the siege of Quebec; a coat which, Mr.
Deacon Brigadier Johnson (as *we* say, Mr. Justice, or Mr. Alderman, so and so) wore there-
after, as in duty bound, on all military days,
precisely as it " came to hand;" with part
of a ragged epaulette, which appeared, some
how or other, to grow larger and more glorious
every year — a great bunch of loose, tawdry,
tarnished copper bullion, dangling with a brave,

slovenly air backward over the left shoulder, thereby proving, what was properly enough called *his* generalship; a bullet hole or two, on the breast, which looked not a little as if it had been scorched, perhaps in the fire of cannon, perhaps in the fire of a tobacco-pipe; a bayonet wound, in the rear, which Peters, after examination, told him plainly, had been made with a pair of sheep shears; and a large equivocal stain upon the white lining, which had always been thrown open to the wind, wherever the Brigadier went, until Peters hinted, not very delicately, that, according to his notion, it was a stain made, not by blood, spilt in the smoke of battle; but by liquor, spilt in the smoke of a country tavern, — the brigadier was three months making up his mind about the matter; nor was he at all satisfied, until Peters had beaten him, over and over again; first, in argument (although the brigadier always had the last word, and left off precisely where he began, with a nod, or a wink, to the bye-standers); then, at fox and geese; then, at morris; then, at checkers, or draughts; a game at which, if you would

believe him, he never was beaten before; and,
finally (as if the Yankee man were determined, if
he went away, to leave the poor, talkative old
brigadier, without a leg to stand upon, as a
lawyer would say, or a single bit of yarn
to run out, as the sailors have it) — finally;
after having beaten him at every thing else,
without mercy, he beat him at his own, his favourite game, the old French war; and, what
was harder still to put up with; before the face
and eyes of the very people, who had been
listening to the brigadier, winter after winter, in
the long, loud blustering nights of a terrible
climate; by the great, roaring fire-side of a
country tavern; while the snow was drifting over
the tops of the door; driving through every nook
and crevice of the board-work; and bellowing up
the chimney, like a tornado; — and all this, if you
would believe him, for the sake of truth; as if
Truth were to be propitiated by such a sacrifice.
Why, it was literally taking away the chief com-
forts of a whole neighbourhood; shutting up the
warm shoe-maker's shop; the best place in the
world, for stories on a cold winter night; and

wasting the happiness, not only of the hearers, who had never a doubt or misgiving, till Peters made them uncomfortable, by making them wiser; but, of a good-for-nothing old man, whose tough stories, like the minstrel ballads of some vagrant harper, were a fortune to all that knew them by heart.

Nor was that all. The incorrigible Yankee, like most of his countrymen, had a way of doing whatever he did, in the shape of dispute, *so* thoroughly. He would always put his finger upon the place; give chapter and verse; prove it all with chalk and compasses; an old map and a tattered " geography;" by bell, book, and candle, as it were; — nor did he give it up, notwithstanding all the cross looks, and pouting of the women people, until he had proved, perhaps, to the satisfaction of everybody but Mr. Deacon Brigadier Johnson, that he, the said brigadier, had been talking for twenty-five years about a matter, of which he knew nothing at all.

But, in the progress of his demonstration, the Yankee had well nigh lost the favour of Edith

Cummin, a little "smart," whimsical Virginia girl; the prettiest one, though, "by all accounts," there " was a goin," as everybody " allowed." Edith had rubbed, with her own little hands, a fine old cherry-tree table; a black, round, queer " tittupping" affair, till she could see her face in it. Jonathan Peters chalked that all over, while disputing about Crown Point. Edith had contrived, after some twenty or thirty experiments, a brilliant red paint, with which, it was her pride and glory, at all seasons, winter and summer, to keep the great hearth stone, as " beautiful," to use her own expressive words, the idiom of old Virginia, " as beautiful" as the red brick hearth of neighbour Nathan Libbey, " all but."

Well; Jonathan Peters took especial delight in demonstrating the capture of Louisbourg, with one end of his cane, charred for the purpose, upon this very hearth-stone. There was no resisting the temptation : it ran so smoothly ; so like a pen, over parchment; a lead pencil, over an ivory tablet; or a stream of oil, over marble; so smoothly, that he could not forbear.

Again; Edith would spend an hour every day; a full hour, in the dead of winter, perhaps, in tracing patterns and flowers (which were imitated all over the country) upon the white sanded floor, with a great hemlock broom. To these patterns, a part of which he defaced with a spiteful emphasis, whenever he came into the room, as he always did, with a shuffle, Peters bore a sort of unconquerable antipathy; in fact, he made war upon them, — open war, — and looked, as if he were glad, in his very soul, whenever the dispute would allow of his drawing the plan of a battle among her " tasty " little flowers, to their certain destruction always; just as much as if he had fought a real battle, in a real flower garden.

And so with many more of Mr. Harwood's visiters, who had an opportunity of sounding, or pumping the stranger. Each went away ashamed, abashed, or confounded; yet, consoling his pride with a belief that he and Peters, after all, were of the same trade or profession. A lawyer, from the Providence plantations, "one Squire Nathaniel Green," so called (after Peters had put

him down, before all the family, for a blockhead,)
put Peters down for a " confounded smart feller ;
'cute in the law, he guessed:" while " Master
Champlin," the preceptor of an academy, to which
boys and girls, quite grown up, would go, in all
weathers, a distance of several miles, through a
dangerous wood, up to their middles in snow,
or half-leg deep in mud ; — this personage observing that Peters, or the squire, as he called
him, " was a pootty partic'lar somebody, or he'd
lose a guess; about grammar, jography, cy-
pherin, pronounshiation, surveyin, hard words,
and all that 'ere sort o' trade," put him down,
the said squire, for one of those New England
people, who go about in the winter, all through the
country ; setting up little schools, for three or four
months or so; wherein they retail out, as it were,
the education, which they had been laying in, at
wholesale, during the summer season before, at
some one of the numberless academies and col-
leges of the country.

Nor was this much to be wondered at. Jonathan Peters, in the first place, was an American ;
one of that singular people, who know a little,

and but a little, of every thing. In the next place, he was a Yankee, the very character of whom is, that he can " turn his hand," as he says, " to any thing." This was the character of a New Englander, half a century ago : it is perfectly true of him, now. It is a common thing, in his country, to meet with a man, uniting in himself half a dozen trades and professions ; having a tolerable acquaintance with many things, that have no relationship with one another, and a pretty good knowledge of some one trade or profession ; but very uncommon, to meet with a man, who is a complete master of any one trade, or profession. The sum of a New Englander's knowledge may be as great as that of another's ; but, in almost every case, it will be found less available, and less wisely apportioned.

Besides ; the squire could have deceived anybody—even a profound examiner, for a time. A man of cool sagacity, a close reasoner, who confines himself to interrogation ; a man, too, like him, of a slow speech, will pass any where, under any circumstances, for more than he is worth.

We give such a person credit for more knowledge, or more wisdom than he shows, by way of
relieving ourselves from the awe that we feel, in his
presence. There is, moreover, as any body may
know, if he call to mind some case where he has
been imposed upon; or, where he has imposed
upon others—no matter for what purpose,—there
is, moreover, a secret leaning toward the uncommon ; a sort of appetite for the wonderful and extraordinary, in every human heart. This appetite
will be fed—on garbage, if nothing better can be
had. We are all, the wisest of us—the best—
always lying in wait, for the purpose; always
ready to assist anybody in imposing upon others
—our best friends—all the world; nay, for
lack of other employment or exhilaration, ourselves. Men feed upon falsehood, as they do upon
opium. They begin with taking it in sport, perhaps; they continue, till it becomes a thing, without
which they cannot eat or sleep. So, too, in their
fondness for the wonderful; they *must* have it,
after a little time, to keep them alive. It is like
flattery: nothing is too gross, nothing too abo-

minable, for the appetite of him who has fed long upon it.

The appearance of this man—we had well nigh forgotten that—was quite of an every-day sort, unless he was much excited by conversation. There was little or nothing remarkable, in his countenance or manner. You might have passed him every day, for a twelve-month, perhaps, without remembering his face, or enquiring his name.

He was only one of a multitude that came out, all at once from the woods, when the trumpet of rebellion was blown; — people who had never been heard of, out of their own little neighbourhood of rocks and mountains, where a dozen or twenty families, thinly scattered over miles of wilderness and water, made what was called a town; —people, who heard an outcry, while they were at work in the fields; threw down their implements of husbandry, even where they stood; left their cattle standing; betook themselves to war; and became, instantaneously—as it were, by inspiration—soldiers, orators, and statesmen.

He was a man of the middling size, hard fa-
voured, and walked, with a sort of lounging
stoop.   His forehead was low, solid, and square;
his complexion remarkable—swarthy—brown—
a colour not easily described.   His head was un-
commonly large; his eye-brows heavy; eyes,
dark and thoughtful, deeply set under his projecting forehead, and surrounded with a purple
shadow, such as we may often observe about the
eyes of a hard student, a severe thinker, or some
poor fellow far gone, perhaps, in a consump-
tion.   His head was rather bald; and his coarse
hair, which had been of a jet black, very like that
of the Indian; or the mane of a young war horse,
if you like, was tumbled about his low forehead
and sunken temples, very much as if he had been
tossing it up, contrary to the fashion of the time,
to cover his baldness; or tearing it, night after
night, in some fierce paroxysm.

No two persons could agree about his age; not
even the women, those infallible judges thereof.
By some, he was thought near forty-five; by
others, not more than thirty-five.   All, however,
agreed in this one thing; namely—that he was

either, an old, a young, or a middle-aged man;
either an old man, who carried his years bravely;
a young man, grown prematurely old, under
some heavy affliction; or a middle-aged man,
with whom study had wrought, like time.

But, while there was little or nothing about
Jonathan Peters, to catch the eye of a stranger,
upon the highway; there were times and seasons, when his hat was off; and the storm of
contention had passed away from his countenance — during which, his head, at least, was remarkable. It was a time of rebellion. A whole
people had become rebels. It was a time of
warfare and sedition. — The face of Jonathan
Peters corresponded finely with it, whenever he
fell back into his habit of profound, stern, solemn
thought, after the heat and hurry of argument;
especially, if that argument related to the political state of the colonies.

A shadow more, or less — a slight fluctuation
of colour — and it would have been that of a rebel,
or a patriot; a regicide, or a martyr. It was full
of serious hardihood; and a sort of determination, such as men do not care to affront, what-

VOL. I.   C

ever may be their tempers. It was a time of
mischief: all the foundations of society were
breaking up; and Peters, himself, was of a
piece with every thing about him; a part of the
furniture of the age — plain — solid — and useful.
He was come of the Plymouth people — the fathers — or pilgrims; the formidable men, with
whose children, every war had begun, for more
than a century; the men, whose descendants are
known, to this hour, by their primitive manners;
their invincible resolution; their quiet, stern
foreheads; and severe eyes. In short, he was
one of those men, who, come when they will; go
where they will, are pretty sure to interweave
their own biography — their own particular
achievements — with some people's history.

The family of Mr. Harwood, who was a wi-
dower, consisted of seven; all of whom, though
two were servants, or ' helps,' ate of the same
fare, at the same table; and sat in the same best
room.

There were two boys, Jotham and Walter;
with a ' man;' so called, because he was hired
by the preacher, for his ' out o'door work;' three

females — Edith Cummin, Lucy Armstrong (a deaf girl), and Miriam Brackett — a 'maid' — so called, because the preacher had hired her, for the 'in door work.'

Mr. Harwood was a great proprietor. He had been a ' speculator;' and was yet — in every thing, perhaps, but land. He was a small, meagre, ' ac-tive,' tidy-looking somebody; a farmer, as the world went, six days in the week; a minister, on the seventh. His countenance was lively and pleasant; but a little distorted; and his eyes had a cast in them — by reason of a malady which had afflicted him, at long intervals, for many years. It was a sort of epilepsy. When the fit was upon him — he saw sights, and heard noises; of which he afterwards made great use.

It was well enough, perhaps; for it gave him power over his people. More than once; while they were about him, he did see — or pretended so well, that no one of his trembling hearers doubted him — a procession of dead people; the fathers, mothers, and little children of his congregation — passing the very windows of the house,

where they were assembled; and looking in, at
such of them as were to die, in the following
year; or, moving slowly through the dim wood,
visible from the door of the meeting-house, in
front of the pulpit, with a new coffin upon their
shoulders — on their way to the grave-yard. —
On more than one occasion, too, while the hand
of the Lord was upon him, he had spoken strange
words of the living, which, in the fulness of time
— so said certain of the people — had become
prophecy. It might be so. — Abraham Harwood was a bold man. He was continually speaking strange words; and continually prophesying,
in a language — so powerful, and so beautiful —
with a manner, so awfully sincere — that — if they
believed in *him*, it was enough to make them
afraid. He had said once, to a number of persons, while they stood about a dead body, which,
on the ' Sabbath' before, had been alive, that, one
more of their little number would soon be required, by the angel of death; and (lowering his
voice) that, of those, who were then alive, in that
small room; wondering over the transformation
of their young playmate; one would be ' want-

ing,' when they should be gathered together, again, for the house of prayer.

Such words might suit any event whatever. But people are too fond of the marvellous, ever to think of that, in such a case. The spotted fever was raging about him, while the preacher spoke; the small pox had broken out; and whole families had been wasted of their little ones, by a cruel distemper.   But who was to remember these things, when the prophecy came to be fulfilled? — After a while, one of those very persons died — one of those, to whom the words had been spoken.   It was a little girl — they had been, for ever, in her mouth; she had been whispering them, over and over again, to her distracted mother, from the day of the funeral, or soon after, till within a few hours of her death.

By a singular coincidence, which gave to the mysterious language of the preacher, a tremendous weight, for the rest of his life, it was found, on making the enquiry, that poor Lydia Norris (the little child) was never at 'meeting,' after the day of the funeral.   She had been prevented, by some accident, or other, on the Sabbath follow-

ing; and before another came round, she took the
fever; of which, after lingering a month or two,
she died.

An event of this nature, would, of course, go
abroad; any where; at any time, with abundance
of aggravation. No wonder, therefore, that it
went forth, like a pestilence, among the people of
the neighbouring woods, and mountains; at a
time when apparitions were seen, at midnight,
walking over the zenith; and voices heard, at
noon-day — with a sound, from the untrodden
solitude, like the roaring of cannon. It went
forth; was believed, on every side, by every
body; and made our preacher more powerful
than ever. His converts multiplied every hour:
a blessing was upon all the work of his hands.
The old stood in fear of him; the middle aged
could not abide his rebuke; while the young
trembled, if he spoke in a low voice — or looked
upon them, one by one; counting them over —
as he did, at the funeral of poor Lydia Norris.

The preacher had a great reputation for sanctity withal; had been a wild young man — a
' store' keeper — a ' speculator' — and a ' lumber

merchant,' all at one time; but, seeing the errour of his ways, he had undergone a conversion, before the eyes of a great multitude; one 'town meeting day;' married; become a preacher of the Gospel; and set off, on a sort of missionary trip.

After many years of trial; and a long absence, in a far country, he had returned; buried his wife; and become a leader of those, who, if they themselves were to be believed, while they were upon their knees, before their Maker, at confession, were a set of precious rascals, to be sure; — the chief among sinners—every man of them; the most wicked of human creatures—hardly worthy of being tormented, for ever and ever; though perfectly willing—for the glory of their Father, above. — In short, Abraham Harwood was now a pillar of light, among those; the greater part of whom—those, at least, who were conspicuous for an austere temper—after having grown old in the ways of the world; in all sorts of 'trickery,' and falsehood; hypocrisy, 'swapping,' trading, and evil speaking; had been changed, all at once—in the twinkling of an eye.

The expression of his face was hardly ever alike,
for three minutes together.   There was nothing
decided in it; nothing permanent; nothing to be
reckoned upon, courageously.   In different situa-
tions, he was like a different person.   At home;
about his own fire-side, with his own family, he
was a pleasant, agreeable, meddling sort of a
man.   Abroad; among strangers; or in his pul-
,pit, he was no longer the same individual : —He
put on the look and bearing of authority.   There
was that in his face, then, which it were a hard
matter—perhaps a dangerous one, to translate : —
changes went over it, when it was lighted up,
from within — like shadows over clear water.
And especially in the pulpit; or, at any time, in
any place, while he was rebuking the ungodly;
or, sorely beset by such a man, as Jonathan
Peters; the rapidity of these changes—or transformations, rather, of his countenance, would be
wonderful—passing all belief.   At other times,
when he was excited, less violently; there were
many fine things to be seen; bright indications
of power, in his little sharp, shining eyes, and
clear temples; a something really affectionate

and warm about his mouth; and signs of genius never to be mistaken, all over his forehead, when it was pleasantly agitated; signs, however, that became alarmingly visible, when there was a bright commotion within; as there would be, if he were overexcited.

CHAPTER II.

VIRGINIA GIRL. — HABITS. — CHARACTER.

EDITH CUMMIN — we shall pass over the rest for the present — was a Virginian; a niece of Abraham Harwood: a creature, so whimsical, so contradictory, that, for many years (until her character changed, all at once, in a single winter), it would have been quite impossible to describe her, so as to give one a true notion of what she really was; without leading her out, making her talk, and showing her off, in a thousand ways, at the same time.

She was little; very girlish, very spirited, and quite singular in her whole appearance; with rich, plentiful hair, always in the way of herself, or somebody else; a pale complexion; large, hazel eyes, full of moonlight and water, never still for a moment:—one hour, she was a woman, the next, a child, a baby, a simpleton; with hardly wit enough to keep herself out of the fire.

Now, she would be found sitting in a corner, alone; purple with cold; poring over some great, heavy, serious book, such as no other child, of her age, ever thought of poring over; and, after a little time, perhaps, cuddled up in a heap, with her loose hair falling about her face; pouting and sobbing over some poor two-penny ballad, such as no other child ever thought of sobbing over. The Babes in the Wood, Chevy Chase, and little King Pippin, lay, side by side; not only in the drawer, but in the heart of Edith Cummin; with an abridgement of Josephus; a part of Chaucer's Canterbury Tales; and the Sermons of Cotton Mather—a very celebrated man, at home.

She had a thousand childish ways with her; innocent, simple ways, which there was no speaking seriously about, absurd as many of them were; a sprightly, sincere temper; without one atom of art, or affectation. She had a knack, too, quite her own, of bringing the water into your eyes, and a smile about your mouth, at the same time; and always (which was the charm, after all) without intending it, or knowing it, or even caring for it, if she did know it. She loved romping; ' *that* she did;' and would go without her dinner any time, for a good long race with her cousin Watty's large dog, under the elm trees; or any thing. else, for a few hearty tumbles, all alone — head over heels—in the long fresh grass; or the newly mown hay, before the rich clover blossoms were dead. And yet, she would never tumble about, romp, or kick up her heels, like any body else, or with any body else. It was always in a way of her own; with 'only herself and Panther,' (Walter's dog;) or a little boy, from 'down east,' whom she was teaching, all one summer, to ride on a cane; herself, the while, mounted on a broomstick.— During these pastimes, it was amusing enough to see, with what an air, she punished all intruders; not even excepting her 'dear, *dear* cousin Watty,' whom, in the language of old Virginia, she loved, 'mighty bad; so she did.' In such a case, at such a time, Edith would look and speak, much more like a dwarf woman, caught perhaps with her night-cap on, or slippers off; than like a sad little tom-boy, as —begging her pardon—she certainly was. — Her large eyes would sparkle,—so the men ' allowed'—like the mischief; and she would stand a tip-toe, with a dignity, quite heroick, for such a diminutive little creature.

She was perpetually doing what nobody was prepared for — perpetually making people jump; and had, if there be such a one, the faculty of unexpectedness, within her; like a Leyden jar, always ready to be let off. At one time, it would really appear, as if she had been lying in wait, like a torpedo-fish, in the water, for an opportunity to set people tingling; at another, as if she enjoyed, in her very soul, the confusion of those; especially if they were grown up, who, led astray by her manner, and size, had mistaken her for a child. A word, or a laugh, was enough; just when some stranger, perhaps, who had been looking at her absurd gambols, with a large dog, was on the point of pulling her into his lap, for a fine romp — only a word, or a laugh; and he would start back, as if he had been playing with an electrical machine; or had put his hand, by mistake, upon one of the little wood-women; the North American fairies, who have bonnets like human hair, and faces like masks,

which they can put off, or on, at pleasure; while
they run about laughing and shouting in the star-
lighted wood; counterfeiting the voices of children that live near; mimicking the whip-poor-
will; and stopping the holes, where the rattle-
snake hides, when she hears them coming.

Between the upper and lower parts of her face,
there was a remarkable contradiction. Judging
by her forehead and look, you would call her
much older; by her mouth, much younger than
she was. Her large eyes were sometimes full of
strange, womanly meaning; solemn and beautiful, beyond any thing that we see in the eyes of
children; while her mouth was always—no matter where she was — no matter though her eyes
were full of tears — her mouth was always just
ready for a laugh.

Her character was like her face; whatever she
did, whatever she said, was full of contradiction.
She was a puzzle. She would say the strangest
out-of-the-way things; now, like a little child;
now, like something wiser than a woman: at one
time, as if she wanted common sense; at another, as if she were inspired. She had, in truth,

all the simplicity of a child, with much of the ✓ woman's loftiness.

Go to the preacher's when you would, you were pretty sure to find Edith squatting in a corner, like a big doll in a baby-house; and, almost always, in the same corner; upon one particular pine-block, which was a matter of contention, with all the younger part of the family, after the winter set in; particularly, when the cider was warming, the apples roasting, the hickory-nuts all ready, and the mince-pie thawing and simmering upon the hearth, before a fire, like the broad-side of a house. No sooner was one off that favourite block, than another was on. But, of all the household, none was more eager and adroit; none, more watchful than Edith, to get it next. Many a tumble, and many a bump was had, in the struggle that followed every rush, after every abdication. Fifty tricks of a night would be played, before Mr. Harwood or the Squire, to seduce the possessor away. Now, his apple would be knocked out of his hand; or the cider pushed beyond his reach: if that failed, another, and another expedient were tried,

until the block was vacated. In these contrivances, nobody was a match for Edith. It was
quite impossible to dislodge her; and, by no
means easy to avoid being dislodged, in some
way or other, if she had set her heart upon the
block.

After the supper-table was cleared away,
Edith would generally be found lolling over the
knees of poor Lucy Armstrong, the deaf and
dumb girl. Edith had pretty feet; and, of course,
knew it. So, on such occasions, if she could
manage it, possibly; one of these feet was always tilted in the air, at the risk of exposing the
other, in a way, that — none but a little child is
ever willing to do. And yet, one hardly knew how
to speak to her; and few persons were able to
laugh at her, more than once, or twice. If you
spoke to her, as if you thought her a sensible
girl; it was fifty to one, that she made you look
like a fool; and if you spoke to her, as if you
thought her only a child, the chances were much
the same, that she made you behave like one.

There were times, also, when her thoughtful
eyes, her pale face — and mouth, like the wet

rose-bud—were brimful of something, like poetry; and others, while she sat in the corner, with a profusion of hair, overshadowing her whole face—when she might have passed for an idiot; so patiently—so stupidly tranquil, would she remain, for a whole hour, together; looking into the ashes, where others were parching corn; or watching the current of sparks, that rushed up the chimney, whenever the " back log" moved, or the " forestick" parted, in the fire. — There was that, also, in her look and manner, while she was reading by herself; or listening, attentively, to the conversation of others, which would have been regarded, by some, as the indication of a soft and submissive temper. But, if any thing happened; if she were taken by surprise; or found, on looking up, that she had been observed— there was, instantly, over all her face, a look of insulted womanhood; a something, absolutely imperious about her clear forehead; and a sort of beautiful petulance about her mouth, which, before one could make up his opinion of her, would be gone — for ever gone — like the shadow of a strange bird, from a lighted mirror.

Having thus given a sketch of the principal characters, which made up the family of Abraham Harwood, we shall now, if you please, take some one evening, such as they continually spent about his table; and report so much of the conversation — paying particular regard, in every case, to the peculiarities of language — as will give the reader a good notion of the people hither-to, introduced; and of the Yankee character, in general.

One Saturday night — In Connecticut, Saturday nights are held sacred; Sunday nights are not: — It is their doctrine that the " Sabbath" begins from the going down of the sun on a Saturday afternoon; after which, they do not work there: — It is a common thing, therefore, on a Saturday evening, for people to assemble at each others houses, under pretence of a prayer meeting, or a lecture, (it being unlawful to visit, profanely) — where, after the " exercises" have been finished, a chapter in the Bible read, and a hymn sung, they fall into serious conversation : — So — one Saturday night, when a " pretty considerable" number of oddities were assembled about Mr. Harwood's little parlour — it was in the summer time — the character of woman was under consideration. A few wise things, and a great many foolish ones, were said; and all was going on smoothly enough, till Peters turned about, very suddenly, upon one of the speakers; put him to silence; and summed up, as it were, much in the following way.

" Poh ! nonsense; you are all wrong, every one of you. You don't know what you are talking about; and as for *you,* Mr. Timothy Archer —"

Mr. Timothy Archer had a " knack o' poetry," and a little, thin voice; made thanksgiving hymns; ballads, about Captain Kyd, Blue Beard, and every thing else, under heaven; with 'a " pair o' varses " every new-year's-day, for the printer at York.'—

" As for *you,* Mr. Timothy Archer, what you say — is no argument at all. You've been squeaking for half an hour, to no sort of purpose. You don't say what you mean, or mean what you say; fine words come to your thought; and you *in* with 'em, whether or no, till you ge-

nerally end, with contradicting yourself, and
bothering every body else. And, as for you,
Mr. Deacon Pepperell, though you have a
plenty of good sense, you don't know how to
make use of it. You wouldn't be able to —
do you know what a syllogism is ?"

" A what ? I never saw one, I rather guess;
have I ?"

" No matter; I have done with *you*. There
is no talking with such a man. — Mr. Harwood !"

" Well; you seem a little out of humour."

" Poh ! nonsense. — You are mistaken about
women. They *will* bear the truth. And I un-
dertake —"

" There they go, now, Cousin Jotty," whispered Edith; shaking back her loose hair; leaning
forward; and slily kicking the shins of " Cousin
Jotty," or Jotham ; a big, lubberly, sleepy looking boy, who sat on the other side of the table,
with his toes in; mouth wide open, waistcoat
falling off; and his great fat head lolling over on
one side, — " Hush, hush ! there they go
again ! hush !"

" Hush, yourself, Edith Cummin," muttered Cousin Jotty; " if you don't let me alone, — By gosh !" kicking over, in reply, somewhat spitefully, as he spoke, — " there, now !"

" Leave me be," squeaked Miss Edith, whose foot, he had caught, in some way or other, under the table.

" Silence there, children !" — " It's Edith, sir." — " It's Jotty, sir." — " I wish you'd speak to Jotty, sir." — " She's kicken my shins, dad." — " He's got hold o' my foot, uncle." — " Children ! children ! — get away from the table, Jotham; go up in the corner, sir; and stay there, with your face to the wall : — go, go, let me hear no more of this. — Proceed, 'Squire." — " Pshaw !"

Away went Master Jotty; shuffling over the floor, so as to obliterate half the sand-flowers, in his path; a malicious thing, which Edith retaliated upon him for, by pretending to cry into her handkerchief; and, afterwards, to wring it out, as if it were dripping with her sorrow, for his punishment.

" No, Abraham Harwood," continued Peters;

nearly shutting his eyes, and speaking a little
through the nose: "No. You are altogether
wrong. This very 'goodness of heart,' as you
call it, sir; this very 'gentleness of temper,'
as *you* call it, Mr. Timothy Archer; 'this jewel
without price, altogether lovely,' as *you* call it,
Mr. Deacon Solomon Pepperell; this obedient,
credulous, trusting disposition, as I choose to
call it, sir — different names, after all, for the
same thing; this temper o' woman (Edith lifted
her head, in alarm), whatever you may call it,
is the cause of continual mischief, to everybody;
to *herself,* more than to all others. Afraid of
hurting the self-love; perhaps, of a fool, — perhaps, of a villain, she is continually doing that,
which bad men take advantage of — "

. "How, pray; how do they take advantage of
it?"

"By misrepresenting her forbearance toward
vice and folly, sir, as a partiality for both."

"Well, well," said Mr. Harwood; "perhaps
you are right. We are all, more or less, liable
to misrepresentation, though; it is the common

lot of humanity. Women, you will admit, are
more amiable, for their charity of heart."

" Yes, taking your definition of the word;
mercy without justice, they are more amiable,
though not so respectable."

"*I reckon!* whew!" exclaimed Edith; looking
about, for Jotham, who was beyond hearing,
" I wonder what he'll say next? — I do love
to hear him talk, though; don't you, Miriam?"

" Well, *if* ever!" said Miriam — the
"help."

" In short, Abraham Harwood," continued
Peters; " in short, sir, it is, and will be for ever,
the destruction of women; this very ' goodness
of heart.' It is eternally leading them to do what
others do, merely *because* others do it; or because it is *expected* of them."

" How so; I do not understand you."

" Probably not; you have never thought of
the matter, before. I have. The character of
woman is my favourite study. Let us try an
experiment." —

While he spoke, he leaned forward, and took
Edith's hand into his own.

" See here," said he; " here is ample confirmation. Take the hand of almost any female,
as I have taken the hand of this child, now; take
it as if you have no doubt of her letting it remain;
as if you expect her to be quiet; and she will
never disappoint you; never !"

Edith caught away her hand, coloured, grew
very pale, and gulped a little; as if there were a
sob or two, in her throat.

" There is further confirmation," said Peters.

" Further confirmation ! how ?"

" She took it away, because it was *expected*
of her; and she saw it."

" How so? poor child ! how could she know
what we expected of her ?"

" Ask her, Abraham Harwood. She is not
so much of a child as you believe; ask her."

" No, no; ask her, yourself. She is your
pupil; not mine."

" Edith," said Peters, " why did you let me
take your hand? you, who are verging swiftly
upon womanhood ?"

" Indeed, indeed, sir, — indeed, Uncle Harwood," answered poor Edith; faltering sadly be-

fore their looks; — "indeed, sir, I hardly know how it happened. I was listening to you, — to Mr. Peters, I mean; I beg your pardon, Sir; and I — I didn't know that my hand *was* there, till you made me feel ashamed; and you, too, Uncle Harwood, you looked at me so."

"Very well. But," continued Peters; lowering his voice; and leaning over the table, toward her, that others might not hear him, — " But, be more upon your guard, for the future. You know what is expected of you; now-; you will never disappoint us, I hope."

Her eyes filled; and he turned away from her, saying, as he did, " Thus it is, with woman. They are all alike. The fountain of tears may be broken up, any time, by a soft word. Thus it is ! — if you show any doubt, when you are claiming her obedience; when you have taken her hand into your, for example, she will withdraw it, more or less gently, as your doubt, is more or less equivocally expressed. Show surprise; and she will snatch it away in confusion : show triumph, concern, or astonishment; and she will either —(it was amusing enough to

watch Peters, while he was ending a tolerable
sentence; he was pretty sure to spoil it), —
and she will either slap your face, for you;
burst into tears; or pass away, like an affronted
queen."—

" *Why !* Mr. Peters !" — exclaimed Edith ;
struck, more at his manner, perhaps, than at his
words; — for he spoke them, with unusual bitterness.

" What I would have said, Edith—pho! pho!
— nonsense. — Don't be afraid. Hold up your
head — push your hair away from your face; and
look at me. — I wish you to understand these
things." — Edith obeyed. — " Very well — that
'll do — What I would say; what I meant, was
this. Observe. When we show astonishment,
at any thing, done by a woman, we, thereby, re-
mind her of her duty. Astonishment, at such a
time, is nothing but reproof. And he, who
shows either confusion or astonishment; concern or surprise, when a woman permits him to
take her hand; — or to do any thing else — no matter what—calls upon her, thereby, to punish him,
and assume another character. — Let us prove

this. — Why did you snatch away your hand, just now, so pettishly?"

"Shall I mince the matter, a little, sir?"

"Mince the matter! simpleton!" exclaimed her uncle; greatly diverted with her simplicity.

"Mr. Harwood! — Sir?" — said Peters. — "No, Edith—no mincing the matter, if you please, now. —Was it not because of something, in my countenance, which, while it made you 'ashamed,' as you say, reminded you of your duty; and showed what was *expected* of you? — Come to the point — you understand my question (she nodded; and bit her lips) — come to the point; yes, or no?"

"Yes."

"There's a brave girl!—you, at least, Edith Cummin, have courage enough, to speak the plain truth — if you speak at all."

Edith drew a long breath; and wiped her eyes. — "Courage, Mr. Evans, courage! Does it require courage, to speak the truth?"

"Yes; do you find it so easy?"

"No; very hard, sometimes."

" And you; how do you manage, then?"

" Manage; I don't manage at all. I hold my tongue."

" The harder of the two perhaps," whispered somebody near. It was the poet.

Peters gave him such a look. — " These flippancies about women, young man," said he, — " were they original, as they are not, would be base and contemptible. When you have more understanding, you will discover, that, under heaven, there are two things, at least, which it is bad policy, if not foolishness, to speak lightly of; the bible and woman."

Certain of the graver men here interchanged a look, almost of horror, at his profane association of two *things*, as he called them — so immeasurably disproportionate, in importance. They were of those, who would rather see women; their own daughters and wives, openly profaned, fifty times over, than the bible. Perhaps they were right.

" Women," continued Peters—" women laugh, *because* others laugh; and weep, for the same excellent reason. Their credulity is the cause of — "

" The innocent are always credulous, I—I believe," said Edith, in a whisper, just above her breath; and shrinking back, into the shadow, as her voice died away; alarmed at her own temerity. She had been taken by surprise.

" Ah ! — do you think so ?" quoth Peters.

" To be sure."

" Why ?"

" Because I have heard *you* say so."

" Because you have heard *me* say so ! — for shame ! Is that a reason for your belief?"

" I can't give a better one."

" Pho, pho — nonsense. You can. — Recollect yourself."

" Why, sir — I — I — What *is* the use of my giving a reason ? — The innocent *are* credulous — every body knows it — I hate reasoning."

" Absurd. You should not only have a reason for every thing; but be able to give one. — How often have I told you, in playing draughts, never to make a move — never to touch a man,

without having a reason. Life is only a game
of draughts. Nothing else will ever make you
thoughtful, serious, or good. Your virtues
will be instinct; and your example of no use,
unless you are able to give a reason, for whatever you do. —How can you believe that the innocent *are* credulous, if you have not been
soberly convinced ? — But if you have been
soberly convinced — in any way — no matter how
— by observation; or by argument; you can give
a reason."

"Why, sir — don't I see it, every day ? Little
children — our little Moses, there; he believes
every thing he hears. He's innocent, I reckon —
There, now ! you are going to ask me for another
o' these abominable reasons: jest as if any body
ever thought o' saying that little children were
not innocent. —— It's in the bible, Mr. Peters."

"Well, well — I am quite satisfied. Only
break yourself, will you, of these execrable
Virginia-isms — (Edith started up) — *I reckon*
— *jest* — mighty bad — leave me *be* —"

"You say *jest*, yourself, sir. — "

"I know it — please to tell me of it, whenever

I do. We all *say* that, which none of us would *write.*— What are you thinking of?"—

" Of— of— pray sir, if women are credulous ; and if — and if— and if the innocent are credu- lous — a — a —"

" Well — go on. Why do you stop ?"

" I cannot — I — I forget what I was going to say."

" Very well. I must help you out. You have a quick, and sure perception of the truth. Your faculty of speech, too, is now disclosing itself.— We should not force it. Your observa- tion was just. The innocent *are* like little chil- dren. Why?— Knowing no evil, they dream of none. Whatever may be their age— they are warm-hearted — credulous. They believe every body to *be* — just what he *appears.* They grow suspicious, only as they grow worse. Wisdom comes only of guilt; as out of a deep foun- tain."—

" Ah! — would you have women wiser, then ?"

" Edith Cummin ! — You are no longer a child."

" Sir."

" You will soon be able to reason like a man."

" I hope not, sir — it is very disagreeable in you, men.—It would be worse, I am sure, in a woman — a young woman — a — a (faltering) a *child*, as you call me. Stay—stay — I dont say what I mean. I should like to be able, when it is proper, to reason; but I dont wish to reason, like a man."

" Very well expressed. But—look this way, if you please. Understand me.—Wisdom, I say, comes of guilt. You cannot be wise, however good you may be—without some knowledge *of* guilt; or some acquaintance *with* it. I would have women less credulous. To that end, I would have them wiser. But I would not have them wiser, by drinking at the fountain head :—nor by a direct participation with guilt. I would only have them acquainted with it — as it were — at second hand — afar off; and only to such a degree, then, as would qualify them better for their duties in life. I would have them know of wickedness, enough to be afraid of it. I would give them as much knowledge, from the experience of others, if I might—as would enable them to warn

their children away from it. In short, I would
have them — they were made for it — women
were put here, for nothing else— I would have
them know what sin is, like the angels, the better
to qualify them for their awful guardianship, over ✓
the souls of their children."

He stopped short; and appeared, by the end
of another minute, serious and warm as he had
been, to have entirely forgotten himself, the
company, and even the argument.

There was a dead silence : all had been over-
heated, and all were glad of a breathing spell.
It was no very comfortable thing, to be in the
same room with Jonathan Peters, during one of
these arguments. All the bye-standers were
sure to become involved, like people standing
over a chess-board ; itching to pop in a word, or
a hint. He was neither loud, nor violent; but
he was cool, positive, peremptory. His very
candour was provoking; his fairness, quite insupportable. His whole manner, in truth, was
that of one, who plays with you, for your amusement; not his own ;— who beats you, as a thing of
course; and who, foreseeing from your first move,

precisely how the game is to end, feels neither
surprise nor pleasure, when he has beaten you,
by involving you in your own combinations.

The consequence was, that, no matter which
side he was on; right or wrong — every body was
glad when he was beaten; every body reckoned
a draw-game, as a victory over him : and every
body lamented, as if it were a victory over himself, whenever the Yankee prevailed.

Besides — and, perhaps, *that* was harder to
bear, than all the rest — his " Yankee notions"
were always either new, or surprising; and sometimes both. Of course, therefore, those who
heard him, would not believe in them, so long
as they could possibly help it. It is no very
agreeable thing, we all know, to be told by a person hardly older than ourselves, in a way that
will admit of no dispute — in a plain, sensible
way; as if it were a truth, which *he* had known all
his life, of some fact, which, if it be, indeed, as he
says, we are blockheads, for not having known
before : no very agreeable matter, for instance, to
be told, after a long life spent among fiddlers,
that we have no ear for musick; or, after we have

grown old among women — the beautiful and
wise — the simple and affectionate — the bold of
heart, or the timid, or fond, or haughty — that
we know nothing of their true nature; nor very
agreeable, to be told by a plain, observing man;
without parade or emphasis; that women always
do what is expected of them; while, it is fifty to one,
perhaps, that we have been of opinion, all our life
long, that precisely the reverse, if any thing,
is the truth.

CHAPTER III.

YANKEE FESTIVALS. — HUSKING. — RAISING. —
QUILTING. — TITLES. —TREASON. — COMFORT.
—HOSPITALITY.

This people; the New Englanders, of whom we
desire to give a lively and faithful description,
yet retain a multitude of their primitive customs,
which arose during their time of necessity, when
they laboured in turn, for each other. To some
of these, we may have to allude, hereafter, in the
progress of our story; at a time, when, if we suc-
ceed at all, we should hope that any interruption
would be thought impertinent. Wherefore, a
word or two of them, now.

They have, — together with certain publick, religious and political celebrations, or festivals there,
some, of a nature, between those of the fire-side and
those of the world; neither private nor publick.
There are three, which now occur to us; — the
Husking, the Raising, and the Quilting.

The HUSKING, which prevails throughout New England only, is brought about in this way. After the maize, or Indian wheat, is gathered into the barn, the farmer, to whom it belongs, puts a good face on the matter; sends round among all his neighbours; and gives them notice, that he is ready to " shell out;" or, in other words, to undergo a husking. The meaning of which message is; that, as he cannot help himself; on such, or such a night, he will permit all the " fellers" and " gals" to tumble and roll about, in his barn, all night long, if they please; eat his pumpkin pies; drink his cider, and waste his apples; under pretence of husking corn.

When the practice began, it was an act of neighbourly kindness; a piece of downright labour, done for nothing. It is now, a wicked and foolish frolick, at another man's expense. Then, it was a favour, which the owner of the corn went about asking of others; it is now a heavy tax, which he would escape, if he could. That, which they are wanted for, is — to tear off the long green coats, from the ear; leaving two or three in some cases; whereby a large number of ears,

E 3

when they are stripped, may be braided strongly together. That, which they *do*, is quite another
affair. Instead of husking the corn, they husk
the owner; trample on the product of his toil;
and push one another about; sometimes, to the
squalling of a bad fiddle.

The RAISING—a word of that, here: it will
save time, by and by. The people of New England live in frame-houses. The frame of any
building, any where, in town or country, being
ready, the publick pour in from all sides; and,
for a mouthful of bread and cheese, or a bit of
mince-pie, and a " twig o' cider" a piece, put up
the frame for the owner, in a frolick.

So too—and here, we come back to the story,
again—so too, whenever a young she-yankee is
" laying out" for a husband, she gives what is
there called a " QUILTING FROLICK." The women
gather about her ; and, for a cup of tea a piece,
or some such matter, " turn out" a handsome
bed-quilt for her, sometimes in a single afternoon.

Edith had been slily tacking little bits of chintz
together, for a year or two; much to the surprise

of at least one person about her; and Peters, himself, who had been watching her progress for two or three months, was just on the point of coming to an explanation with her, when, as he came into the parlour one warm summer after-noon, — there wasn't a breath of air stirring — he saw a large wooden frame resting upon four chairs; placed in the four corners of the room, precisely so, that, for his life, there was no squeez-ing himself in, but by crawling under the frame; or along by the wall, behind some eight or ten young women, at work; not one of whom stayed her needle, or chalk-line, for a single moment — or lifted her head—except Edith; and she, poor thing, though she had no sort of reason for it, burst out a-laughing, in his face.

Peters made no reply. Something — a strange thought appeared, all at once, to have risen up in his mind. He looked at her — at the preparation before him — grew pale — appeared, for a moment, as if undecided whether to go, or stay; and then, without speaking a word, he turned off, and went hastily out of the room.

Edith followed him, with tears in her eyes; overtook him, just as he was tapping at Mr. Harwood's door; and assured him that she was very sorry for having laughed, and hoped — "indeed she did — please — that he would come back."

He did not appear to understand her. He was thinking evidently of that, whatever it was, which made him grow pale, in the room. At last, however, he recollected himself, and spoke to her, in a voice, and with a gentleness, that set her crying.

" My dear child," said he; parting the hair upon her forehead, while he spoke; and stooping reverentially toward it, as if to put a kiss, there; " I had quite forgotten your age, some how or other; how old are you, pray?"

" How old am I!—Why, surely *you* know, sir." He stood waiting the reply; — bending patiently over her, like a father over his own dear child. — " Nearly sixteen, sir — if you please."

" If I please!"—He took off his hands from her forehead, as he spoke, and stood upright; " Upon my word, I had well nigh forgotten my own age, Edith—you had better go back to your friends—your uncle, I perceive, is not within."

" Won't you return with me?—do, sir— do, till he comes back—do—do—he's only gone out for a walk, sir."

" No, no," said Peters; bowing—she had never seen him bow, before—and passing out, as if he knew not whither he was going.

" *Edith, Edith,*" said the poor girl; wiping her eyes, and looking after him, with her lips apart, as he passed on toward the wood; " I wonder what *is* the matter, now. Something bad, I am sure. I *do* wish Walter was here—he doesn't call me Edith, for nothing—I know."

" Edith, Edith !" cried Jotham; opening the door of the room, where the "quilting" was under way; and bawling after her, with all his might; " This a-way, Eady Cummin !—ye hadn't ought o' be away from your com'many."

" Edith—everybody calls me Edith, now;— I wonder what I have done, to-night. Comin', Jotty !—lubberly Jotty—comin', as fast as ever I can !" cried Edith; wondering the while, how it could happen that Jonathan Peters, who had been talking to her about her age, only two days before, should have so soon forgotten it; and how he came to stoop down, as if he were going to kiss her forehead — a thing that he had never done but once before, in all his life; and go away without kissing it, after all; as if he had forgotten what he was about.

She returned, however, to the quilting; and Peters, after a little time, to the study of Mr. Harwood, who, on opening the door, found him in his usual posture — one, common throughout New England, even to this day; if not universal— his chair tilted back; and both legs thrown up, over the fire-place, within which, two or three lighted pitch knots, a substitute for candles, were burning;—his lips compressed—forehead lowering—heavy shadows over the face; and all the light of his dark, luminous eyes, apparently turned inward upon his own heart.

" Ah Mr. Peters ! how do you do ?" said the preacher.

Peters made no reply, for two or three minutes; and when he did, it was after the fashion of the

Yankees, anything but what might have been looked for.

" Nearly sixteen," said he. — " When does Walter come back ?"

" Ah ! what has put *him* into your head ?"

" Will you answer my question ?"

" Will I ? — how can you put such a query ?"

" Abraham Harwood ; is there no such thing, I should like to know, as getting a direct answer out of you ?"

" Pray, did you ever see one of my countrymen, out of whom you could get a direct answer ?"

" Will you answer me ? will you try ? When does he return ?"

" Will you be kind enough to tell me what has disturbed you ; and why you put your question to me, as if it were a matter of life and death ?"

" It *is* a matter of life and death," said Peters : —a shadow fell upon his face while he spoke ; a shadow that arose from within — his forehead shook ; the loose hair trembled upon his head ;

and his mouth was agitated; like the mouth of a woman, with untold sorrow.

The preacher was awed by his manner. It was new to him. He had followed the mysterious man through all his changes, for many a month; he had seen him serious, gloomy; stern as death —melancholy; and, more than once, judging from his looks—for he made no complaint, whatever— unspeakably wretched; but never before, had he seen him in this humour; so full of authority; so unreasonable; so impatient; so hot and imperious.

A long silence followed. For nearly half an hour, neither of them opened his mouth, or hard- ly moved in his chair; and each seemed to have entirely forgotten the short angry questioning of the other. Mr. Harwood sat, in a sort of revery —smoothing his black, rich, glossy hair; which, being divided in the middle of his forehead, flowed back behind his ears; and fell, in pro- fusion over his shoulders, like the hair of a woman. Owing to the position of the strong yellow lights; intercepted as they were by the legs of Peters; the white wall, clean sanded floor, and sky blue ceiling of the apartment, were covered with great

flaunting shadows—a troop of prodigious apparitions, that issued from the strange gloom and
brightness of the fire-place, in a continual procession.

"Soft hair and a white hand, Abraham Harwood," said Peters, looking up—losing all patience when he saw the preacher coquetting thus
with his own tresses; and watching the shadows
on the wall as if they were alive; or had really
been conjured up, out of the fire, by some great
Indian sorcerer—"Soft hair, and a white hand,
for an American farmer, at a time like this!"

"Men of a contemplative habit, you know,
Mr. Peters, are somewhat prone to these peculiarities."

"Not if they have ugly hands, or coarse hair."

"Squire Peters!"

"Abraham Harwood!"

"Well."

"How dare you call me squire?"

"Not yet reconciled, I perceive, to our customs. Surely, my friend; after the town meeting,
t'other day—"

"The town meeting!—Don't make a blockhead of yourself. I like a title as well as another, when it *is* a title; when it will not give the lie to all that I have said, or done, for years. But I won't put up with a nick-name. If I must have a title; give me one that has meaning in it — a high one — the highest. No titles for me, that imply subordination. *'Squire, 'squire!*—I'd as lief be anointed ' moderator;' ' se-lect-man,' as you call it, or corporal, or deacon."

" You are unreasonable. Something has put you out of temper. These titles are given, as a matter of course, to every stranger. It is only a way, that our people take, of sounding him."

" So! were *you* sounding me, too? Look me in the face. Do you remember what I told you, when that lank-haired, hypocritical chap — I forget his name —

" Overseer Pendleton."

" Overseer! the rascal! I told you then, that he was pumping me. Had I known it of a certainty, as I do now, he should have eaten grass where he stood, like his name-sake of old."

" You mean Zachariah, perhaps, or Zekiel; not Nebuchadnezzar: neighbour Zekey *is* rather

meddlesome; but, as for overseer Nebby, he's
only one o' the committee of safety. He came
here, thinking you might be one o' the innemy;
that's my guess."

"Pho, pho! Nonsense. We have no inne-
mies now, as you call them. I wish you'd learn
to say enemy."

"Between you and I"—"You and *me*, if you
please."—"Well, well; between you and me, I
consate."—"*Conceit*, sir"—"Well, well, I
conceit; upon my word, your notions of the
matter—"

"*Notions*, Abraham Harwood! men of my
temper are not over likely to have *notions* about
any thing. Look at me; (facing about, and fixing
his bright eyes upon the wall, behind the preacher), sir!—I am an American; a native born Yankee. We have begun a war upon titles. It
will end—mark me, Abraham Harwood; mark
me; it will end yet, in bloodshed."

"I hope not, sir; but, if it should; and if we
should prevail—and if—and if—"

"And *if*—and *if*—peace! You are darkening
counsel. If we prevail, we shall have no king in

America. We shall never be able to agree upon a person, for the office. Our form of government will not be regal : we shall have no fountain of honour — no titles: therefore, the sooner we begin to make war upon them, the better. Cut off the attributes of sovereignty, one by one, without noise; and we shall strike a vital part, before any body can guard it."

" I do not well understand you. I have never thought of this matter, so seriously. You seem to calculate on something more than warfare; perhaps on a separation."

" Peace ! you are not a man for me to speak with, freely. Your avocation is unlike mine; your temper, soul, heart; every thing — peace !"

" But surely, my good sir — if this unhappy dispute should end, as you seem to foresee, what harm would come of a title so humble as that of squire. It confers no distinction."

" Pho, pho ! — why is it given ?"

" As a title of courtesy."

" Ridiculous ! why is it not given, like that of master, to everybody; or, as we call it now, *mister ?*"

" But we must have judges, generals, and governors."

" True; call them so, then. Call them whatever they are, while they *are* so. Call them
judges, and generals, and governors; but if you
are an American, don't call them honours,
esquires, and excellencies — for ever — in office,
and out. All these people may be wanted in a
republick."

"God help us ! á republick ! what have we
to do, with a republick? our king alive; we,
only a part of his great empire."

" King, *king!* Abraham Harwood. Have you
forgotten; or have you never heard, how this king
hath permitted his ministers to treat us? We
have been slaves, for a whole century. We have
never been regarded as Englishmen: our treasures
have been wasted, and our blood poured out —
in war after war, made by him — not by us.
Look you ! thousands of our young men have died
in the West Indies for him : thousands are now
manning his fleet: many thousands have perished
in our wars with the French *here ;* on *his* account,
not on ours ; for it was our policy to be at peace

with our formidable neighbours: alone, single-handed, we captured Louisbourg for him; the Dunkirk of North America: and what has been our reward? This very Louisbourg, which we, the men of New England, carried for him, *alone:* this very Louisbourg, which was the only valuable acquisition made by the British in the whole of that long war — an acquisition which gave peace to Europe—this North American Gibraltar was thrown up, without any sort of regard for *us,* in exchange for a foreign barrier to the Dutch; leaving us precisely where we started from, to fight all our battles over again, with our martial neighbours, and all their Indian allies. — I know something of this matter, and I advise you to be prepared for a change. The hour is at hand, sir, when we shall become a confederation of states;—or nothing. Have you forgotten the congress at Philadelphia, in fifty-six? Observe! Another congress will be heard of, yet, where traitors will sit in the high places; and give judgment, as it hath been before, upon all the kings."

" I tremble to hear you."

" Very well; tremble, if you please."

" Republicans—I hardly know how to understand you;" said the preacher, pondering over
what he heard.   " Surely, sir; surely—there
may be titles, under any form of government;
among the Greeks—"

" Foolishness—hear me.   I will give you the
substance of all that *can* be said, in this matter—
all that should be said, in two minutes.   No
government should have the power of taxing a
people, but by their own consent.   The power of
conferring titles, I say, *is* a power of taxation,
beyond all comparison, more exhausting and mischievous, than every other.   It is unrighteous.
You cannot raise one man, without lowering other
men.   You cannot endow any one of a multitude,
with rank alone—rank, without privilege or
power (if *that* were possible) — but by taking it
away from the rest of that multitude."

" But when it is only a sort of precedence,—"

" Well; precedence, itself, is power. It is the
power of going before other people : and, in some
cases that power might be worth disputing, to
bloodshed."

" But in a monarchy,—"

" Pshaw! Never talk to me about such things. I know all that can be said for it, in a monarchy. The power of conferring titles, they argue, is the power of rewarding merit, in the most economical way. It is not, sir. It is the power of taxing the people *indirectly*, beyond what any people would bear, if it were a *direct*, open, visible tax. Hence it is, that, however they may talk, wise rulers are unwilling to use that power. They know well that it impoverishes a people; subdues them; lowers their manhood, more than all their other taxes. Hence it is, too, that men of rank are so vehemently opposed, in their hearts, to the exercise of this kingly prerogative. Every new peer must be made up, they all know that, chiefly out of the old peers; a part of *their* supremacy and privilege must go to the making up of *his*; and what is then wanting, must be contributed by the multitude. There is only so much rank, and no more, to be expended by any government. The smaller the number that share it; of course, the greater is the share of each. A duke, in a country, where there is no other duke, is greater than a king, where kings are a drug. Look at Germany, — France, —

Italy, — Europe, — what has become of their peer-
age and chivalry? Subdivided; until no man has
enough to distinguish him from another. The
blood-royal, itself, is found in the common veins
of common men. So — you are thoughtful."

" Yes; I am watching your countenance."

" You are ? —"

" Shall I never be able to comprehend your
character ?"

" Probably not. I don't like being sounded
with short lines, or a common breath."

" Sir ! — Jonathan Peters ! — I begin to be
afraid of you. Your looks are no longer the
same. What has happened? Letters, perhaps?
— (No answer). — What is to come of this convulsion through the colonies, think you ?"

" War — war — war."

" With Great Britain, sir ; — with our *home ?*"

" Yea — yea ; — with our *home*, if they will have
it so ?"

" We shall be destroyed."

" Probably."

" Gracious God ! sir, — how you speak of it !"

" I speak, as I feel. If they drive us one

inch further, we shall do something that cannot
be forgiven : after which, we must prevail ; or die
—to a man."

"You frighten me ; what am I to believe ?—
would you promote a separation ?"

"By no means ; we are not prepared for it.
Our strong men — our good men — are afraid of it.
Confusion would follow, — we have so many jar-
ring dispositions to reconcile. And yet—yet—
confusion, death, any thing—were better than such
vassalage. What! are we to be taxed, without
being represented ? No, no ; Abraham Harwood — no, no ; if they will have our gold, they
shall have it : if they will have our blood, they
shall have it — in our own way."

"But, concerning titles ; I am not convinced.
I cannot see why titles may not be—ah !"

"Not convinced !" cried Peters ; getting up,
leaning over his chair, and planting his foot, —
"Not convinced ! will any thing convince you ?
who are our nobility? men, Abraham Harwood ;
men, called out of the coarse earth, like Adam, by
the will of Jehovah ! what have we to do with
ensigns and armorial bearings — the blazonry of

an old people, any more than he had; he, the un-
titled Adam? We are a new people; we have
no fathers, no progenitors; we are disinherited;
banished; cut off by our fathers; and our progenitors—where are they? Confounded with all the
rubbish, of all the earth. Whence are they? From
the four winds of heaven.—Squire—*squire!* I
will strike that man to my feet, henceforward, who
shall dare to insult me, with such a title. Am I
to be honoured by a nick-name, which anybody
may have, with his Majesty's commission? or anybody, who can poach with impunity among our
women, squirrels, and rabbits.—No, Abraham
Harwood, no; you are one of the priesthood.
You are appointed by the Maker, to mount guard
over this people, with a sword and a trumpet.
How will you answer it hereafter, should they be
taken by surprise?"

" I never saw you in this mood, before."

" So much the worse; I have been a hypocrite. Is Edith going to be married?"

" Edith going to be married! what can have
put such a thing into your head, pray? our
Edith—"

" Yes — our Edith ; whose quilting is that ?"

" Her's to be sure ; but —"

" Supper! supper! dad, supper!" cried Master Jotty ; running through the passage, and
bawling out, as if the house were on fire. So the
preacher was fain to lead off, with his cold, stately
uncomfortable companion, to the little parlour ;
neither of them speaking a word, on the way.

A new England supper-table ; and a genuine
Yankee supper may be worth a moment of our
time, and half a dozen sweeps of our brush ; a
supper and a table, such, as were in fashion, half
a century ago ; and such, as are still to be met
with, all over the " Western Country ;" throughout all the woods and " back parts" of America,
—with a few variations, from " hasty pudding and
molasses, to hog and homony ;" from sweet corn,
pumpkin pies, and *sarse* (vegetables) ; to buck-
wheat cakes and goose's gravy, — in many of the
smaller towns, and over all the country parts, of
New England.

We all know the value of these fire-side habits,
in making up our mind, about the social and
moral character of a people.   It is the household

virtues, that chiefly distinguish one set of men from another. To know a man well, we should see him at-*home*. People are very much alike, in their out-of-door habits; their dress of ceremony and fashion, before all the world: they are not half so much alike, at home; in their old coats and big slippers; lounging over the tables and chairs; each after a fashion of his own—more or less dignified or sloppy, as he is more or less afraid of being caught. Abroad, people are seen afar off, as it were, through an atmosphere, which, while it exaggerates the whole, confuses every part. Distance in space, like distance in time, never fails to confound the minutiæ and peculiarities of all men, however they may loom through it, like a great ship, in a fog.

At home, it is, and only at home, as everybody knows—(Then, why tell us of it? Because men will have it so. Books, altogether new, put people to the trouble of thinking—perhaps)—At home, it is; and only at home, that we show the "natural man;" the real temper of "the beast" —perverse or sociable; overbearing, stern, or affectionate; cross or cruel; gentle or severe;

our infirmities, whatever they are; our virtues, whatever they are; the kinder pulsations
of the heart; the wickeder emotions of the mind.
If there be any bad blood in a fellow, he will show
it—whenever he dares—wherever he can : but,
where can he shew it more safely, than at home,
where his wife and children cannot help themselves;
and his " people" are paid so much a-week, to
bear it. See him at home, therefore; whoever he
may be; whatever he may be; good or bad; great
or little; if you would know his true value. Is it
a pyramid? go near to it, if you would know its
real strength;—it may have been built of pebbles.
Is it a ruin? go near to it—nearer:—it may have
been richly sculptured; it may be a treasury of
ornament.

A man may be a hypocrite all his life long,
before the publick; but no man ever was, before his
own family. His true disposition is that, which
they see, however it may appear abroad; over his
wine; or, on particular occasions.

For this reason it is, that we love to follow men
home to their own fire-sides. The table itself;
apart from every thing else; that alone, is a crite-

rion, by which the refinement of a people may
be determined.   There is no better one; or, at
any rate, only *one*—the condition of women ✓
among them.   The rude, barbarian virtues; the
coarse hospitality; and substantial fierce welcome,
of every people in a savage state, are all of a
piece.

The black broth of the Spartans; the raw
frozen fish, and sea-blubber of the Laplander;
the sour crout of the Germans; the fish-and-
potatoes of the Yankee; the corn bread and
homony of an old Virginian; the oatmeal cakes,
bannocks, and crowdy, of a Scotchman; the train
oil of the Esquimaux; the substitutes of a
Frenchman; the horse flesh and mare's milk of
a wild Arab; the brave, coarse meat of the
North American—that of a strangled bear, perhaps; the potatoes and point of an Irish peasant;
the live, quivering steak of an Abyssinian; the
buck wheat cakes of a New Yorker; the lion's
meat of some people; the broken glass, brick
bats, and old iron of the ostrich; or, worse than
all, perhaps, the abominable plum pudding of
an Englishman; that which, if he were not

"brought up" on it, the ostrich himself could not manage: what are all these things, but so many infallible measures of refinement and character. They are always detestable to strangers, and always agreeable to the "natives." Those who are "brought up" on them, love them : those who are not, bring them up—with a curse. They work upon us, nevertheless—all of them — like our mother's milk; and keep us yearning toward our home, even to the last.

Now for supper. There being " a pootty consid'r'ble snarl o' gals, I guess," the supper was bravely furnished. As usual, in America, puddings and pies, vegetables and meat, were all on the table, at once. " We aint proud, I guess." Here were " sweatmeats," *i. e.* preserved plums; there was a fine goose; here, was a pumpkin pie, nearly three feet in length, baked in a milk pan; there, a quantity of long, short, and round sauce, or " sarse," *i. e.* carrots, turnips, and potatoes: here, were dough nuts, a kind of sweet cake fried in lard; honey comb, new butter, cheese, rye and Indian bread; *i. e.* a bread, baked in half-peck loaves, made

partly of rye meal, and partly of Indian meal—
the meal of Indian wheat or maize; there, a prodigious pumpkin, "right out o' the oven, by faith;"
perfuming the whole house, while Miriam stood
stirring up the "innards;" pouring in the new
milk, with now and then a handful of "ginooine"
maple sugar; a spoonful or two of "turrible
good" corn-stalk molasses, and a little nutmeg,
till every body was impatient for a dip, while
it was bubbling and smoking; his neighbours all a tiptoe; and *a* silver spoon, "the only
one about," going the rounds; with a pretty
"respectable" Indian pudding, a plate of pickles,
a tub of milk porridge.

It *was* a genuine Yankee supper; and such
a one as might be met with, now, at a Quilting, Husking, or Raising, of the northern states.

CHAPTER IV.

CHARACTERS. — READING. — TALKING. — MIRA-
CULOUS ACCOMPLISHMENTS. — MARRIED 'LIFE.
— TOUJOURS PERDRIX. — FARMER. — PURE
YANKEE, WITH MUSICAL NOTATION.

" BE quiet, Edith; Watty 'll be here, soon,"
quoth Mr. Harwood. — "But, how happens it, my
friend," addressing himself to Peters, with whom
he had been holding another talk, about certain alarming movements on the sea-board —
" how happens it, I pray, that, ever since our late
conversation respecting the affairs of our country,
you have held aloof, as it were? — You do not
speak so freely with me, as you did."

" No matter, now;—I have my reasons. After that
boy returns, we may talk them over; at present—"
He stopped short, and smote his arm on the table,
as if something had occurred, all at once, to him;
something, which made him desperate with im-

patience. — " Will that boy *never* come back, I wonder !" said he.

" Never !" — answered a low voice, at his elbow.

The preacher started. So did Edith, who was half asleep in her chair; Miriam — everybody. Even Lucy Armstrong, who sat apart from the others in a corner, sideways toward Peters, with a little strange-looking baby at her breast — even she lifted *her* head in alarm, as the table sounded with his blow. They looked into his face, all of them, even the baby; but stern, cold, and pale as it was, they could see nothing in it — no change whatever, to confirm their terror. The blow had been given by accident, perhaps; or, perhaps, with no other feeling, than that of surprise, or anxiety.

The child alone was disturbed. On seeing the countenance of a man so near, it began to cry; turned away its little face; and cuddled more closely into the mother's bosom. The preacher put forth his hand upon the great family Bible, which lay near; coughed; and was about addressing Peters in reply, when, as he turned for

the purpose, he found him entirely lost, in
thought — absent — wandering away; perhaps
among the stars; perhaps among the nations.

The preacher forebore. There was a something in the look of Jonathan Peters, at such a
time; a something, which no person of common
humanity would have been willing to disturb;
a look of sincere sorrow; of piteous, mournful,
profound abstraction.

These fits of strange revery were not uncommon
with Peters. More than once, they had seen him
stop short, in the middle of a sentence; lose himself entirely; forget where he was; and leave it,
unfinished:—as if, during all the previous argument, however serious — or anxious — he might
have appeared, he had been whiling away his
time with children; amusing himself with "make-
believe;"—and had, in truth, no sort of concern with any thing, or any question, which
he might have been disputing, a minute or two
before; perhaps, with all the warmth of his heart,
and all the power of his understanding. Many a
time, too, they had seen him, while raising the large
brown mug of cider to his mouth, as if he "loved"

it; as if it were a comfort — many a time, they
had seen him stop short; relapse into a fit of
musing; and pass it on, to some country
neighbour — the squeaking poet, perhaps, whom
he abominated — without swallowing a drop.

A stranger, at such a time, would have thought
him a little disordered; a little — so suddenly
would he stop, in the warmth of dispute; and so
steadily, would he rivet his large eyes, for half an
hour at a " go," upon some part of the wall, or
fire-place; or, perhaps, on a large empty chair.

Even while in conversation with you,
Peters would not appear to be conscious of your
presence; or even to see you, though he were
looking into your eyes the while. It was more
as if he saw through you — beyond you — into
the eyes of somebody else, behind you. He
would hold on his course, too, very oddly; sometimes, for a full hour; in the same voice; the
same tone — rather nasal by the way; with eyes
nearly shut, and a continual glimmering in the wet
heavy lashes; very much, as if he were only com-
muning with himself, aloud; or in conversation

with something — a spirit — invisible, for ever, to all but himself.

The clock sounded — a cumbrous old affair, with a bell-metal face; and, before the noise had entirely died away, the preacher sprung the silver clasp of the Bible; and opened at the regular chapter for the evening. It was a habit of his, to read it entirely through — every word of it — aloud — in his own family — about once, every year. We say nothing of his good sense, in doing this; we speak only of the fact.

He began to read; but read, in such a style; with a puritanical whine, so insupportable to Peters, that he could hardly sit still. The rest of the family were still enough, to be sure, before he had read five minutes; but most of them were asleep, and the rest were nearly so.

" What !" said the preacher; ceasing abruptly, and looking up, " What! all of you asleep again, while the Being, who spoke to Moses out of the burning bush; and unto Saul from the great sky — asleep! while HE is appealing to you, by the mouth of his minister —"

" Abraham Harwood! I wonder at your courage," quoth Peters.

" They are asleep, sir. Would you have them sleep, at such a time ?"

" It is your own fault. If you would read properly, naturally; neither sing nor whine the word of the Lord, sir — it would keep anybody awake. The chapter, which you have there, is full of magnificent language. Read it, as it should be read ; and, instead of sleeping, as they do now, *while* you are reading it, not one of them would be able to sleep, for the whole night, afterwards. They would sooner fall asleep, to the noise of trumpets."

" Can *you* read it better ?"

" Yes."

" Allow me to proceed, for the present."

Peters nodded, and fixed his eyes upon the wall, again. The preacher began, anew ; but, long before he had come to the end, the little family were lolling and sprawling about, on the settles and chairs; blocks and benches; all over the room ; all asleep, or near it ; and all pretending to be wide awake.

Here was Jotham, lubberly Jotham, as Edith
sometimes called him, leaning upon both elbows,
with all his might; his prodigious head supported — partly, by his great, red, sprawling hands,
through which it was continually slipping; and,
partly, by his loose, ragged locks, which had caught
in his fingers. He was dead asleep; his ponderous under-jaw had fallen; his tongue was out;
and the weight of a pound would have tumbled
him, head foremost, into the fire-place, among the
pitch-wood, the blaze of which was close to his
face. Yet, even Jotham, if you would believe
him, had never missed a word.

There was Edith, mounted upon her favourite seat; a tall pine block, the end of which was
not sawed square; one shoe off— her bright hair
afloat upon the table; her arms abroad— one
sleeve pushed up to the shoulder, quite up; *her*
mouth half open too—her neck—with a Testament
lying open before her; the chapter for the night
carefully indicated by a folded leaf, though the
book, itself, was wrong end upward. Still Edith
Cummin was not asleep; no, indeed, she had no
idea of being asleep; no, not even while her

pretty hand lay over the arm of Jonathan Peters;
her sweet mouth, so near to his face, the while, that
his coarse hair stirred in her breathing, faint as
it was; and every beat of *her* heart could be count-
ed in *his* temples.

And yet, Edith Cummin, the disciple of truth,
would never own that she had been fairly asleep;
not she, indeed. She had only been meditating;
lost in thought, like Peters; or listening, like the
rest, with all her heart and soul.

And so, with every one of the household. All
were very thoughtful — *very* — and very attentive.
Yet, nevertheless; at every pause, in the reading;
at every sudden change of the preacher's voice;
at every unusual or forbidden sound; such as
the falling of a leg, or a foot; a book, or a hand;
the bumping of a head, or two; or the loud
breathing of some *very* attentive auditor; such as
Jotham, for example, whose every breath was a
hoarse blubber, at last, as he went, balancing on
his way, into the fire-place; up would go
all their heads together! — a sort of paroxysm
would follow among their legs and arms; part of
which were asleep, it may be; and part, sadly

abroad, on their own account and risk.   Then,
they would rub their eyes, all of them, with
particular emphasis; make faces; put on a de-
vout, pondering expression; change feet, very
much as if they weighed half a ton a piece; and
lean forward, each with his chin upon his hand,
just long enough to be seen of the preacher;
cough a little, to catch his eye, and convince him,
if he would look, that all was fair and above board:
—after which, it was delightful to see their ma-
nœuvres.   Each would gradually turn away, by
little and little, from the light; shadowing his face,
more and more, from the preacher's eye; and
sinking his head, lower and lower, at every sob,
until he was again fairly lost, in that rich, drowsy,
luxurious meditation, which people find so delicious, whenever or wherever—as in God's own
house—it is either indecent, or improper; wicked,
or foolish.

The preacher saw it, and was wroth.   He
lifted his voice, and shut the book with unbe-
coming violence, while he was repeating the last
words;—pushing it away, as if, in his own
heart, he had no real veneration, either for it, or

for that office, into which he had been put, as he would have men believe, by a " call" from above.

" Have you no decency left? are you not afraid of the judgment?" said he, in a loud angry voice; looking about him, as he spoke.

" Abraham Harwood! Abraham Harwood! have *you* no decency left?" cried Peters. " Are not *you* afraid of the judgment? It is your own fault; and you know it, if they fall asleep, sir, while you are reading the Bible—repeating the words of the Almighty after him; why do you not learn to read?"

" Railly, Mr. Peters; you progress at a strange rate, in these—"

" *Railly!* why not say, really? *progress!* why not say *get along?*"

" Well then, *get along*," said Edith; " why don't you say so, uncle? *Do* say so. You *do* read well; don't you?"

" Peace, child," answered Peters; " reading well is no such easy matter. Your uncle reads miserably."

" Ah! but you never heard Mr. Archer — the poet."

" Pshaw."

" Ah, but he does read well, though, for all that, I reckon. Mind your har, Jotham; be all a-fire in a moment. Thar you go."

" Edith; will you never break yourself, pray, of these abominable Virginia habits? Come, come; don't fly in a passion. Will you never be done with *I reckon?* must you continue, all your life long, to say *har,* for hair; *stars,* for stairs; *far,* for fair; *thar,* for there?"

" You often speak of good reading, sir," said the preacher, gravely, " as if it were a thing of great importance. One would suppose, to hear you talk, that you thought more of the manner— much more—than of the matter."

" I do. A good reader will make nonsense, beautiful: a bad one, the language of heaven, itself; that of inspiration, foolishness: poetry and prophecy, ridiculous."

" How do you like the reading of Mr. Archer? We allow him to be about number one—here— among us?"

" Like it! like his reading! the reading of a chap, who squeals, at prayer; sings through his

fore-teeth, shut close; walks on his heels; reads
with all his might; pshaw!"

Edith began to giggle. "I can see him," said
she; "I can see him, this moment. It's jest his
way; ain't it, our Jotty?"

"Isn't it, you mean, Edith. How often am I
to tell you, that ain't is from aren't; arn't from are
not; and, of course, never to be applied, in the
singular. You still say *jest*, instead of just, I
observe; and — but no matter, now. This, Mr.
Archer, you are absurd enough to call a good
reader; a fellow, whose voice, you know, is like
that of some little animal, in a trap: he reads
poetry, with a whimper; and prose, with a whine.
Mr. Harwood — Edith — let me give you a simple
rule: observe it, and it will make you what otherwise you never will be — good readers. Always
read as you would speak—or *talk*, rather—to the
same people, upon the same subject, in the same
place. A few, to avoid what we call a *tone*, read
poetry, as if it were prose: others read prose, with
a regular sing-song intonation. Avoid both.
Some people, seeing others laugh, when they
tell a story; by way of avoiding that, run off into

a worse habit; one, more unnatural, and—*therefore*—worse. They tell you a story, no matter how droll it is, without moving a muscle. They are like the readers. It is a foolish piece of affectation, sir, in both. As for Mr. Archer, I have no patience with him. He uses big words; and reads the superb language of Job, with his little voice, very much as if he were sounding a charge, with a tin whistle; or a twopenny trumpet."

" I am sorry to hear you speak of a natural infirmity, in this manner," said Mr. Harwood.

" Pho, pho; you don't care a fig about it. You only think it proper to say so. I have nothing to do with his infirmity; the blockhead. You call him a good reader. I have only spoken of his voice; because that, alone, would prevent his being a *good* reader, if there were nothing else. Besides; he never changes it."

" I reckon," whispered Edith; " how can he change his voice."

" As you change yours, Edith, at every breath; as everybody will, in conversation. Observe *me* now. You'll not hear me pronounce a dozen words, without as many changes of the voice.

Watch your uncle. He preaches in one voice; talks, in another; reads, in another; prays, in another. This would be right, if, while he was *reading*, for example, he changed his voice; not because he was *reading*; but *because* of the language; or the subject; or the sentiment; or the character of his audience."

" Very well."

" Do you understand me, Edith ?"

" No."

" Let me make it plain. This very chapter, which yonr uncle has been reading, is partly dialogue; partly narrative; partly declamation. Yet, he has read it; *you* have read it all, sir; every word of it, in the same way. You have read it, without any consideration for us; or the language; or the sentiment; in your *reading* voice; not, perhaps, with such an abominable whine; or with so much ridiculous pomp—"

" Plain dealing, Mr. Peters."

" Very, Mr. Harwood; not, perhaps, with so much ridiculous pomp, as you would have read it with, in the pulpit, before a large congregation; but, in a voice, which is never heard while you are talking. I wouldn't have you, like some fools that I know, *act* a dialogue, in the pulpit; much less, would I have you *act* a narrative—the common fault of ambitious readers. It is not a dramatick performance that I go to see, on the ' Sabbath,' as you call it. I do not go to see the characters of the Bible *played.* I would not have you mimick them, or counterfeit any thing else. I would have you read firmly; with simplicity and power; changing your voice a little, and *but* a little, in dialogue or narrative. I only require of you to *describe* them—to tell a plain story, like a serious man; as if you believe it, in your own soul. It is one thing to *say* what you have seen; another, to *be* what you have seen. I remember a man; a great man, too—a great reader, he was thought by his congregation – who put himself into the place of every speaker, while he was reading the Bible; not only changing his voice a little, as everybody should, when repeating the language of another; as we all do, in a parenthesis; but changing it altogether; aye, and what was harder to bear, actually *performing* the piece. If he read of the poor publican, for

example, he would go ' afar off;' as far as the
pulpit would allow; and smite his breast; and
call out, in a piteous voice, ' Lord have mercy
upon me; a miserable sinner !'—thus playing the
character. . And if he spoke of the more righteous
pharisee, he would come swaggering bravely up, to
the front of his pulpit; and give out the words, in
a blustering, loud voice.   Remember what I say,
Edith; I address myself to you: among the wonderful operations of our mind, I know of none so
wonderful as two, which are continually overlooked.   They are indeed miraculous; the chief
among our miraculous properties.   Talking is
one; reading is another. My opinion is very
decided on the subject. I would rather talk well,
than do any thing else well — any thing else,
under heaven. It is more difficult, I believe.
Talk, therefore; talk, whatever you say; for, other
things being equal, he who talks most, will talk
best."

" Ah ; then, why do you make poor Jotty hold
his tongue? You won't let him open his mouth,
when you are by."

" Because; although he never can talk well,

without continual practice, it is not pleasant for
me to be near, when he *is* practising. I may like
to hear a person play finely upon a bugle; but I
should not like to be near, while he was learning
to play." Edith laughed; and gave Jotham a
hunch. " As for you, Edith," continued Peters;
" you may talk, as much as you please. You
have made some progress; and are learning to
play, not so much on a bugle, as on a flagelet.
Persevere."

" But, sir — about reading; you have entirely
forgotten that," said she; seeing him relapse into
a brown study.

" True; learn to read well, and you have the
power of entertaining every body, in every situation;
more persons for a longer time, in a more delightful manner — if you read well — than if you were
to play ever so well, on a musical instrument; or
sing, ever so well."

" There now; there he goes, again; if my New
York master only had hold o' him; he'd make
the feathers fly, I reck — hem — I believe."

" It is all very true, nevertheless. Out of a
large company, there will be found hardly one

who loves musick; and, out of a multitude, who love musick, there will be hardly one real judge of it.   Not so, with fine reading, or conversation. They are understood and relished, by every body.   Besides; musick soon grows tiresome." " No."— " Yes; we cannot feed long on dainties. Nobody can bear to hear a favourite song, or a favourite piece, over and over again, the same night; so that a musician is easily exhausted. Not so, with reading, or conversation.   Judge for yourself. Sometimes, too; one is not in a humour, to sing or play.   She is out of health, voice, or temper; the musick is mislaid; or one is travelling; a-foot, or on horseback; in a carriage, or ship. At any rate, we cannot play, or sing always—for ever—all day long; but only for a little time, just now and then.   How different with conversation ! Try it when you please.   Go into company; and you will be sure, if your conversation be trifling, or common-place, to meet with repeated invitations to sing or play."

" That shows that people do love musick; does'nt it, sir ?"

" No; it only shows, that, little as they care

for musick, they like it better than poor conversation. Besides; if there be one of a large company able to sing or play, they must invite her to show off; or they pass an affront upon her, and her parents, never to be forgiven. You don't hear a sensible woman, or a clever man, thus invited — while in conversation — to leave off talking, and go to singing."

"But musick is an accomplishment, of which we know little or nothing in the country," said Mr. Harwood; "and, as for Edith, if she had staid in town, till this time, I doubt if she would have made much proficiency."—Edith coloured.

"I am glad of it. Little as we know; it would be well, if we knew less of such tawdry, miserable, accomplishments. Our daughters may be better employed. I have no objection to musick. I would have them learn it, *after* they have learnt what is better; not before. I would have women able to manage their household; men, children, horses. I would have them know how to cypher, spell, read—and put a stop, or a capital, in the right place. I would have them learn to talk well; read well; walk well; ride well; before they

learn musick, dancing, painting, or embroidery.
They should be able to breed men — grown men —
for the harness, or the plough ; the field of battle,
or the field of grass." Edith leaned forward ;
her eyes flashed fire. " I would'nt have them
suckle nasty animals for the ball-room, counter,
and shop-board ; creatures—things—made of bad
material, put badly together ; built by the job.
You are laughing, Edith."

" I can't help it, sir."

" Why do you hide your face? — are you
ashamed of it ?"

" Yes."

" These accomplishments too, as you call
them ; learnt as they are, at a most unreasonable
cost of time and money, with us ; to say nothing
of their interference with substantial knowledge ;
what are they, after all ? wicked lures, nothing
more ; lures, like those of the eastern girl. They
are thrown aside, after marriage. One half the
time, which is wasted by women ; by all of them ;
in frivolous accomplishment, if spent wisely,
would enable them to pass the season of peril in
safety ; the season of trial — of danger — that which

follows their delirium, after marriage. Whatever
was necessary to the young, beautiful, unvisited
girl, must be yet *more* necessary to the woman.
That accomplishment, whatever it was — however
frivolous or vain — which was of any value to the
maiden, while winning a husband, will be of
much more value to the wife, in keeping him."

Edith had grown very serious. Her eyes were
full, and her mouth trembled, as if her thought,
for a while, was that of a woman.

"One word more," continued Peters. "Just
when these accomplishments are most wanted;
just when every earthly aid is required; just when
the woman, or the wife, cannot spare one jot or
tittle of the sweet allurements, that made a wonder
of her; just when she cannot wisely—nay, just
when she cannot safely, forego a single one—
the least of all the mysteries that *were ;*—even at
such a time, are they all thrown aside, for ever.
What miserable infatuation! These accomplishments, which, if mothers are to be believed, were
the charm of her high maidenhood; all these are
to be thrown aside, for ever, in the same hour, with
all her untasted beauty and freshness; her

sanctity — her innocence—the great mystery of
her being."

" Well! darn his buttons, our Edith !"
cried Master Jotty, on opening his great eyes,
while Edith was leaning forward, with her
face opposite him ;— " well! darn his buttons,
if she aint as white as any thing."

" Peace, muttonhead ! — Just when the newly
married are weary and faint with happiness ; while
the deep, holy, and affectionate quiet, which is
to follow their delirium—the sacred love, which is
to be born of their convulsions — are yet a little
way off; while both are afraid and ashamed of the
alteration, which they feel within their own hearts;
just as if that languor and weariness were not a
wise and benevolent provision of our nature, to
keep ourselves and our love, whatever we may be,
alive; just when both have begun to perceive the
uncomfortable truth — made forty times more uncomfortable, by their mutual want of candour, courage, and common sense — that something more
than the perpetual society of one another — after
all— is necessary to their happiness ; that fondling,
fuss and foolery, though lawful, may be tiresome ;

at such a time — while they are most wanted —
away go all these accomplishments together; all
in a heap.   That is the time of trial; wo to the
⌡ husband; wo to the wife, then, whose colloquial
powers have not been cultivated.   A fine reader
would·be worth her weight in gold, at such a crisis; a fine talker, more.   Confectionary won't do;
musick won't do.   The jaded appetite is dropping
asleep with sweetness; like an over-fed infant, upon
the bosom of its own mother.   All the senses are
weary and faint, with luxury,   No—no—musick
won't do.   Something more homely, more substantial; food, of a more household nature, is
wanted.   Wo to the wife that cannot furnish it;
⌡ wo to the husband, who, when he requires it — as
all men do, soon after marriage — requires it in
vain; wo to the lover, when he comes to watch the
woman of his worship narrowly — continually —
in spite of himself; to tremble, whenever she opens
her mouth; to feel that his own heart — not only
his head, but his heart — indulgent as it is, blind
as it should be, has begun to number the
transgressions of her, whom he has chosen out of
all the world, for the mother of his little ones;

wo to him, if she is unprepared for it; if she
cannot abide her trial time, after the tempestuous
brightness of their joy is over — hark!"

" It is Walter! it is!" cried Edith; jumping over
a chair; as the heavy door opened, with a loud
noise; and a stranger walked in — a Colossus —
one of the giants — wearing the dress of a
North American savage.

" If that aint a Mohawk! I'm darned — that's
all!" cried Jotty; pitching, head foremost, into the
fire-place. The Mohawks were a terrible race
of Indians; a tribe, of whom all the other sa-
vages were afraid.

The preacher jumped out of his chair. —
Peters looked up; and put his right hand into his
bosom. Edith took to a corner. Away went
all the other women folks, into such places of
concealment, as they could find in their hurry;
and, away went a couple of the hardest listeners;
one, who had been listening a good hour — with
his whole weight across a rickety light stand,
whereon, if he had not been so deeply engaged,
he would'nt have trusted his leg, for a nap;
with one, who had been listening, the whole time,

through his nose, like a bag-pipe; away they
went—" all of a heap — a power o' legs an'
arms; — right into a fur corner o' the room —
sleek enough — I guess !"

> " Come all ye brave Figinnyans,
>   I'd have ye for to know,"—

cried the stranger; singing a favourite ballad of
the day, in a voice like a whirlwind ;—

> " That for to fight the inne——my,
>   I'm goin' for to go !"

" Law, corporal ! if that aint *you* ! — *Well,*
as I'm alive ! I reckon !—a trainer too, or *I'm*
darned ! where's Walter? corp'ral, corp'ral,
where *is* Walter ?"

" Taters and codfish !"

We shall now give two or three short, faithful specimens of the language, or dialect, of this
people; as it is heard even to this hour, in the
country parts of New England. We can easily
do it. A page or two would contain all their peculiarities— not only of words, but phrases; most

of which, by the way, can be traced, with little
or no variation, to their English ancestry, whose
other children still speak the same language:
while of this proportion, about nineteen twen-
tieths are now, or have been the provincialisms
of a single county in Great Britain—the county,
or kingdom rather, of Kent. Nothing denotes
the precise origin of a people, so unequivocally,
as the peculiarities of a common language.
They are so many ear marks.   Keep in mind,
however, that, when a fellow talks Yankee,
it is always through the nose, with a sort of
swing to his voice; a drawl — a tune — a regular intonation, that changes every two or three
minutes.   But, above all, keep in mind, we pray,
that such passages are never to be read aloud,
unless by a capital reader.   Like the incoherent,
broken language of deep tragedy; that of broad
farce; or that of superb and powerful poetry —
though it may bear to be read in a whisper,
the talk of a real Yankee, will never bear to be
read out, by a common reader.   The men of New
England speak the very language of their fathers;
in the very tone of their fathers; placing the

emphasis, oddly enough, sometimes; where nobody else would ever think of placing it; as we
shall indicate, by putting a few of the words, on
which they lay the stress, in italicks.

" Taters *and* cod fish!—rattle sneks *and*
ring'ums! *what* a hubbub!" continued the stranger; taking off a large bear skin cap; wiping the
paint away, from one side of his face; and bursting out, into a long, loud, noisy laugh; " *What* a
hubbub *here* is! ye was'nt skeered, nor nothin',
was ye, tho'?"

" Scared!—we!"—" To be sure"—" What
could possess you tho', neighbour 'Lijah, *for*
to come over here, *in* that 'ere tarnal?"——

Out broke a dozen voices—" O, Walter!
Walter! are you come at last? where *is* he?
where's the injunn? what's become o' *him?*
What luck a' gunnin? any bears? any beaver?
any wood-chuck? *Be* the niggers railly up, or
no? rather ryled, I guess, in Carrylynee?—Dod
burn *his* hide!—what's *he* laughin' at?—*why* don't
he speak up?"

" *One* at a time; one at a time, if ye last the
longer! hul-*low!* marsy *on* us, *what* a gabble!

flock o' wile geese—*in* a harrycane.   *What* a clatter, *to* be sure !"—" Where's Watty ?"—" Close by;"—changing his whole manner—"Bald Eagle's runnin' for his life; and Watty's in the woods yet, I ruther guess."

" *Why?* you *don't* say so ! not *in* the woods !"

" Guess he *is,* tho'; *be* here soon—see'd him jess now, comin' over the smoky mountain there —sun about an hour high."

" Gracious God !" cried the preacher ; "what is the meaning of all this ?— out with it—peace, children, peace ! who is that crying there ? what has happened ?"

"Why; darn it all, parson Harwood, can't ye let a feller get his breath.—Hole still, Jotty, boy; can't ye hole still ? Ony lass Sabba'day"—glancing at Peters, who sat, with a portentous frown over his brow," ony lass Sabba'day, 'at ever was, *me* and Bald Eagle—what a feller *he* is ! and Watty, boy, what dooze they do; but, *in* they goes, both on 'em, by gosh ! *plump*—into a snarl o' Mohawks campin' out; *in* they goes ! *feered* o' nothin', them are fellers — *not* they ; by'm by—told 'em so, long aforehand: you know, Watty's way; no *whoa* to *him,* I guess : what dooze *they* do? but

Watty, he knocks up a wrastlin' among 'em;
Watty's nation sleek, at arm's length, you know,
parson Harwood. Well—and so, I sees what's
a-comin', I do; and Watty, he throws 'em all,
one arter tother—same as nothin'; which Bald
Eagle, he dooze jess the same. So that *mads*
'em; and I clears out.—*Bym* by; *naiteral* enough;
there they go! *all* a qurrellin'. A word and a
blow with Watty, boy; chock full o' fight, I
guess; proper chap too, in a tussle; seen him
afore *to-day*, I guess; haint *you*, Mister? turrible
sharp feller, as ever *you* seed; as *big* as you be;
don't care for *you;* dozen more jess *like* you—with
all your stuffy looks."

" No more of that," said the preacher; " no
more of that, if you please; tell us what has
happened."

" Well, and so; Watty, boy, *he* knocks 'em
about; *fust* one side, then tother; faster 'n sixteen
more'll pick 'em up. So, one o' the tribe; he *outs*
with a knife; and he *ins* with it, into Bald Eagle,
chock up to the hilt; slick enough!"

" The old one!—he didn't, though?"

" Guess he did, though; but our Watty—he
walks into one o' the rest, *I guess*, about right. Then

for it ! *away* they go ! *off* like a shot. *Bald* Eagle ; *he* runs *like a deer ;* an' Watty—*he* takes right into the woods ; an' then back again ; which, when I seed him next, he had his face painted—and so I paints mine. " Oh, my !" — " *nation* !" — " yah ! how they pulled foot, when they seed us commin'. Most off the handle, some o' the tribe, I guess."

" God forbid !" exclaimed the preacher, " we shall have the Mohawks upon us !"

" What a 'tarnal shot he *is,* tho' ; that 'ere Watty—*hits* where he likes, *when* he's *arter* squrrls ; picks 'em off, like a daisey ; seen him pop 'em off many a time ; that's what I have — with ony *one* leetle buck shot — when he could only see the tip eend of a nose ; *right out* of a clever white oak-tree ; jess like nothin' at all too ; allays hits 'em in the eye ; heered the nooze ?"

" What news ?"

"Niggers up in Viginny !" —"No !"— "Yes ;" — "Ah !"—"Injunns out, all over the wood ; whew ! tories risin,' all in a buzz ; pocket full o' bumble bees. We'll have a tussle soon ; or I miss *my* guess."

" Well ; if ever I heern tell o' sich a feller," cried Miriam, who had caught his eye.— " Haw,

haw, haw !" added Master Jotham; " he's ony
pokin' fun at us, all the time, I know!" — "Scoundrel !" said Peters, growing pale, as he spoke;
and grinding his teeth. " Scoundrel ! how dare
you come here with such a pack of lies, to fright
our —"

" *Find* out, by *your* larnin', squire; never seed
a wood chuck in a toad-hole, I guess? I know
you; don't care for *you;* land o' liberty; walk *into*
you, any time, for half a sheet o' gingerbread.
Out with you, Jotty ! out with you ! come along,
I say ; What are ye arter there, squattin' so ; jess
like a cub in a bear trap? Well, well; how
goes it, Maryam? how do *you* carry *yourself,*
now ?"

" Why; none the better for you."—" There
— take that" — giving her a smack. — " Ye great
beast !" — " Hope you're the same."

The preacher — accustomed as he had been to
these frolicks of the farmer — hardly knew how
to forgive him, for throwing his whole house into
such a flutter. " I hope," said he; after a little
consideration; " I hope that you have not, as Mr.
Peters very properly said—ahem !—that is, I hope,

sir, a—a—you have not been telling us a pack of
—a—a—*lies.*"

" There it *is,* now ! twould'nt be you, if twa'nt !
pretty feller *you,* for a parson ! you'd like to have
'em *true;* would ye?—Niggers up; Mohawks out;
a feller stabbed, and Watty boy runnin' for his
life ! *tor*-ment us all !"

"But, something,"—the preacher could hardly
keep his countenance — " you seem to forget who
I am, sir," said he ; " something *has* happened.
Your clothes are torn, — dreadfully torn; your —
surely, (lifting his frock), surely there *has* been
a desperate struggle.   Here is blood — fresh
blood. — Elijah ! you are not wounded, I hope ?"

" *That's* what I be, tho'; tight squeezin', for
all that.   Skin o' *my* teeth, *I guess,* If't hadn't
been for Watty, boy ; you'd never a' seed my
face agin ; look o' there, now ! (showing a bullet
hole in the flap of his jacket ; and one side of his
leather " over alls" torn badly ; as if by the claws
of a wild beast) look o' there, now !"

" Lord ! Lord !"—" Possible !"— " How you
do talk !" — " I say ! You, corporal ! I say !
twar'nt a cattermount tho', was it ?"

" No, nothin' but a bear; a pooty clever one
too — I guess." — " Nothing but a *bar!*" said
Edith; gasping for breath. " Here Jotty! here's
the paw, ye sleepy houn' — there!" — throwing one of the bear's great fore-paws at him —
"*there!* that'll keep him awake, I ruther guess;
what say *you*, squire ?" Peters made no reply. " If
it sarves *him*, as it did *me*, twill keep'im awake,
I know; that's the very fore-paw, he tickled *my*
trouzes with; so, I chops it off. There it is, agin!
there ye go! can't hold still a minnit" — seizing
a large brown mug of cider; and emptying it, with
a single draught — " gi' me you yet, parson; *you*
know."

" Finish your story, I beg of you."

" Right away?" — " To be sure." — " So I
will; and so, arter that, says I, speakin' to Watty;
Watty, says I, Watty boy, he was a good ways
off then; makin' up to me, through the durned
bushes, Watty! says I, I've gut 'im!"—
" Ah!" — " Yes; that's what I did! Watty,
boy, says I, jess so; Watty boy! I've gut him."
" Railly !" — " Why, how you talk!" — " And
Watty, jess then, he was jest about where them

'ere gals be now" — throwing his cap into their
faces; — " and I, I was pooty near about where I
be, now. Here was the bear, as a body may say;
jest *here;*" — putting his hand, as if by accident —
without any appearance of design or drollery —
upon Peters, who pushed him off—rose up; and,
fixing his eyes upon the farmer, told him, in a
low voice, that, if ever he did any thing of the sort
again, he would give him a lesson, that he should
remember to his dying day.

" Somethin' I can't eat," said Winslow, with
a good-natured laugh. " Well; and so, says I, to
Watty, says I; fire away, says I. Wait a minnet,
says he; and I'll be there, says he; and smash his
head for him, says he. Don't you lose another
minnit, says I; fire away as quick as wink; if
you don't I'm darned, says I. We were jess then
at a dead clinch, both on us."—" Ah !"—" To
sure; sort o' close hug."

" Who — Walter and you ?"

" No; bear an' me. Stuffy feller that, as ever
you see'd; big as all out o' doors; we'd cotch
hold o' one o' t'other, kind o' unawars; while I
was a little a-head, scrabblin' over some rotten

logs; an' Watty, boy, a long ways off. I've gut
him, says I; fire away: I'm a-feered, says he.
Fire away, says I; I shall hit you, says he. Fire
away, says I, where you be, says I; never you
mind me, says I: I daz'nt, says he. If *you* don't,
says I, I'm up a tree, says I; jess so, says I;
that's all, says I; and if you aint spry about it
too, I shall have. to let him go."

  ." Let him go !"

  " To be sure.   I'd gut him jest here, by the
wayzban' of his breeches."

  " But how had he got *you ?*"

  " How should I know ? I was tryin' to strangle
him, a few; and he was tryin' to squat me. Fire
away, Watty, says I, darn *your* hide; I shall
not, says he. I'll do as much for you, says I;
I hope not, says he; with all my heart, says I;
I'll see you darned fust, says he."

  " Zounds !" cried Peters; losing all patience;
" will the blockhead never make an end of this !"

  " *To* be sure ! All the time, *there* was Watty,
makin' his way, *through* the bushes, *half* leg deep;
thrashin' about; an' *tumblin'* over the logs, *like* fun
—well, arter that; now for it, says he; by 'm by —

now, *for* it; stand out o' the way. I can't, says *I,*
—Move a little, says *he.* *I* can't, says I—I can't
see nothin' at all o' *his* eyes,—what's that 'ere
bobbin' about afore 'em, now? says he. That's
my head, says I; fire away."—"Well, *if* ever!"—
" Great sulky beast he was, too; would'nt wrastle
fair."—"How so?"—"How so! begins to bite
and gouge; an' trip an' scratch, afore I was half
ready—if that's what you call fair—did his best, I
tell you—would a' turned my trowzes inside out,
if he could, I know."—" The great nasty crittur!"—" Yes; an' every time *he* slipped; why,
burn *your* hide, if *his* great — *cold* nose — didn't
go — lollopin' over — *my* neck —jess like a dead
fish."

" Will you never finish?"

" Hole on your grip! says Watty, says he;
bawlin' so, you might 'a heered him a mile. Hole
on your grip, says *he.* *I* can't, says *I.* I'm gettin'
tired, says *I; my* hands are poottily fixed; cramped
like any *thing,* I guess; *and* slobbered all over.
So, says he, hold still! says *he.* I can't, says *I:*
jess let *me* get a good *aim,* says he. If I *can,* I'm
darned, says I. Why don't you kick his shins;

and make him lay down? says he.   I have, says
I; over and over agin, says I: but he wun't lay
down.   He's *too* plaguy stuffy for that, says I.—
In făct—*I* thoŭght—*mў* tĭme—*hād* cŏme—sŭre
enŏugh—I guĕss."——We preserve the last
line, as a gem of pure Yankee; and, as a sort of
key to the language, have marked the quantity.

"Why didn't ye trip him up? the great ugly
tejuss crittur," said Jotham, who had grown
very attentive in the progress of the story.

"Trip a bear up! trip a cat up, more like!
May be you'd like to try.   Take a fool's advice,
Jotty; and when ye git sich a kind o' cattle on
their backs, look out for your innards, that's all;
if you aint plaguy sharp."

"Well, well; *did* he fire?"

"Did he fire! *to* be sure.   Fire away, says I,
and I'll hole still."—"Ah!"—"Yes."—"Well; and
so Watty, he lets drive, while the crittur's lickin'
my mouth —whizz! twent by my head, *like* fun;
through it, I thought, fust: an' so, *up* he comes,
and whacks away *at* him, while I hold on by his
two fore paws, — there's one for Jotty; here's
tother for you, (throwing one toward Edith,) and

so—and so—and so you've got both eends o' the story, now.   How do *you* like it, Mister a— a—what's your name?"

"Another of your lies, I dare say," said Peters. "Abraham Harwood; are you not ashamed of yourself, to permit such an abominable outrage upon our better feelings, before your face, in your own house?   Come out of that corner, Edith; what business have you there? Have you no more command of yourself, than to cry and skulk, at the bidding of such a blockhead : come out, and put him—and your uncle—and me—and all of us, to shame !"

CHAPTER V.

CUNNING. — SIMPLICITY. — THE CHURCH. —
GRAVE-YARD. — A MURDER. — SUPERSTITION.
— HABITS. — APPROACH OF REBELLION. —
CHARACTERS. — IDIOM. — SUNSET.

" Corporal Winslow;" otherwise called
"neighbour Winslow"— the particular and especial abomination of Peters, next after the
" squeaking poet," already spoken of — was a
giant; a giant, even among the people of New
England, whose children, the " western countrymen" of North America; the frontier settlers—
are, probably, the largest and most powerful race
of men upon our earth. He stood six feet four,
bare-footed; was built every way in proportion;
was very good humoured; rather comical, in his
own way; and played with men, as men play with
children. He was not " over spry," (active);
but nobody " thereabouts" could match him at
a " dead lift;" so that he was a sort of champion

at all the raisings, trainings, and huskings of the neighbourhood; and, of course, at all the country taverns; the chosen places, everywhere, for the trial of championship.

" You were angry, the other night; I am sure of it," said the preacher to Peters; alluding to the occurrences, which were detailed in our last chapter; " you would not have staid away so long, else."

" You are right. I was angry; I am yet. Your little parlour is no longer what it was—a place of comfort."

" I am sorry for it; have you seen Walter?"

" Yes."

" You find, of course, then, that Bald Eagle and he really did have a scuffle; and, what is more, that, on their way through the woods, they did encounter a bear, which they slew."

" Winslow is a liar. Were it not for Walter, I would not believe one word of the story; and as for you, I am ashamed of you. Why do you encourage these things? Why do you permit such behaviour? It is'nt a month since he threw your household, yourself, and all your family, in-

I 3

to consternation, by one of these frolicks : — eternally romping with your women, too, before
your face. For my own part; when I think of
your huskings and quiltings ; your musterings and
your meetings, I wonder that you have a decent
woman left among you. The very " bundling"
of the Dutch settlers; that mischievous, wicked
habit, which is now spreading through the frontier settlements ; even *that* is hardly worse. You
are a minister of the Gospel. It behoves you to
look well to these things. They are at your door.
What will you say for yourself, when you are
charged with having encouraged falsehood, licen-
tiousness, or what is worse, a —— Upon my
word ! you appear to take all this in very good
part; have you no veneration for truth ?"—fixing his eyes on the preacher, with a sharp, severe
look.

" Forgive me. I cannot help smiling to see
you so carried away by prejudice. About six
months ago, if you recollect, you called neighbour Winslow, to his face, a foolish blockhead."

" Well."

" You believed him a blockhead ?"

" Yes."

" You were mistaken. Blockhead or not, he has been making a fool of you, ever since."

" You are imitating *me*."

" Well ?"

" Well, sir — you overdo the matter. But Winslow — let me know the truth of him. Is he, or is he not, a blockhead ?"

" By no manner of means." — " Pho; talk English, will you !" — " By no means; that'll do, I hope." — " Yes; proceed."

"· Well ; he is far from being a fool. He is, in fact, a very shrewd fellow; with a plenty of mother wit; as you would have perceived, but for your prejudice."

" You appear to believe what you say."

" Believe it; I know it. I have permitted him to carry on the joke, a little too long, perhaps; and a little too far, sometimes : But you gave the provocation." — " Yes :" — " You have deserved it." — " Yes." — " And I have been willing to see how far, such a man as you, could be imposed upon, by one whom you have thought a natural fool."

ɪ 4

" I never thought him a natural fool ; never."

" Well, well; a blockhead."

" Why not say so, then ?"

" All the same."

" All the same — is it ! — Then, why not say so ? why change the words ? — All the same — are they ! — Are truth and falsehood all the same ?   Look you,   Abraham Harwood;   I don't half like these variations.   They are a bad sign."

" Besides," continued our preacher, smiling; " besides ; I have been expecting you to discover the truth, for yourself. Your knowledge of the human heart is quite wonderful.   I have known you read off the character of a man, at a look, as if it were actually written out, upon his forehead."

" It *is* — in almost every case — fairly written out upon his forehead; — why do you turn away your eyes ?"

" In short, I have been willing to see, if such a man as you, could be played upon, so grossly; week after week ; without learning the truth ; by a —— you are not angry, I hope ?"

" No; and if I was, I wouldn't own it.   You

have been permitting this brutal familiarity, therefore, on my account?"

" Yes."

" I don't believe it. He has imposed upon you, twice, to my knowledge. *He* may play tricks with me; but you cannot — shall not. I have had no reason to watch him; no motive; nothing, at risk. If I had, I would have known his length, and breadth — as I knew yours — in a single hour."

" Jonathan Peters."

" Abraham Harwood."

" Your deportment is altered of late."

" I know it — I —— but no matter. I have no time for explanation. Do me one favour — say nothing to Winslow; nothing, to any body else, of this matter. Give me an opportunity of watching him. I should like to understand how I have been played upon. The character of man — whatever it may be — wherever it may be found — is my favourite study. This fellow may have something in him, that we shall turn to account, by and by."

" How — I don't exactly comprehend you."

"Of course.   I have tried, over and over again, to awe him; as I do others — everybody; but I have never been able.   Do what I might, he never appeared sensible of my superiority, in any way; at any time; for a single moment.   His rough, coarse freedom; his rude, simple ways — have never altered, for a moment.   Perhaps I have been a little mistaken.   If so, sir — although I have never given the matter a moment's consideration before; never thought of him, except while he was here — if so, he must be above the rabble about him."

"He is a likely fellow, you may depend."

"Pshaw.   It is a common trick of my countrymen — I know that, very well; — a very common trick, when they have any object in view — to overreach other people, by their simplicity.   I have seen it, many a time; but never any thing of the sort, equal to this."

"You will see him change it, every hour. Sometimes, you would really take him for an idiot."

"No — never."

"He will be here, I ruther guess." — " Rather." — "·I rather guess, to-night, sir; wun't you stay?" — " Won't I, you mean." — " Well —won't you ?"

" No."

" Had'nt you better."

" No. Some other time, I may — or —— yes; I will. If he should come, I will. It is a kind of humour, that I like. It enables one to put almost any question; do almost any thing, without risk; and, in some cases, to set all wisdom and authority, at open defiance. In a time of trouble and warfare, it might be turned, I am sure, to good account."

" I observe, my dear friend — Ah ! the clock — I must be gone — will you go with us ?"

" I don't care, if I do."

" I observe, my dear friend — excuse me — but, I observe a continual reference, of late; in all that you say, or do; to a season of trouble and warfare."

" In *all* that I say, or do.   Pshaw !"

" Well, well — I never saw any body so scrupulous, in all my life," said the preacher; lugging out a prodigious watch — of silver — with a brass dial; — and flourishing about with it, somewhat ostentatiously.

" Then, you have never seen a truly honest man, sir, in all your life. Put up your watch."

It was a delightful day — " Sabbath ;" or, more properly, one of the Lord's days. Owing to the distance, at which a great part of his congregation lived, from their place of worship, the preacher was in the habit of giving them only one sermon a day. To make up for that, however; he began early, and left off late, in the long warm days of summer; allowing a short intermission for those — who came a great way, and had no friends in the neighbourhood, of whom they could get a dinner — to take their lunch, under the old apple trees, in the grave-yard.

The " church," as he called it, repeatedly, on their way — to the great annoyance of his companion, was a homely piece of architecture; painted red; with white window frames; black roof; and large doors, of a brimstone colour. It was a school-house, on six days of the week; and a meeting-house, on the seventh. It was an academy also; a court house; and, after a time, a sort of

town hall, where the transactions of the British
Parliament were ponderously reviewed: so that,
besides the alphabet, and multiplication table;
the sciences of law and government; politicks
and theology, were taught there.

" How ridiculous !" cried Peters, looking
toward a crowd, in the grave-yard.

" But how strongly it shews their veneration
for the house of prayer."

" No such thing, Abraham Harwood; and you
know it. But you are one of those, who never
call things, by their right names. The more I
see of you, the more am I convinced, of this.
The people come into their Lord's house, rigged
out in all their dirt and finery; not because of
their veneration for him, or it, as *you* know; but
because of their miserable vanity. How much
more becoming were clean, bare feet, in such a
place, before Him, who is no respecter of persons
— the Everlasting? how much more, than beautiful raiment, over that which is unclean ?"

" True, brother Peters—true; the whited
sepulchre."—

" For shame. Why play the hypocrite with

me? Why change your voice? Why hail me as your brother, when you are going up to the house of the Lord? Is it because your people are nigh?"

The preacher groaned.

" Yes — yes — tell them of it. You will never have a better time, — brother Harwood. Speak to them — tell them that the ground, whereon they tread, is holy; command them to put off their shoes."

"Yes — yes —" thought Mr. Harwood. " Yes; there can be no doubt of it, now; none at all. He is, — he must be — one of the ' more righteous' than other men. He has the gift, indeed — if man ever had."

They were going by the grave-yard; — a barren, bleak, and savage-looking place; dreary, as death. It had been, at one time — not many years before — a place of remarkable beauty; full of large apple trees, known all over that part of the world, for the size and flavour of their fruit. It had been, a nursery: it was now, a burial-ground; — a place of common sepulture. It had been, rich and fertile; — green, to a proverb; it was now

quite overgrown with patches of juniper — ground
hemlock — mullein — thistle — and sweet briar.
It had been a smooth, wide level: it was, now,
broken up into graves; their wooden tablets moul-
dering away on the damp earth; or half buried,
in the harsh, wild grass. Of the great orchard,
and heavy stone wall, which had been, there was
nothing left, but a few miserable trees, blackened
with fire; spoiled of their branches; and stripped
of their bark; as if they had been blasted from
above; — with a loose, irregular hedge, of black-
berry-bushes, and briar, which had come up, of
themselves, among the stones of the old enclosure,
after it had been utterly overthrown.

The cause of the desolation was this. The
manslayer had been there: blood had been shed,
unlawfully, upon that land, in the time of its fruit-
fulness. A murder; the only one, that had been
heard of, among this primitive people, for more
than twenty years — was perpetrated, under circumstances of thrilling peculiarity, in this very
orchard. It was done, without noise, or outcry,
upon a youthful stranger; — by one, who had
never been found out — in the summer-time —

day, in the woods; and heard, every night in the
sky,—no man would have eaten thereof, in all
that part of the world.

It *was* frightful, though, to see this green branch
flowering forth, suddenly, in the desolation of the
place—flourishing, as if the murderer was near;
the common weeds underneath it blossoming up,
in their savage luxuriance; the herbage of death
breaking out, all at once, with a bright, unnatural, fierce bloom.

While this had been, there were few able to go
by the place, unmoved; and long—long after it
was over, when the war broke out; many a serious
man spoke of it, as one of the numberless prodi-
gies, which, when they happened, had been gazed
upon, by the believers, on every side, as the fore-
runners of that war.

Peters and our preacher were passing this place,
when the observations were made, which led us
away for a moment. Under the trees; and upon
every grave, within reach of a little quiet brook,
that ran through the middle of the inclosure;
shining like silver, through the coarse, long, rich
grass — were a number of young women; their

bonnets off; their faces flushed; and hair loose; wiping their feet, on the turf; washing them, in the little stream; or pulling on their shoes and stockings, to wear *in* church;—those, which they had carried in their hands, perhaps, half a dozen miles, that very morning, while on their way *to* church; — walking barefooted, over bush, and through briar, every inch of the road. It was this; the sight of their large, flashy buckles; ribbons; leather shoes; and white " boughten" stockings, put on, at such a time; not for comfort, or decency—but for show — this, which provoked Peters to speak of these young women, as he did.

On the approach of their minister, the people became still, and serious; left off talking; and poured into the meeting-house, with looks of habitual veneration, for the time, and place. The preacher went up, into his high seat; — for it was nothing more; and Peters, into a far corner, which commanded a view of the grave, wherein the preacher's beautiful wife lay — a place, about which, he—Peters — had been met, over and over again, early and late, since he had been among them. The service began. A more than usual

spirit of unction was upon the preacher; a more
than usual solemnity, in the congregation. Suddenly, they heard a sound of horses' hoofs, clatter-
ing over the stones of the grave-yard — a shadow
went by the windows; — and, before they could
recover themselves, a man rode up to the door,
on horseback — the animal hot and smoking —
called out, with a loud voice; threw in a folded
paper; and set off, again, at full speed.

   Peters, who was at prayer, when the horseman
dashed by the window, uncovered his face;
turned pale as death, when he heard the voice;
and stepped hastily forward, as if to secure the
paper. But he was prevented by " our deacon"
Pepperell, who, notwithstanding the alarm and
agitation which followed, went, leisurely, from
his place, a step or two, without hurrying himself
at all; or even removing the hat from before his
eyes — it was in prayer time; and set his foot
upon the paper—accidentally. Peters appeared,
for a single moment, as if undetermined whether
to knock him down, or not; but, after a short
struggle; and a very hard one; he drew up; set

his teeth; folded his arms; and stood, as if awaiting the issue.

The preacher, by way of shewing how superiour he was to the carnal influences, at such a time, was rather more "lengthy," perhaps, than usual. The sermon was delivered, with a more wearying deliberation; more emphatick pauses, and more of every thing, that was insupportable.   The hymns were longer, than usual — the prayers— the very benediction.   But all the time, *there* stood " our deacon ;" quiet and motionless, even to the last— maintaining his erect, strong position; formal aspect; and look of especial godliness, until the very echo of the preacher's voice—the last reverberation of his protracted blessing—had actually died away; the people had risen to go out; and were only hesitating, until the severe decorum, and grave, cold sanctity, of " our deacon," should permit him to see the paper under his feet.

Peters drew back; and, after a prefatory groan, the deacon recollected himself, as it were; shuffled with his feet; appeared a little surprised; picked up the paper; ran it over, without any visible emotion; — Peters watching him the while, with

K 3

intense anxiety — and gave it up to the preacher,
whose hands, while *he* read it, shook : — The people were breathless. His countenance fell :—They
saw it; and were afraid.

It was a printed circular, from the " Brother-
hood of Safety;" informing all the ministers of
the land, after a short preamble, that a petition
from the colonies — " their last petition" — had
been treated, " at home," with contempt and laugh-
ter; that preparations were on foot, by them, who
made war for the majesty of Great Britain, to
waste all the rebellious colonies, with fire and
sword; that a season of trial was near; that
something decisive was likely to take place, before
long, in the province of Massachusetts' Bay — the
chief port of which, Boston, had been put under
the ban of the empire.

The preacher read it aloud. Then, calling upon
all the people to accompany him, he went, once
more, down upon his knees; and broke out, into
fervent prayer, to the Ruler of the universe; be-
seeching Him to have compassion upon the
afflicted of all the earth —

It grew dark, while he was praying; an evil

omen; though it was in the summer; — yea,
thundered and lightened, while he was upon his
knees; another prodigy, of the time, which has
not been forgotten.

— To restore the nations thereof, to a right understanding, one with another; to put away all
thought of rebellion from the hearts of men; but,
more especially, to bring about a speedy recon-
ciliation between the people of Great Britain; or
the king thereof; or the parliament; or the mi-
nistry thereof; and the people of America.

Not a murmur of disapprobation was heard —
not one. It was the sincere prayer, not only of
the minister; but of the congregation; aye, not
only of them, but of all the people — of all the
colonies. Nobody was prepared for independ-
ence. Nobody had come to think of it; however
wild, or ambitious he was; or, however foolish —
as an event either likely to happen, or proper, to
be desired.

" It may be well," said ' our deacon;' as he was
putting his foot over the threshold of the door —
" it may be well," said he; without lifting his eyes,
or looking to the right or left; and speaking, as

if he could not have any concern, with any sort
of worldly business, on the Lord's day, until the
sun had set — " it may be well for them, whose
consciences are not *so* tender, I opinion, to no-
tify such, as they may see their way clear so to do,—
of a ' town meetin'; to be held, here;—the Lord
willin'; say — to-morrow arternoon, if you like;
between the hours of three and six." .

That was enough. The people, having got
outside of the meeting-house,—within which, no
one of them would have shown a sign of recognition, to the dearest friend of his heart, under
any circumstances whatever, — shook hands with
one another all round, as if they were indeed
members of the same household; come together,
after a long separation — making the usual inquiries, and showing all their new clothes — took
horse; and rode off in every possible direction, to
alarm the country; their way being clear before
them; their consciences not " over tender"— like
" our deacon's."

" Another specimen of your sneaking, hypocritical temper, here," said Peters, to the preacher,
after they had returned. In all that congrega-

tion, there was not a man, but myself, with courage or honesty enough, to give publick notice; . fairly and openly. What! are works of necessity, and of mercy, alike unlawful, in Connecticut, on the Lord's day! as if the ' Sabbath;' a sweet and solemn festival, from the first, were only a day of suffering and misery; a day set apart, for lying, with a sterner aspect, in the Lord's house."

" You mean our deacon," said the preacher; waking out of a trance-like revery. " Pray, sir; were you not greatly disturbed, by the circumstance, which took place, at meeting? It appeared — I beg your pardon, sir — I — I — ahem!"—

" Out with it, Abraham Harwood! out with it. How came you to see me? Were you only pretending to be at prayer, with your face covered? Out with it, like a man! I never take a hint; I never give one."

The preacher was going to reply, with some sharpness, when Miriam, hearing the tread of many feet, arose, and threw open the broad folding doors of the porch, just in time to prevent a party of Mr. Harwood's people, from catching him in the fact — a serious one, to be sure; that of being wroth, on the Lord's day — before the sun had fairly set.

They entered, one after the other, in due form; declaring, with a bow, or a bob, that " nobody needn't plague themselves; for they'd no 'casion for a cheer, as they know'd on; hadn't come over to tarry, more 'an a minnit, or so; and—" making their manners, once more — " and, whether or no, they sot down, or not, Mr. Parson Harwood — you see — they hadn't come sich a *tor*-mented long piece, but what, if the door wan't shot arter 'em, they could push on, a pooty, tedious, clever bit furder, cross lots—they could — sich a han'-sum night, as 'twas:"—each one taking a seat, nevertheless, while he spoke; and plumping himself into it, all of a sudden, as if he were shot through the head: all the women, as usual, in this " land of steady habits," getting as close to the wall, as they could; sitting bolt upright, in their high-backed, perpendicular chairs; and wearing unspeakably prim faces; their hands crossed in their laps; their feet cuddled up,

under their petticoats—or put.aside ; save, in one
or two cases, where their new brass buckles, or
" boughten" finery, would bear the candle-light ;
—and all the men, of course, away from the wall,
as far as they could get, without falling — heads
back—feet forward —balancing out, on three legs.

The summer wind blew into the house, with a
delicious coolness. The flame of the pitch-wood,
which had been lighted, as usual, and set in the
deep fire-place, during the darkness of the shower;
now that it had gone over, and all the doors were
open, began to fade away, before the beautiful,
strong light of the western sky, which came
slowly into the room ; taking, and holding possession of it — like a spirit — as if it were something that would not ; and could not be shut out.

A part of the preacher's house was very old
and " awful," for that portion of the world ; having withstood, for nearly fourscore years, the
revolution of empires, and of seasons. The older
part of the pile ; that, which the cattle now occupied, was built of solid square timber ; and had
been a " block-house;" or fort,—in the early Indian
wars, of that colony. The whole was overshadow-

ed by great, overgrown trees; a part of the ancient
wilderness of the country;—and, of course, a part
of the red man's original inheritance, of which
the white men had been spoiling him, generation
after generation.

A dead silence followed, soon after this abrupt,
and superb disclosure of the skies. The sun was
going down, with great splendour, even for the
new world — North America — where a sunset is
frequently one of the most glorious and wonderful exhibitions of God ; leaving the whole atmosphere of a luminous purple ; the tree-tops, of a
changeable crimson ; the skies, coloured up to
the zenith ; and all the waters flashing below.

Every voice died away—even that, of the angry
preacher, who had half risen from his chair, in
the hurry and heat of his reply; yea, even that
of Jonathan Peters, who was not a man to be
awed, easily—into a solemn, profound, affecting
stillness.

It grew darker, abroad; bluer — and colder.
The silence became yet more holy. The shadow of a prodigious tree, that stood by the porch,
and overhung the door-way, like a huge canopy—

shedding, even at noon-day, a sort of twilight into the little parlour; and covering the white sanded floor, with a continual quiver, and sparkle; a shadow, like that upon the green earth, when a shower is coming up, on a hot afternoon — slowly entered; and filled every part of the house, with a quiet, religious dimness; and overcast all the youthful and stern faces there, with a temporary cloud, until they were all afraid, or unable to speak, for the awe that was upon them.

They were perfectly still — perfectly — their very breathing, for a time, was like that of little children — asleep, in their untroubled innocence. The strong, fierce yellow, and crimson light, which, a few minutes before, the pine torches, in the fire-place, had sent up, in broad, angry gushes, through the turbulent vapour, had now died away, into a pale, faint, bluish mist; hardly visible through the heavy smoke, which rolled with it, up the large chimney. The tree branches, that overshadowed all the door-way, were motion-less, in the quiet, solemn splendour of the hour: the wet leaves, where the hot, yellow, sunshine came through them, were like amber; the warm, fine rain sparkling over the old, rich, mossy-bark, as if the whole tree were encrusted with molten jewellery; and lighted up, from within. A bright momentary delusion followed — strange and beautiful as the operations of sorcery. The room opened, as it were—the whole house, to the light of the western sky; and where the sunshine fell upon the solid walls, they appeared, like the sunshine, itself, to tremble.

By and by, however, this quiet became insupportable to our boisterous young country creatures: a timid cough or two was heard; with a little accidental shuffling of the feet, which the minister took in good part — as a hint for him to break up the sitting.

Winslow and four of his brothers were there; each, with a flaming calico waistcoat on, gorgeous with many colours; and each, with his chair tilted back; both hands in his trowsers; and one leg over the other.

"Nation sleepy—tarnal sleepy —" said neighbour Winslow, addressing himself, with a chuckle, to Peters, who sat, as if he heard nothing of the remark, or noise; and saw nothing, but a por-

tion of the far sky. " Tarnal sleepy, there; all
on 'em—ever seed a snarl o' black sneks thawin'
out—in sugar time—under a pooty smart rock
heap? winkin' away; winkin' away, jess like so
many milk adders, at a frog pond"—laughing.

" Milk adders at a frog pond!—cow's teat,
more like, our 'Lijah."

" Shet your clam, our David. You never seed
a mess o' young cubs, arter a-hard frost;—e'en
jest a gwyin'—like so many tejus great Niggers, with *all* their noses byled"—another laugh.
" *That's* in to ye, our David! I guess; aint it?"

" Whisht! whisht!" whispered one of the girls
—" whisht, our 'Ijah: he's a lookin' this
way."

" *Hul*-low!—who cares for him—I guess."

" There it is, agin! that are nation grand feller; he can't bear a joke, no more'n a—there
he goes, now! as naiteral, as *can* be; *tor*-ment *his*
hide! pooty con-sider'ble proud, he is, too."

Forth went Evans. The splendours of the
firmament had abated; come down, to a steady
flame colour, on one bright spot, where it was
impossible to look. It was like the mouth of a

furnace — fading off — cloud over cloud; slowly evolving, up to the very zenith, into gorgeous purple — deep crimson — pale, quiet apple green — rose, violet, and clear blue — clear, as that of the finest Italian sky.

" I don't like him — that air feller," said one of the girls, to her next neighbour; — " nor you, too, I guess ?" — " Ah, but I guess I do, tho'." — " He haint got no more heart — no, that's what he 'a'int," said one of the ' boys;' a strapping fellow named Isaac, who was whittling in the corner; — a favourite and serious occupation of the Yankees, who make all their bargains, with a penknife and shingle — " No more heart, as the Nigger said, than stick your head in the fire; and pull 'um out, agin."

" No heart !" — said Edith; flushed with anger — " No heart ! He's got a heart as big as the world — he has !" — " Well ! — if ever !" " No !"

" He's a likely sort o' man, tho', to my notion," added an elderly looking maiden. " Oh my !" answered her companion.

" Big as the world ! — Whew !" — said Isaac

— holding up the bit of pine wood, which he had been whittling — " whew ! — not bigger ; darn me, if'tis, than the leetle eend — o' nothin' — sharpened; as the Irishman said." — Another laugh.

Peters heard nothing of this. He was an altered man. He saw the sky; and had gone out, like one of the ancients, to meet it, with a lowliness of manner, wholly unlike any thing, that he had ever shown before the same people, during all the time that he had been among them. The preacher followed him with his eyes ; wondering at his forgetfulness of the farmer, about whom, he had been so anxious, but a little time before ; at the awful abstraction of his look ; and, above all, at the deep humility of his carriage. It was that of a broken-hearted man — a believer — bowing his head, with submission, to the last.

He walked out, patiently — meekly — into the midst of the greenness before them; and put away, reverentially, two or three of the great, heavy branches of the old, overgrown, motionless tree ; with all their encumbering weight of matted herbage, and creeping wild flowers, that shook and sparkled high up in the shadow; and stood very quietly there, for a long time, with his arms uplifted, pushing the verdure aside, and look-·ing into the great sky — the habitation of God — as into a sanctuary, of repose and brightness; more like a good man, going to be translated before their eyes, than like the cold-hearted, severe, intolerant being, whom they had seen, hitherto, scowling upon their innocent, rude hilarity, as if it were a crime.

"Upon my word! he is very tall—much taller, than I thought," said Mr Harwood.

But he was not a tall man; certainly not, —for that part of the world. He looked so, to be sure, when he stood forth, as now, above his natural stature; rearing himself up, on tip-toe, before the clear, bright sky; his long arms yet higher up; and his very palms extended, fervently, toward his Father's abiding place, as if he were one of them, who do their worship, midway between the skies and earth, assured and steadfast; without stay, or support, from either.

Let us leave him at his devotions.

CHAPTER VI.

COMMITTEE. — ARTICLES OF ASSOCIATION. — CHARACTERS. — COSTUME. — LANGUAGE. — TOWN MEETING. — ORATORS. — REBEL- LION — WHY —WHEREFORE.

THE town meeting was now at hand. Mr. Dea- con Pepperell's notice had run through the woods like wild fire; and a multitude were as- sembled, hours before the time, in front of the meeting-house. But, before we go in, or take our friends there, a word or two more of our farmer, whose behaviour, dress, and appearance, are well worth a little of our attention, before we throw him by. Such people are gone out of use, now, in America. The husbandman there, of late, is hardly to be distinguished from one of the town-rabble; either by his plain dealing, ho- nesty, or sobriety; or even by the quality and fashion of his clothes.

L 2

His " go-to-meetin' " coat, as they call that, in America, which a farmer wears, on training days, and Sabbath days, had been, some thirty-five years before it came into his possession, of a strong, bright, claret colour. It had been, moreover, the only coat, otherwise called, the best coat — of a militia captain; a shopkeeper; and a Puritan — the last of whom was Winslow's father. It was never worn, by either, but on particular days; and when, by reason of its age, the seams, collar, and elbows came to be alarmingly visible, a short quarantine through the family dye-pot, made all right, again, till a few more thanksgiving, Sabbath, and muster days; or an exposure to a hard rain, made another dip expedient. — A family dye-pot, we should mention, is a convenience, for ever in the way of those, who travel over New England, or the country parts thereof; the smell is insupportable to those who have not been brought up to it.

Fifty years ago, a coat of this kind; like the stone walls, which were then piled up, would have outlasted several generations of substantial American farmers. It is not so, now. It would have begun ; — the history of such a piece of cloth would be curious — it would have begun to see service, belike, in the shape of a loose, great coat, or double-breasted surtout ; and, after a series of transmigrations, would have still existed, no doubt, in the shape of pincushions, coverlets, or carpets ; having, meanwhile, gone through every species of coat—long and short—breeches, and waistcoat— double and single breasted, with and without flaps ; for men, youth, and boys. It is not so, now. The country people are quite as extravagant, fashionable, and foolish as they can be ; and who are more so ?

The corporal wore, beside, in all weathers, hot or cold — if it were a day, on which it was proper for him to spruce up — a heavy spotted swandown jacket, which had also been the property of one or two progenitors ; — under another, of chintz, flowered all over ; and a pair of nankeen pantaloons, rather tighter than his own skin — of a burning flesh colour ; which, altogether—being a good deal too tight, and a little too short for him—were quite an abomination to the maiden lady, spoken of, in our last; who; whenever she spoke to him, always turned away her head.

Yet — yet — corporal Winslow, awkward as he was, and stupid, as he appeared, in these absurd habiliments, on a warm sultry summer evening, after a shower, was one of the very men, who did the heavy business of the American Revolution.   Would it have been as well done, think you — you, his countrymen of this age; if he had been brought up, as you are, in ruffles and gloves, purple and fine linen?   After a little time, this very man was remarkable for his bold, free, military carriage :—so easy is it, for a *man* to be made any thing of; and of so little substantial disadvantage is that rude, awkward manner, which the country people are so anxious to throw off— to their destruction, always.

We have alluded once to the calico waistcoat, in which he appeared before the preacher.

" My stars !" cried Miriam, when she saw him in it, first ; " My stars ! — well, *if* ever !"—wiping her fat hands very carefully; approaching the showy " trade;" and venturing upon a part

-of the flap, as if it were leaf gold. — " Bran-fire noo, as I'm alive !"

The farmer shifted his posture; threw open his coat; and leaned away for her accommodation, with a look of perfect self-complacency.

" They'll have him up, afore the committee for that 'air ; if they don't — why ! — dod rot him, that's all !" said Jotham.

The farmer's countenance fell; and, sure enough, on the very next afternoon, Peters, while on the way to the place of meeting, was overtaken by our preacher, who informed him that Winslow was on trial, with several young farmers, for having appeared, with certain outlandish finery on the Lord's day ; contrary to the articles of association. " You had better follow me," continued Mr. Harwood; " and see to what account, he will turn his low humour, and simplicity, here. My word for it, sir, that he baffles them !"

They entered; and found Winslow under examination, with his waistcoat in his hand; before six evangelical, stern-looking men, at a table; or board.

"How came ye by it; ye vain young feller?" said one of them, just as Peters appeared.

"Had'nt ye better ax our Sammy fust? He's got one o' the same, I guess; aint ye, Sammy? —Hold up your head, Sammy—what are you afeer'd on?—hey!—aint ye, Sammy?"

"Why is it, corporal Winslow, that you never answer a question?"

"Darn it, Mr. Deacon Pepper-all; don't I al-'ays arnswer your questions?"

"Do you ever? did you ever; can you do such thing, under any circumstances, whatever?" said a third of the committee.

"There, now! aint you doin' the same thing —your own *self?*"

"Silence!—I allow, that in these ere evil days —ahem"—fixing his eyes directly upon Peters —not a muscle of whose dark face trembled— "Strangers are invited—a—ahem—a—to —to withdraw."

Several byestanders took the hint, and walked off; but Peters!—he planted his foot, more peremptorily; and eyed Mr. Deacon Pepperell, with a more cool and wary determination.

" Humph !" said Mr. Deacon Pepperell —
" humph !"—still keeping his eye upon Peters —
" Humph ! — Strangers will be accommodated
with a place in the other room — till the publick
meetin' is opened." Not a foot — not an inch
would Peters budge. " Give that man a hint,"
said Mr. Deacon Pepperell. " I never take a
hint," said Peters. " Will you bundle out ?"
said another, who undertook to give him a hint.
" Will I bundle out ? — No." — " Shall we bundle you out ?" — " If you please." — " Humph !"

· " Let him remain; proceed — brother Libby."

" Where did you buy that air trade ?" said
one of the examiners.

" Will you let me tell my story arter my own
way, Mr. Cappun Libby ?" said Winslow; putting on a look of sheepish awe.

It is amusing to see how adroitly; and, for
how long a time, a genuine Yankee will evade
your question. Put it in what shape you may —
though you believe it impossible for him to escape,
he will either pass it over, entirely, without any
appearance of design; or answer it, by another
question—urged, in a serious, or pleasant, or droll

manner, with singular promptitude, and a great
show of simplicity.

" Shall we never be able; never — to get a
direct reply, to our interrogation, brother ?" said
a little man, with a fat, angry face; addressing
himself to Mr. Deacon Pepperell, with unex-
pected vivacity, as if determined, whatever else
might happen, to surprise *him* into a reply.

" Shouldn't you like to try *your* hand with
him, our Ebenezer ?"

This habit of evasion would seem to indicate
a shrewd, conscientious, inquisitive people.
Among the Brother Jonathans, however, it is a
sign of something more; the sign of a suspicious
— cool, keen, cyphering, thrifty temper; with
little or no heart. Every thing is a matter of
serious calculation with your genuine Yankee.
He won't give away even his words — if another
should have occasion for them. He will
" swap" any thing with you; " trade" with you,
for any thing; but is never the man to give anything away, so long as there is any prospect of
doing better with it. If you put a question, to
a New Englander, therefore; no matter what —

no matter why — beware how you show any solicitude.   You will make a bad bargain, if you do.
He is pretty sure to reason thus; generous and
kind as he is, in some things. — " Now; this information is wanted. It must be of some value to
him, that wants it; else why this anxiety? — Of
course, it would be of some value to *me*,
if I knew how to make use of it, properly.
At any rate (a favourite phrase, with him); at any
rate, he wants it; he knows the value of it; he
can afford, of course, to pay for it; and will
not give more than it is worth.   Therefore I
shall get as much as I can: if he gives too much
for it; whose fault is that? — His; not mine.
Therefore, he shall have it; if he will — *at any
rate.*"

We would not have it inferred, however, concerning this people, that, with all their faults,
they are either sordid, cruel, or wanting in real
hospitality.   By no means.   They abound in
virtues; but abound more, perhaps, in a most
unrighteous, disposition for bargaining; swapping; trading; trafficking; a curious, prying,
inquisitive temper, which cannot be put aside, or
baffled, or evaded; and a provokingly sober

business-like way of doing matters, which would
be " sentimental," or affecting, if they were done
by any other people, under heaven; or, in any
other way, under heaven.

" Well; and so, you see," said Winslow—one
more short specimen of his Yankee, as it was,
and *is*, yet, among this people, away from the
sea board :—" well, and so, you see," dropping
his head; leaning over, on one side, with his right
foot forward; and swaying his ponderous body,
like a great school-boy, repeating his lesson;
" well, and so —I sot myself, down; saying, says
I to the marchant, says I; how'll you swap
watches — how'll you swap, says I ?— So then,
says he to me, says he; sharp off the reel ; — as
'cute a feller that, as ever you seed, I'll wage a
cracker, our deacon,—corporal, says he—corporal ! if you ain't a funny feller, for to come here,
says he — none o' you slack, says I — and *up*, I
riz; none o' your pokin' fun at me, says I—feller
like you ; — hope I may never speak agin, if I
didn't; feller like you — don't know a pitch-pine
hay-mow from a sugar maple-tree, says I, to let
sich a spec — he knew what I was a-drivin' at,
all the time — to let sich a spec, says I, slip

through your fingers, right away, says I—like a
ball o' butter, says I — through a cabbage leaf,
says I. — Well, an' so—"

"But what has all this long, lockum story to do
with your trade?"

"Never you mind, Mr. Major Greenleaf.
Never seed a flock o' pigeons — did you?—
workin' up — workin' up — through a clever hail
storm; all a flyin' — right in eend?"

"Come to the point, immediately, sir," said
one of the examiners. "Come to the point; or
we'll have your name put up, on all the boundary
trees, for having broken the laws of our association."

"Well; and so;" continued our corporal —
nowise intimidated by the alarming threat;
"Well; and so, I happens into that air store o'
his'n;" it was a room over a tavern; — "so, says
I—speaken' to the marchant," a Boston pedlar
— "so, says I — lookin' him right in the face;
keepin' a good stiff, upper lip, all the time; like
a nigger lookin' 't a gingerbread; ever seed him,
any of ye, on a trainin' day? Ye needn't go for
to think o' ketchin' me, says I : — I know your

tarnal rigs, inside and out, says I. I don't want
none o' them are notions; that's what I don't,
says I: and so — he begins for to wheedle, ye
see — right away; sleek enough too, I guess;
and so; bein' afeerd he might ryle my blood, I
begins for to whistle a toone or two; I dooze.
Yankee doodle, says I — that was into him —
I guess — haw, haw, haw : —

> "Yankee doodle keep it up —
> Yankee doodle dan — dy;
> Mind the musick and the step;
> And, with the gals be han — dy."

"Possible!" cried one; — "that beats all
nater!"—"Down with his name," said a third. —
"Softly, softly," cried a fourth: "fair and softly:
he is not a man to be driven, to terms."

"Well, and so; don't be sulky, neighbour
Neezy, I keeps whistlin', I dooze; and he; he
keeps lookin' about—lookin' about, like a squir'l
in a raccoon's nest; whereupon; arter all that—
in I crams both o' my two tejus hands right into
my trowzes; and up, I goes to the counter —
right away—and what dooze I see, there, but one

eend o' this 'ere trade"—lifting up his waistcoat,
and flourishing it before their eyes—"one o' these
'ere hangin' out; and so, I fetches it a rap, with
my goard stick. Our Barnaby was there; ax
him, if I didn't, or anybody else, that's all. And
so, what d'ye think?—our marchant—*hē* nĕver,
sō mŭch, *ās* tŭrns, *his* nŏse—*nōt* hĕ, *tō* bĕ sŭre:
jest 'cause another somebody was there, with a
great heap o' goold in his pocket. And so,
bein' a little miffed, or so, from the fust, I gets ryled,
by-an-by, like any thing. I' ins with my hand
arter that; and I outs with a handfull o' the
right stuff; old continental"—paper money issued
by the colonies;—"and up I jams it; right up,
into his face. There's a snórter for you! says I.
Match that, if you can, says I. Whereupon,
he outs with his; and I outs with mine;—he
shows, and I shows—valley for valley. So, dod
butter my hide, if he don't show most, arter all!
So, I couldn't bear that—not I!—and he,
a-grinnin there, all the time, like a wolf in a bear-
trap; and so, I outs with my jack-knife, without
sayin' a word, more; and I rips open the waistband o' my breeches; and I shows him a double

handful o' the rayal goold; the ginooine yeller stuff — wheels; and so; he wouldn't believe they was mine: he dares me to lay 'em out; and so —and so — I do lay one of 'em out; jest a joe — right away—and — and so — and so — that's all."

" Down with his name!" repeated one of the board; a younger man; evidently better educated, and less forward than the rest. " Down with his name! we must make an example of some-body."

" I'm a leetle afeerd," quoth one of the rest; " a leetle afeerd. He's a man o' substance."

" Afeerd! afeer'd of what!" cried Peters; coming out, and speaking with a voice of authori-ty. " Afeerd of what !—of doing your duty? It is only the other day, that we rose up, as one man, against a paltry stamp-tax; a few pennies a-piece, for the best of us. But a little time before that, our fathers threw themselves, headlong, into the sea; lashed, as it were, to a single plank; yet, having faith—holy faith, enough—to walk the great waters of the Atlantic, dry shod, if that one plank were wanting: and why? — why was

it ! — why? Because they were brave, good men;
determined, serious men ; believers — created in
the image of One, that will not be dishonoured
— will not ! — even by royalty !"

As he spoke, he set his right foot upon the
plank, with a sound of such convincing power,
that all of those, who were going to lay hands
upon him, but a little time before, drew back
afraid; leaving him alone — holding forth, in the
middle of the room, like a prophet; with a low,
strange voice ; and cloudy, dim eyes, nearly shut.

" No — no — ye men of little faith.   No! *They*
were not of a temper to compromise their salva-
tion — to sell their God, for a few pieces of silver!
They were not a people, to barter away their
birth-right, for a mess of pottage ! — to abandon
the Lord God of their fathers, for a few shekels
of gold or silver !"

" Who is he — who is he ?" whispered one of
the board.   " That man should be watched,"
added another, in a low voice.   The people
were afraid; and he, to whom they looked for
explanation — even the minister — he was utterly
confounded, amazed, and overborne, by the un-

expected boldness of Peters. He looked, as if
he had never seen him before. He denied *his*
master.

" Yea, and your brave brethren of the East;
a part of the same race ; the men of Massachusetts — they, who have inherited but a portion of
the strong blood, which distended the veins of
their fathers ; and made their great hearts bold ;
even they have lately answered, in a voice of
thunder, to him, that came upon them, with
many ships — in the roaring of the sea. Fear !
— afraid ! — I wonder that ye are not afraid
even to say the word, at your age ; assembled
as ye are together now — here — in the house of
God — in the name of God — with God in the
midst of you. Is this a time, or this a place ; are ye
the men, to be afraid, of any thing ? If you are —
down from your high seats ! down with ye ; and
begone to your hiding places ! Away with you,
to the holes of the rocks ! Look at him ! —
behold this man ! A giant; a Goliath — able
to make head, alone, if he would, against a great
multitude of ordinary men. Behold him — a
strong man; a mighty man — casing his broad

chest; not with a harness of iron — but with a breast-plate of painted cotton; wearing a badge of servitude — openly — bravely — before the people — into the house of the Lord — into the very presence of Jehovah — while the great skies overhead, are darkening, with his displeasure; and the thunder is falling, on every side of him. Man! — Men! — I would rather see a sister of mine"—his voice trembled—" a wife; a beloved one" — it was very low — very — " a beloved one, swathed in her burial sheet; a *son* of mine" — it was a loud hoarse whisper — " a son of mine—dead upon the scaffold, fifty times over, than clothed in a material, spun by the fingers of them, that have become to us, and our little ones, even what the Egyptians were to the people of God, in their bondage; pitiless and abominable. task masters. Hewers of wood, and drawers of water — slaves and bondmen, have we been all our lives long: wherefore it is, now, that we are bidden to make bricks, for them, without straw. But—for this wretched slave ——"

" Slave! Who's a slave!" cried Winslow; coming stoutly up, with a stride, that shook

the whole house; facing the "stranger;" and
striking his powerful arm upon the table, as if
he would split it asunder. " Slave! who's a
slave! I'm a free born American, that's what
I am; no more of a slave, nor a Nigger, than
yourself! — there! take that! I know ye,
ropped up, as you air; never clamb a tree, for
nothin—arter owls;—that's into him, I guess —
our deacon!"

" Be quiet! We have no time to lose.
The people hear the noise outside; and are getting impatient," said Mr Harwood. " Peace —
throw open the doors!"

All were eager to obey the voice of their
preacher; and, of course, a " pootty consid'r-
'ble" uproar followed. " Silence, there! —
quietly — quietly."

Away they went; each man to his place, on
tip-toe. The doors were thrown wide open;
the people, seeing their minister, became instantly still; took off their hats, and poured in,
without noise or confusion; almost without being heard — like a multitude of shadows; until
the whole house was crowded, up to the ceiling,

with heavy, solemn faces; the doors blocked up;
and all the windows full of men — men, who had
never met before, in all their lives; and would,
probably, never meet again, till the day of judgment.

The town meeting was opened with a prayer;
" a pooty tejuss good one, it was too;" said one
of the elders, " though 'twas ruther lengthy."
That over; a chairman, or moderator, as they
call him, there, was chosen; a plain fellow, with
little or no experience in such matters, who never thought of telling his fellow citizens that he
was wholly unprepared; quite incompetent; altogether unworthy of such a distinguished honour — wherefore, he should keep it, as long as
he could; but, being only a plain man, he took
the chair without any sort of parade, or fuss;
very much as if he knew they had shown their
good sense, by choosing him; and opened the
meeting. His words were few; and exceedingly
to the purpose. " We are here," said he, " on a
serious matter. We want information. Let
him that hath it, speak freely. The less talk, the
better. The men of Massachusetts Bay are in

trouble. Are we to go all lengths, or not, in
aid of their cause ? Every man here knows what
cause I mean : — therefore, I need not speak
more plainly."

"It is the cause of rebellion !" said Peters :
"And ye dare not speak it, aloud," added somebody
else; no man could say who.   The voice came,
out from the midst of them. Every eye was
turned upon the place; but no lips were seen
to move — no countenance to betray itself.

"Proceed," said Mr. Moderator. Several
speeches followed ; chiefly from the lawyers, who
had collected from all the county ; and made —
as they always do — a plenty of talk, to little or
no purpose. Most of them ; the younger and
more clamorous, were for war, open war, at
once; first, upon the people of Great Britain ;
then, if they took it, unkindly, upon all the people of all the earth, who should be foolish, and obstinate enough, after due notice, to call their fellow men, Lords, and Kings. Why ! it was
downright blasphemy !"

"Mr. Moderator !" murmured some one of
the multitude, in a far, sweet voice. — "Yea !"

answered another; a very tall man, through his
nose; "Yea; there is but one Lord, and one
King! even the Lord of lords; and King of
kings! Wherefore; wo — wo — wo, unto them;
that bow down to ——"

"Mr. Moderator!" said Peters, putting the
people aside; and mounting a bench: "Mr
Moderator! — I have only a word or two, for
you."

The orator saw his face; and his courage
died away. The people saw it; and, while he
turned his head slowly about, from one side of
the house to the other, as if numbering them, all
for judgment — every one; man, by man; the
crowding and pressure; the tumult; and cries
of order! order! order! — all died away, even
like the courage of the orator. Peters was very
pale; his bald, broad forehead, was like hewed
stone; cold as a rock. His eyes were full of
wrath; his bony frame agitated with a strong
inward convulsion; his hands clenched. For a
whole hour, had he been standing still, in one
spot; not an inch, had he moved. Nobody
saw him; nobody cared for him — nobody heard

his voice; though he had striven many times to
speak out, in his natural tone — but he could not.

. The tall men, that were about him; they, who
had overshadowed him till then; looked around
among themselves, when he stood up; wondering
who he was — and what — and why they had not
seen him, before.   They could not believe, that
he, who was then above them; standing up, like
one of themselves — a tall man — among the wise
and powerful of the place, and speaking, too, as
one having authority; — they could not believe,
that he was the same, quiet, common-looking
man, who had been standing behind, and below
them — any where — any how — so patiently;
for a full hour; and speaking, in the voice of a
child — feebly and petulantly — four or five
times.

    " Mr. Moderator !" said he. — The multitude
leaned forward, and held their breath.   He spoke
in a strange voice; it was that which had come
out from the midst of them, a little time before;
a whisper only; but a whisper, that every man
heard; and a whisper, that no man forgot. " You
are talking treason. Go to — go to ! You are

doing treason. Recollect yourselves. There may be spies among you : besides — what know you, or any of you — concerning this matter — a parcel of blockheads ! Are we to have war ? — war ! — with whom ? — when ? — where ? — why ? — are we prepared ? — have we money ? — No ! — men ? — ships ? — No ! — officers ? — plans ? — military stores ? — *No !* — Have we even a government of our own ? — or a common interest ? — *No !*"——The silence had grown awful — oppressive.

" Our sufferings," continued he — " our sufferings — what are they? weigh them, sirs. They — you know what I mean — they, the British Parliament — George, King of Great Britain — whose groan was that ? — Let him come forth, like a man ! — Let him be a friend, if he dare — now is the time ! Let him be a friend; if he dare, to the King of Great Britain ! Oh ; ye begin to be afraid, I see ! there's a bustle among you now. Ye begin to recollect yourselves. You are skulking off. Abide ye in your places ! Every man that passes over that threshold before I have done, shall be marked for ever. What ! will ye

do treason; while ye dare not speak it? Are
such men to lead us, by and by, when the legions
of Old England are upon us? Look you. I
am the friend of George, King of Great Britain.
That ye have heard me. say" — a man passed out
of the door — obstructing the light, for a single
moment.

"Amos Pepperell!" cried Peters, in a loud
voice; "Amos Pepperell! otherwise Deacon
Amos Pepperell! I proclaim you, for a trai-
tor!" The people rose, tumultuously. "Peace!
peace there!" he continued: — "for, unless ye
hang me up; unless ye crucify me — within the
hour — wo to him that lays the weight of a hand
upon me!"

"Order! order!" cried several persons. —
"Order!" cried Peters; and lo, the multitude
rolled back from the place; and were, again, still.
"Hear me patiently. I know almost every man
of you, by name. I have a list of every father;
and of every elder son of this whole assembly. Go
out, if you will, therefore; and escape me, if you
can! What! afraid and quaking at my voice!
afraid of a single man! afraid — one of yourselves

— unarmed ! How will ye stand, by and by, the voice of armies — of multitudes — the neighing of horses—and the roaring of artillery ?— Go to — Go to. — I am a friend of George — King of Great Britain. Yet — I dare to *do* that, which no man of your whole number dare to think of. I dare to wage war, with him — open war — face to face. On whom, shall we depend, for succour and council, by and by ; if your strong men turn pale at the *name* of danger ; and your wise men dare not *speak* of treason. — Our sufferings ! what are they ? weigh them ; number them. Ye are a prudent, calculating people ; ye are not of a temper, to be surprised into any thing. They will permit us to trade, with nobody, save themselves : — But what of that ? They tax us, at pleasure, without permitting us to be represented : — But what of that ? They take our citizens over three thousand miles of sea-water, for trial ; they provoke the nations upon us ; they use our young men to conquer the French — one year in the West Indies ; another in the Canadas. They put slaves upon us, in spite of our prayers : disgorge their jails and hulks upon us ; conquer,

with our men, by sea and land;—or, when we conquer for them;—laugh us to scorn; insult us, in
full parliament; and refuse all indemnification;
slander our loyalty, even to the face of our so-
vereign; turn our victories, to a reproach; prohibit us — God help such legislators ! — prohibit
us from hammering out, so much as a tenpenny
nail, in these colonies. But what of this ! —
we can bear it. Are we not a *prudent* people ? —
Do we not know, precisely, how much of insult,
wrong, and outrage, it is *profitable* to bear ? —
out with all this idle bravado ! Break up your
meeting ! Home to your houses ! Let each man
take a slate and cipher it out. Verily, verily,
but ye are a valiant people ! Mark my words,
nevertheless ! You will have to fight for this —
fight, knee deep in blood, for what ye have done,
this day ! It is rebellion ! —(His words were like
heavy thunder)—it is rebellion, I say ! These
clamorous young gentlemen will have to go to
battle for what has been said here, this afternoon.
Yea — yea — remember ye all my words ! They
must prevail too — or hang."

As he ended, with a cry, that made every

man's blood in the house thrill — he came away
from the bench; — and walked off; the multitude making way for him, on either hand, as if
he were a wild beast, — or had some deadly sore
about him, that no man might ever touch, and
live.

The crowd were left, in a state of unspeakable
perplexity and alarm. " He was a spy — there
could no longer be any doubt of that." Hardly
another loud word was spoken, after his departure.
The young men — the lawyers — the talkers —
were mute as whipped spaniels; the old, were
cowering, in their seats; but certain of the
middle aged men, with hard-favoured visages;
long foreheads; portentous eyebrows; and wea-
ther-beaten hair; men, who were not much given
to talking; they held a consultation, apart, in a
heavy, serious whisper; broke up the meeting;
and went away, each one to his home.

Peters took a direction to the parsonage; out-
walking everybody, on the road; leaving the
preacher, Jotty, and one or two more, a long way
behind.

CHAPTER VII.

FIRE-SIDE FROLICKS. — ROUGH DROLLERY. —
SPIRIT. — PLUCK. — VIRGINIA GIRL. —SCENES.
— WALTER HARWOOD.

JONATHAN PETERS, after he came out of the
meeting, went straightway to the house of Mr.
Harwood ; — only for a minute or two however ;
just long enough to shake hands with poor Edith,
who was frightened, half out of her little wits, at
his look ; enquire for Walter Harwood, who had
gone out again, she knew not whither ; and pass
away to his own desolate abiding place — a miserable hut in the woods — where, in the old Indian
wars, much blood had been spilt ; " sights of
people" seen, who had no business upon the
earth ; and voices heard, in the dead of night,
like those of little children, lost in the wood. —
Peters, himself, had once heard something of the

kind; but he knew it, for the natural cry of the young female panther; although he was assured, every where, by the country people, that it was no natural cry; but a lure, to decoy the way-faring man, aside, from his path. A thousand frightful stories were told him of this creature; — of mothers and fathers; and of little children, that had been led into her very jaws, by the plaintive, sick moaning of her voice. A thousand more might be told; a thousand, which are true.

It was nearly a week from the night of " meeting," before he showed himself at Mr. Harwood's, again. They had almost given him up; — having sent repeatedly into the wood, without finding him—and were truly sorrowful, at his long absence; when, one evening, rather later than usual, he entered, abruptly; without knocking or calling; and, after a question or two, precisely as if nothing had happened, went into his favourite place; took possession of his favourite chair; tilted himself back; threw up his legs, over the chimney; and sat, a full hour, without speaking a word.

" Where is Edith?" said he, at last.

" Gone to a quiltin'."

He made no reply; but his breathing changed — his chair creaked; and he grew trebly impatient, under the noise and absurdity of Winslow, who, as the devil would have it, had come that evening too, for the only time, since they had met before, in that very place.

" Where is Walter ?" said Peters; after another long silence, on his part. " How very thoughtful, you are !" was Mr. Harwood's reply. " You ask for him, as if you. were angry ?"

" Where is Walter, sir? you have answered one question to-night. Perhaps"—drawing his breath, as if there had been a dead weight upon his heart, for the last half hour; and speaking through his teeth; — " perhaps you may be able to achieve one more. Where is Walter ?"

" Will you permit me to ask, why you ——"

" Pshaw ! Answer my question first. — Where is he? — gone with her, I dare say ?"

" To be sure." —

" Fools !"

" Why so? Edith had a quiltin', herself,

'tother day and 'ts no more 'n fair, for — ah! that's Walter's voice! Here they come!"

"Burn my buttons if 't aint her!" said Winslow; making a sign for them to be still; and placing himself behind the door, ' for a leetle bit o' fun,' as he said; ' cŏn — sarn it all; there!'

While he spoke, the outer door opened; Walter and Edith were heard; both in high spirits, talking and laughing. "No, no, Watty, don't go," said she. "It's mighty bad, huntin' o' nights." — "I shall be back in half an hour — if nothin' happens." — "O, but somethin' *will* happen." — "Pho, pho — here, panther, here!" whistling to his dog; taking down his gun, which always hung up, loaded with ball, over the doorway; and setting off, at a slow, steady trot, by the windows; like a young savage, after his prey.

"Off to the woods, again!" said his father; looking after him. "Off to the woods! Loitering there, all day long; trampoosing about, all night. I wonder the boy's not afeard."

"If he aint got some Injunn blood, in him, bad, I'm darned — right up a tree!" quoth Jotty,

"Blockhead!—will you?" said his father, reach-ing over, to lend him a cuff.

" My stars, dad ! if ever I see'd you make sich a face, afore !" said Master Jotham ; dodging the blow, adroitly enough ; and pitching over the tilted pine-block, just as the door opened ; and Edith came bounding up, with her whole heart in her eyes.

" O, Jotty, Jotty !" cried she ; all out of breath, as if she had been running for life. " O, Jotty, Jotty !" pushing away the hair from her eyes : — " O, Jotty, Jotty ! sich fun, you can't think ! Why, you great lubberly feller, you !" — capering up to him — " what are you sprawlin' there, for ? what is the matter with you ? what's the booby laughin' at ?"

Jotty could hardly keep his countenance, though he held it between both hands, with all his might ; nor hardly help anticipating the joke. There was Peters, on the left, unseen of poor Edith, while she was in her " tantrums ;" with Winslow on the right, moving out after her — little by little — on tip-toe. Poor Jotty had enough to do ; — chuckling in his very heart, all the time ; and sat, with his head projected; mouth clenched; eyes rolling; and every feature convulsed with expectation.

"Mister Peters! I declare!" cried our little heroine:—off went Jotty, like a two-and-forty pounder—"O, I am *so* glad!—I didn't see you, sir—I beg your pardon, sir—I—a—a—a—I was afeard ye might be gone, sir—I was. Indeed—*indeed* Mr. Peters, we did want to see you mighty bad, once more; only once, afore you went, for good an' all; we did indeed, sir, mighty bad—O, so bad, you can't think!"

"I can't think! You can't speak, I believe. Are you crazy?'why do you talk 'Virginny'—that vile gibberish—whenever you are in high spirits?"

"It's my mother-tongue, sir; and when I'm very happy—*very*—I can't speak any other—I can't; and *so*." It was a critical moment; Winslow was just within reach of her. Jotham could bear it no longer; he threw up his heels; hurraed; and rolled over, in a sort of ecstasy; just as the corporal sprang at poor Edith; and caught her in his arms, with a war-whoop, so

like that of a North American savage, when he
gives the tomahawk, as to make even the preacher's
blood run cold.   But—weak, little, and frightened, as she was — Edith freed herself, instantaneously; and, uttering a faint scream, darted into a
far corner: looking at Peters, who got up from
his chair, with a tremendous expression of wrath
in his eyes: Winslow followed her; wiping
his mouth on the flap of his coat, as if he intended
a kiss for her. It was only another " bit o' fun,"
perhaps — nothing more.

" Uncle Harwood! uncle!" cried Edith;
" speak to him; dear, *dear* uncle!_do speak to him."

" Well done, Figinny! hourra for Figinny!"
said Winslow; stretching out his arms; and approaching her, slowly, as if he were at blind-man's
buff. Peters appeared half ready to spring at his
throat.

" Uncle! uncle! — I won't be kissed."

" Hourra for Pickinninny! Don't you be fractious. Give us a buss — ony *one* — any where —
jest one — that's all — an' say no more 'bout it."

" I'll see you hanged first! I will! — Sir! —
Sir! — Mr Peters! will nobody take my part!"

" No," said Peters — " *no*" — glancing at a pair of sharp scissors, that hung within reach of her arm. " No!—every daughter of Adam, if she will, can take her own part, in the paws of a wild ✓ beast. Where the rattle-snake haunts, there grows the plantain."

" O; if Watty was only here !" cried Edith ; " ye great nasty bar." — " Bear," said Peters. " Ye great nasty bear, then! Oh! Oh!"—snatching the scissors ; and retreating to the very wall— —" Oh; uncle Harwood! uncle! speak to him! I will certainly do it — I will! It's no frolick, for *me*, to be rumffled or slobbered; or towzled up, as he calls it, whatever you may think. I *will*, indeed !"

" What !" said her uncle; gasping for breath; and reaching forth his hand, with a faint, helpless cry.

" Right, right !" cried Peters ; " right, girl ! stab him to the heart, if he put so much as the weight of a finger upon you."

" I will, sir !" — " Edith ! Edith!" — " So help me heaven, I will !"

" Winslow !—far—far—farmer !" cried the
preacher; " have a care! you do not know her.
She means it! she means it! I see it in her
eyes."

" Fiddle de dee, then; I'll venter it !"

" Man! man! beware!—she will do *his* bidding, I tell you, whatever come of it."

" So! why do you interfere, now, Abraham
Harwood! — why, now ?" quoth Peters.   " Let
him do it; let his blood be upon his own head!"

" Blood, blood !" repeated the preacher,
shuddering at his dreadful calmness; or at somewhat within himself, till the table, upon which
he leaned, gave way. " Blood, Jonathan Peters !
blood is easily shed; but ——'O ! ————
Oh ! —— forbear !"

Winslow faltered : he had never heard such
a voice, before.   His extended arms fell down ;
he had never seen such a face, before, as that of
Edith Cummin; so sorrowful; so serious.   It
was pale, too; like the face of a dead woman ;
dead, in resisting some outrage, — the very name
of which, would have broken her heart.

" Why ! *our* Eady; ye wouldn't, tho'," said

he. " Ye wouldn't 'a let a feller's blood out : jess
for that ; hey ?"

" Yes, but I would, tho' !"

" Is it possible, Edith, my dear, *dear* Edith !"
said her uncle ; big drops of sweat standing on
his forehead, while he was trying to smile. " My
dear, *dear* Edith ; I tremble for you. Such a
temper—in one so young — so beautiful, too — a
child — a woman-child. What will become of
you ! Would you really have drawn the blood
of a fellow-creature, for such a trifle ?"

There was that, in the voice—in the look—in
the sharp, unspeakable agitation, of the preacher,
beneath whose two hands, the table shook, while
he strove to appear composed ; a something,
which, while it frightened every body else in the
room, as if it were the prelude of another fit,
such as they had seen before ; only provoked
Peters to move up nearer to him ; to lean forward ; catch his breath ; and peer into his dilated eyes, with a look—partly of savage exultation ; partly of grief—pity—and awful seriousness.

The preacher saw it ; and, after a struggle,

N 4

turned away; while Peters withdrew into his corner; placed himself, in the shadow; leaning upon both hands, with his forehead contracted, fiercely; and sat, watching him, without opening his mouth; or taking off his eyes from the preacher, who, after a minute or so, asked Edith again, if she would really have drawn blood?"—" I! — I! uncle — I! blood! — O, no — not for the world."

" No sobbing, child," said Peters. " Why did you threaten it? Why did you lift up your arm? Why swear, as you did, so help you heaven — to stab him; if you did not mean it!"

" O, but I did mean it! I did; I would have stabbed him; but I — I — a — a — a— I never thought of the blood. Oh, sir, I — I — Indeed, indeed, Mr Winslow, I would have done it; and I am sorry for it; but if you ever provoke me again, I certainly will do it, sorry as I am, now, tho' I die for it. I've told you so — over and over again— I have — I hate your great ugly ways; I do, so. But you won't let me alone—you—you" — sobbing; " you are eternally pestering my

soul out; making fun o' me; calling me names,
you are, as if 'ole Virginia weren't as good as a
great, abominable Yankee; always pulling and
haling me about — so you be; won't let me
have any peace o' my life, when Watty's away;
you are afraid o' him — you know you are:—you
needn't laugh;—you are afraid, as death of him,
though he *is* nothing but a boy; and you know
it. If I was to tell him o' this, he'd put a tomahawk into your head; that's what he would, before you slept. You know this, very well; and
you know, I'm afraid of telling him; and so are
we all; and that's the reason, ye great slobbering beast, why ye plague me, as you do, when his
back is turned. I'd rather be whipped, fifty
times over; and I have told you so, than have
you put your great nasty paws on me. I won't
be tumbled about, by any body; that's what I
wont — let alone a Yankee. —— Ah ! — hush !
hush — there comes Walter. —— Now, look out!
you'll buy it !"

" Winslow; leave us — leave us. Take a
round about path; do — do; there's no knowing how this may end. Edith ! — I command you

— all — all — every one of you ; if you wouldn't see blood spilt here—here—upon the spot, never to speak of this."

"Enough," said Peters ; reaching forward with his lips apart; and catching the preacher's eye, with a slow, mysterious motion of the hand. "Enough! —Abraham Harwood !"

"Well — What would you with me ?"

"Abraham Harwood !"

"What is the meaning of this, pray ?"

"*Thou art the man !*"

The preacher sunk into a chair, as if he had been shot.

"Read you ever, this passage, Abraham Harwood? ' Here, Lord ! here am I !' or this — ' Am I my brother's keeper ?' "

As he spoke, he would have passed out; but, on his way to the door, it opened hastily ; and Walter Harwood came in, flushed with anger. Winslow got away; without being observed ; and Peters came back to his chair ; saying to the preacher, as he passed, "Keep your own counsel ; be quiet ; play your old part ; fear nothing."

He was not well understood, even by the preacher; but he was obeyed, — with all the submissiveness of a child.

" Hul-low !" said Walter — " hey ! what !" looking about him. " What's to pay, now, father? How pale you are — not another fit, I hope — hey? — What's the matter with you all? why don't you speak? — Edith !" — going up to her, — " what's the matter with you ?— What ails you? Another argument, I guess, between father and —— Hul-low !" — coming round, just opposite Peters; planting his foot; and looking him ' right in the eye ;'—" what is the matter — what ails ye? Don't all speak at once."

Walter Harwood, if one might believe in his countenance, which was exceedingly fierce and beautiful, had somewhat within him, which is not common with boys.

He was tall — strong; well proportioned; with a broad, clear, ample forehead; and a noble chin. His hair was parted before, like his father's; carried behind his ears; and let loose, below, upon his broad shoulders, where, at every motion of his body, it played and shook, with a changeable brightness, not altogether in character, with his fine, large, masculine head.

" I know, Mr Stranger," said he, addressing Peters; " I know well enough, when you've been here. We are all out o' humour, for a week arterwards. I wonder what such people are good for." He stepped forward, as he spoke; and supported himself, with both of his large hands, upon a wide board, which ran below the ceiling, just over the heads of the family, from one side of the room, to the other; a hanging shelf—such as may be found in every New Englander's farm-house, to this day; loaded with cheeses; ropes of onions; dried apples; seed-squashes; rennet bags; indigo dittos; and heaps of blue, woollen yarn; laid in, for the winter's knitting.

" Stand back, Walter Harwood !" said his father; beginning to recollect himself. " Stand back — I tell you ! what is the meaning of this ?"

A tall, shaggy, wolf dog, of the rough, Mohawk breed, followed after the boy; eying every motion, like a cat.

" There — *there !*" exclaimed the preacher; springing up — " There ! — *there !* — ye'll have the shelf; and all the lumber, down upon our heads ! — That beast ! — begone, sir — begone ! — why don't you mind ?" Walter took off his hands. " Why do you let him follow you, into the house — every where — any where — even to church ?"

" Why not, sir ? He knows how to behave, there; he never made so much noise, in all his life, as that 'ere Deacon Pepperell."

" Be quiet ! — You'll sleep with him next, I dare say ?"

" I do, now, sir."

" Be done playing with him, sir; be done, I say ! — Do you hear me, sir ? — Be done playing with him; or ——— your hands upon that shelf, again ! — Take them off: begone Panther — begone."

" Lay there," said Walter; (" Lie," muttered Peters ;) — " Lay there !—I won't say lie, for you, nor nobody else." — Panther walked off, to a far corner of the room.

" Very well," continued Mr Harwood; " very

well, sir; — so far — so good.   But now, Master
Watty; one word for you.   Learn to command
your temper.   I shan't have my friends insulted
by you, under my roof; nor my house turned
out of doors, again, by you, in a hurry.   You are
getting quite ungovernable, of late; — you are. —
It won't do, sir; it won't do. — Your haughty
temper must be curbed, sir; shall be curbed, sir.
This long indulgence of mine — what are you
laughing at?" ———

"I wasn't a-laughin', sir."

True. — The boy smiled a little; a very little;
but he did not laugh.   He looked more as if he
could not laugh; as if he had never laughed, in
all his life. — The smile, too, was a smile of bitterness, pride, and sorrow; such as few people
can bear to see in a boy; fewer still, to think of.
There was a forlorn, high, disconsolate expression about his mouth — haughty as it was—which
betokened a bruised and suffering spirit.   He
was hardly able to stand, without holding on, by
a chair.   His colour came and went, with every
breath; and every thing, upon which he laid his
hand, shook, as if it were under the paws of a

wild beast. He stood awhile, regarding his vulgar, heavy-headed, square-built, round-shouldered brother opposite; with his mouth curling, face flushed, and eyes full.

"O, Jotty Harwood! O Jotty! Jotty!" said he, — "if ye'd half the sperit of a man, ye'd 'a held him a tug, for your life, when I was away; afore ye'd 'a let him crow it over the whole family, as he dooze, now. You're a coward, Master Jotty—I won't call ye brother, agin, if I do, —God forgive me!"

"Walk out of the room, sir! walk out, if you can't behave yourself."

"Yes, father; but ony to think! a great, lubberly good-for-nothin' feller; with no more pluck, than a skim-milk cheese ——"

"Boy! — boy! why, what a rash and headlong temper is this! coming in here; with your great eyes wide open, — like a young wild cat's, near a fire; — and your whole body trembling with rage."

"Yes, father."

Very true.—There was a ferocious brightness— a live lustre—in his dilated eyes, which appeared,

somehow, to change colour with every sob; while
his whole frame — his face — feet — hands —
were convulsed with passion.

"Be still, there; be still.—How can you ever
hope to get along, through the world, with such
a temper?"

. "With such a temper, sir!" — said our boy;
falling back, abashed, into the shadow; faltering,
in his voice; dropping his head upon his bosom;
and his arms, poor fellow, as if he were overcome
with a sudden sickness; "with such a temper,
sir!"

. "Yes. It will be the death of you! — I am
sure of it!"

Forth came the boy, with a new face. The
cloud had gone over the landscape. His heart
bounded; his brilliant hair flew out, behind, with
a sudden glitter, in the current of the open door;
and he walked up — up — to the very table;
with his face illuminated.

"The death of me, father; is that all?"

"My dear boy!" said his father; quite overcome, by the change that he saw. There was
no affectation at all, in it. He saw plainly, that,

whatever might be the reason, death was no longer terrible to the lad. He spoke, therefore, with unusual kindness.

" Father — *dear* father; I am sorry — I was wrong. Please to forgive me. I am only a boy, to be sure — only a boy; but Jonathan Peters won't cow me; I tell you. He's a spy, and I know it — I do so. The tree did'nt flower for nothin', arter all !"

Peters had been grinding his chair, into the floor. He stopped short, when he heard Walter's charge; and, straightway, began to enquire, with a keen, cool, determined look, into the meaning of it. Walter met his gaze, without any visible emotion. The preacher was confounded; he knew not which way to turn, or where to look. The family were still, as death. Up rose the dog; and came forth, as if he understood the cause of what he saw; and the meaning of it; up he came, to the side of his master and remained there, for a while, surveying the faces about him — leisurely — one by one — as if he knew that he should soon have to interfere.

" I am, as you say, only a boy, sir; — a mere

boy" — continued Walter; speaking, in a low, quiet way, to his father, and looking at Peters; " I know but little o' these things; and I — I —I won't deny it, sir; — I can't, sir — I do find people get along better, sir; much better, sir — I do so."

A drop fell — a tear. — The dog started, as it passed him; looked piteously up, at his master; wagged his tail; thrust his head under his arm, a little further; and pressed more decidedly, toward him. —

" Much better, sir — by a sneaking — abject — base, crawling temper; what you call a — a — a meek temper, sir — in the pulpit — o' Sabba' days. People make money, sir — I know that, sir — by being patient, sir; and submissive under insult. I — I — It pays well — I know, that, sir; it pays well, to put up with kicks, an' cuffs — like a Christian. — I — I haven't lived long, sir — I know that; nor seen much — I allow that, sir. — But — but — I have read — felt — and studied it out, when Jotham has been dead asleep; and every body else, in this world, I believe : — that's what I have; till my own heart, sir — a — a"

—nearly sobbing— "my own heart, sir,— I was afraid even to draw my breath; afraid 'twould ketch fire, if I did."—" Boy !—boy !"—" Don't call me so, sir, pray.—I am not a boy. I'm no great shakes at braggin' — I never was; but I know this; I know I aint a boy; or at any rate, I'm not, like other boys. You need'nt laugh, sir; — nor you, nyther, sir; nor *you*, jolterhead; nor you, nor you: — and you — and you needn't cry, Edith Cummin. — I aint afeard of 'em all.— No, no; ye needn't laugh; it's no laughin' matter, I can tell you that, sir. — The time 'll come yit. You'll believe what I say, by'm by. You'll remember it, one o' these days, father: So — I tell you agin, that I am not like other boys. I don't know why, to be sure. I don't railly know what makes the difference; but I feel it, sir—all over, sir — through every limb; through every joint, sir — through all my blood. I feel it in every part of me; body and soul; that, I am not like other boys ! — I can't crooch, as they do. I never did — I never will—to any body. — No, father, no ! I'd sooner die — die, like a dog — that's what I would, — right away."

" So you shall, Watty; I know," whispered
Edith, " so you shall ! *you* are made o' the right
stuff, Watty !"—" Be quiet, Edith Cummin — be
quiet !—So sir ! you have no respect, I see, for the
opinion of those, who are older than yourself !"

" No, sir; — not much; without I think so,
too; nor you nyther, I dare say — that is — for
my part, I can't see any great odds between old
and young—lay still, Panther !—not much—when
old folks are foolish, or wicked; can you, sir ?—
Howsomever — to make short work o' this; if
the great world is, what some people, would have
me believe — why, then, father — I don't care how
soon I'm out of it."—" My poor boy !"—" The
sooner the better; that's all !" — " So I say,
Watty !" — " Edith ! — Walter Harwood."

" I can't help it; so there ! It's the solemn
truth. But, after all, it ain't, sir — this world
ain't, sir ! I know better. I know right well,
who made it. Somebody, father; I'll swear —
somebody, that never meant me to be a slave; or
a coward. Some folks may be made for slaves
— they're good for nothin' else; but some, I ruther guess, are made for dominion. If there

must be servants, father — why, there must be masters. — I choose to be a master."

" Miserable boy ! — What are you talking about ?"

" I don't know, sir; I can't say what I think; — I allow that, sir. It requires great practice — I lose myself, you see, right away."

" All men are created equal."

" I don't believe it, father."

" How dare you, sir ? — never let me hear you speak of slaves, or slavery again, with such a ——"

" Very well, father — very well; it may be so; mind — I don't say 'taint so." (" T'aint; pshaw; 'tisn't, or, it isn't, or it is not," whispered one, whose observations we will put into a parenthesis, for a page or two; merely to show the provoking coolness and accuracy of the man, at such a time — while others were in a transport.) " Very well, father; very well—it may be so — I don't say it aint (*isn't*). But, I say; father !"

" Well."

" How can all men be equal, father, when you never see two men alike ? You pity me, now; I

see it, in your eyes; but I'm right, nevertheless;
I know I'm right (I know *that* I'm right). There's
you and Mr. Peters. (There *are*.)   Here's
Jotty an' me. (Here *are* Jotty and *I*).   Are we
equal now, father ?—I guess not.   Were we ever
equal ? — ever alike ? — any of us ?—no — never
— never — not for a single day, since we were
made !"

   " Pho, pho, my poor boy; though you're musical enough, in your own way, (musical —
pshaw — *clever*) very well; thank you; tho'
you are clever enough, in y'r own way, you confound matters here; mind, with body; things,
with appearances; moral, with physical equality."

   " No such thing, Abraham Harwood; no such
thing — the boy is right; perfectly — perfectly."

   " Then, I'm sorry for't; I'd ruther be wrong,
than agree with you." — (*Rather*.)

   " No, no, my poor boy; we shall never learn
you to argue.   (*Teach*). — Thank you, Mr.
Peters — ahem — you will never learn to argue;
as if____"—" Another of your evasions, Abraham
Harwood. You'll not own yourself in the wrong,

if you can help it. So — to avoid saying teach, for learn, where you had been convicted of saying learn, improperly, you change the whole phrase ; and carry it off, as if you were in the right, after all."

" Father !"

" Well."

" Why don't you knock him down ?"

The preacher laughed. " I am a minister of the Gospel, you know ; and ——"

" Shall I ?"

" You are not serious, I hope ?"

" To be sure, I am. He talk about putting you *in* the way; he's eternally putting you *out* ; he is. But, sir; you were a sayin',' jess now (*just now*) — *I'll* knock you down, by gosh ! Mr. No-body-knows-who, if you don't let me alone. — Well, sir; you were a sayin' jest now (*just*); you were a sayin', that I ——"

" Yes — that you can't argue."

" I'm glad on't, sir — (*of it*) I never saw any use in't. I don't see as it makes people any better; or wiser. It only makes 'em a little more

o 4

plaguy tejus — that's all. I can't argue - I allow that."

" You deceive yourself — young man," said Peters. " You *do* argue; *can* argue; *will* argue. Be quiet; your mind is now breaking out; a little time, sir; and we shall see *your* sky lighted up."

" There now, Watty! that's into you!" whispered Master Jotham; " he's pokin' fun at you, now." —" Hush there, Jotty!—I can't argue. I allow that —(*allow—admit—pshaw!*) I can't even talk long. I can't say what I mean; or what I think, or — or — in short, if I begin to speak at all, words keep comin' to me, that I can't use; words too, that I never want, while sich as I want (*such*) I'm never able to find. But I can make you understand me; all of you, about one thing — I ruther guess."

" Well — what is that?"

" Only this father; nothin' more. I have made up my mind; I have, now. I wun't be bullied, by any body - old or young; never — (*ever*) — never, while I draw the breath o' life.

I'll never give up — no — not so much as a straw,
to nobody (*to any body*) without I like."

"Ah — but if the straw ain't your own,
Watty," said Edith — putting her arm affection-
ately about his neck: — "It would'nt be right, you
know." — (*isn't.*)

"I don't care — not I! — Right or wrong.
— I won't be driven to do what's right. I've
made up *my* mind. If any body likes; let 'em try
it; (let *him*) — let 'em cross my path, if
they like (if *he* like); they'll find a bear in it;
or, I lose my guess!" — (*He'll* find a bear in it.)
—— Panther growled. "I have made up my
mind, father; I have nothing more to say. I will
keep my word, if I die for it — here and hereafter
— body and soul!"

Panther barked. His master's voice had been
growing louder and louder, till he concluded;
when it was like the voice of a trumpet, or a
bugle. Every body in the room, but Peters, had
been ready to cry out; and all were so carried
away by the bold enthusiasm, of the passionate,
froward, strange boy; as he stood before them —
breathing like a war-horse — the angry, fierce,

torch-light flashing over his pale face — that
Panther escaped; not only without being rebuked,
but, without being heard, perhaps.

Edith was in tears; Jotham, powerless with
amazement; — Miriam, in a " plaguy pucker."
The preacher had risen, without knowing it,
from the great arm-chair; and stood, leaning toward Walter; resting all his weight upon the
table; his countenance full of alarm, sorrow, and
perplexity; holding his breath, and gazing upon
the apparition before him — the face of a young
man — as if it were the face of a spirit, a vision
of sleep.—What wonder ?—The eyes were sunshine; the mouth, blood red; the large, noble
neck, which was open to the bosom, full of solid,
strong beauty; like marble sculpture.

The rest were wholly carried away; but Peters watched him, for half an hour, without any
visible emotion; yea, without speaking or moving,
save when he corrected him, for his bad language, in a low, firm voice; or encouraged him,
with a cold, positive look, which made the boy's
heart heave.   Peters could endure any thing better than false grammar; false English; and false

pronunciation.   They fell upon his ear; like false notes in musick, upon the ear of one, who is all alive to the delicate combinations of harmony. They galled and fretted him.   Wherefore, he lost no opportunity of correcting people, no matter who they were; no matter what they were talking about.   He was continually interrupting them; in the heat of their conversation, perhaps, when every body else was carried away; and ready to forgive any thing; or incapable of perceiving any errour : at such a time, he was for ever popping in, with little words, and phrases — uttered in a low voice; much as if he were talking to himself; or inwardly repeating what he heard; and correcting it — for himself; not for others.   If spoken to, his answer was, "I never correct any body, whom I believe to be incorrigible; whether from ill temper — age — or situation.   I never correct any body, whom I despise.   Of course, therefore, these interruptions are a compliment.   I choose to correct people, if they are worth it, in a way that will be of use; in a summary way, too.   Whatever is worth doing at all, is worth doing effec-

tually." — " But, why interrupt us, while we are
talking? Why mortify us, before a third person? Why not speak to us, more kindly; or,
at another time; or, while we are alone?" — " I
do not seek to please the mob; I seek to reform
it. I would make you wiser, in spite of yourselves. If I interrupt you, while you are talking; a dispute is avoided, concerning the word or
the phrase, to which I object: if a third person
is by, you are sure to remember the reproof.
You are ungrateful, perhaps; or angry; but who
cares for that? By interfering as I do, the mischief is counteracted, before it has time to oper-
ate; either in the way of example, or habit."

So much for Jonathan Peters, who watched
our hero, as if he were nothing more than a piece
of capital statuary — having the gift of speech; a
piece of wonderful workmanship; the most com-
plicated movement of whose machinery, he understood, and was able to regulate; and yet, after the boy's manifestation was over; and Peters had grown thoughtful again, there went a
sort of shadow — a sorrowful, dim shadow— over
his eyes, and over all his face; much as if, while

he had been contemplating the beauty and power before him, he had only been comparing it — in the solitude of his own spirit — with some departed beauty and power, in which he had long held a deeper, and a livelier interest.

The dog had grown very troublesome, now; and Mr. Harwood was preparing to drive him out; when, as he turned for the purpose, he caught Walter's eye sternly fixed upon Peters, who did not observe it.

" Walter Harwood! Why! — Walter Harwood! I am astonished! What is the matter with you? What is the meaning of all this? You are paler than ever. Your hair too, is wringing wet — your ——. What, sir! caressing that beast, while your father is talking to you!"

" Would ye have me beat him, father, jest for puttin' his head into my bosom for breath?"

" Send him out o' the room, this instant, or —— and begone with him, yourself, sir, if you prefer his company to ours." Walter moved away. — " Where have you been, ever since day-light, sir? Why do we never see you, at your meals? nor ever know where to look for

you?—Speak, sir. Do you hear me? Why
don't you answer?—Where are you going?
Come back, to me, this moment!—Walter
Harwood!—come back, I say!—another step
—and I'll——"

That other step was taken. Over the thresh-
hold, went he—the disobedient boy—as if he
never desired again to cross it: walking away,
in full view of the open window; Panther keeping proud step with him—side by side—under the double row of trees; both catching bright
glimpses of the sky, at every motion, through
the overshadowing foliage, till they were out of
sight.

" Sir—Sir!—that boy will break my heart!"
said the preacher; as they disappeared, in the
obscurity of the wood.

" No doubt of it," answered Peters. " Hearts
are easily broken—for those, who talk finely."

" So rebellious, too, after all my care of
him."

" You deserve it."

" Deserve it!—Sir!—Jonathan Peters!—But
—no matter—we must bear and forbear."

" Humph."

" Deserve it, sir! I do not; or — or — that is, I hope I do not."

" You hope, therefore; you hope that HE, who made you, is unjust."

" Jonathan Peters."

" Abraham Harwood."

" That was a sneer."

" No ; it was a rebuke."

" Never mind — I pass it over. Tell me, if you please, how I deserve it."

" If I please ! You are wonderfully courteous."

" Your look, just now, when that boy walked out of the door, was frightful. It made my blood run cold."

" Pho, pho; keep that style for the women."

" You have been surprised, I rather expect, (*suspect*,) into a premature avowal of your opinion : you have been thrown off your guard ; you ——"

" No such thing. I was not — cannot be thrown off my guard."

" There never was a parent fuller of yearning solicitude; or fuller of affectionate anxiety for his children."

" Talk to me, in prose; will you?"

" Well, then — how do I deserve it."

" Keep your temper."

" Speak plainly. What have I done?"

" What have you done! — Pack off your people to bed, if you dare. What have you done! Would you have me tell you?"

" Certainly," said the preacher; turning very pale; " certainly."

" Are you serious? are you bold enough to encounter the trial? If you are; prove it—away with your people, to bed. Remain here with me — if you dare — alone."

" Trial! I fear nothing — care for nothing. — Speak to the purpose. Speak to the purpose. My people may remain. Speak out."

" Is it possible! Have you the desperate courage—you—*you*, Abraham Harwood—so to face me down! How dare you look me in the eyes; knowing, as you do, now, that I know you! So!—we understand each other, now! Compose yourself. I shall speak only of your boy, now; but beware how you provoke me, again. I shall not be satisfied, with words. Think of your child, now; forget everything else. The treatment of your brave, resolute boy — this evening — before all the family — think of it! Why, sir! if you could have your way, you would make him as base, and pusillanimous a reptile, as crawls the earth; you would make him a coward.".

" Nay, sir; hear me — hear me, for a moment; will you ?"

" No."

" I will be heard !"

" Will you ! — try. You shall raise your voice above mine — above the noise of a trumpet — if you do, before I have done. Look, Abraham Harwood — look ! — there goes your boy. Lo ! I will expound for you, the hand-writing upon his forehead. It is you — you, yourself; you, alone, sir, that have destroyed him. You have set your foot upon his proud neck; misunderstood — misrepresented, his generous, fine temper, for that of a rebellious blockhead. Look; look !"

Walter was just outside of the window —

hardly a pistol-shot off; his face up-turned, bravely, to the heavens — bravely; — a thousand stars were reflected in his large eyes.

"Look, look! The great and good Being, above, never made a finer head : — You would mutilate his proud workmanship. See ! — it is full of exaltation ; you would extinguish it. You beheld his heart, a few minutes ago — his naked heart ; you saw us all take fire, at the sight — all of us ; and yet, you were wicked enough to set your foot upon it, before all our faces. I am talking, to you, now, in your own language — poetry — noisy, vain poetry."

"Lower your voice, I beseech you."

"Lower my voice ; I am speaking hardly above my breath."

"True ; but, some how or other, you fill the house with it. It sounds very awful, to me."

"To you ! I am glad of it, sir. It will save many words, by and by. It will make you understand me, perhaps, when they do not. Of the boy, though" — turning to the clock — "a word or two more, if you please, before we part. He

loves the dog, and you know it; nay, if he did
not love the dog, after the brave animal's behaviour to him, while they were among the wolves,
he, himself, would be hated. You would hate
him; we should all hate him; and he would
richly deserve it. You know this; and yet, how
did you receive the noble outcry of his young
heart, a few minutes ago? It was like the onset
of battle to me. How did you receive it? — As if
he were alien to your blood. How reward him? —
As if he and his dog were both hateful to your
eyes. The boy is a hero. You should have
thrown your arms about his neck; you should
have wept upon his forehead — wept upon it, like
a father; proud of your unconquerable boy.
This — you should have done; this, you would
have done, sir, had you suspected a tythe of his
great value. But you did nothing. — Did you go
to your closet? — no; or kneel down? — or
cover your face? — or weep and pray? — or bless
the Maker of all men, for having put a soul into
one of your lineage, like the soul of David, himself, when he set forth, unarmed, unaided, quite
alone; a boy — to encounter the giant, who was

built round about with iron; as it were, with a wall
thereof. Did you this; or any thing of the sort?
No. But you mocked him; you met his valour,
with derision; you rewarded his courage, with a
sneer. Think of that, sir; think of that; a
father sneering at his own child. You told him
to go away from before us, and associate with
dogs. He obeyed you. I honour him for it.
Farewell!"

" Sir; sir!"

" Why do you stay me? The clock is now
striking. Farewell."

" Your manner is new. It scares me. I — I
—we shall see you again, I hope."

" Hope!—Do you desire it?"

" I!—desire it!—certainly."

" Beware. I am not of a temper to be trifled
with. Precisely one week from this hour, you
shall see me again. Farewell."

CHAPTER VIII.

DESCRIPTION. — SQUATTERS. — HOW TO SMOKE
THEM OUT. — MISCHIEF. — MOHAWKS. — MO-
HAWKING. —STRANGE MALADY.

It was precisely one week, to an hour; — to a
minute; as Jonathan Peters had promised, before he gave Abraham Harwood an opportunity
of speaking to him, again.   The Yankees are a
very conscientious people—in such matters; and
he was very conscientious—for a Yankee.   In the
mean while, strange whispers were abroad; wars
and rumours of war: the whole of New England was up; and Walter, anticipating the crisis,
began to talk mysteriously, about going to seek
his fortune.   His father was alarmed; he could
neither eat nor sleep; and symptoms of his old
affliction had begun to show themselves, in the
occasional twitching of his haggard features.

The noise of preparation; the voices of a warlike
people, mustering with a heavy tread, over all
the land, grew louder and louder, every day —
every hour — every minute. Artillery was heard
in the solid earth; trumpets, blowing in the
mountains; the noise of battle, overhead —
everywhere; subterranean musick — the neighing of horses — and a wild, solemn harmony in
the sea breeze, night after night; by serious ve-
nerable men, who are yet alive; and, if required by the unbeliever, will swear to it.

Meanwhile the neighbourhood were all up in
arms, about poor Jonathan Peters. He had no
peace of his life; night or day. He was beset
on every side, again, very quietly; waylaid, as
before; and watched, more narrowly, than ever;
but, without noise or stir; — so that he had nothing
to complain of; nobody, to quarrel with. Look
out when he would, from his wretched log hut —
which he slept in, because no other man could
sleep in it; — a place, abandoned of all the
world; a habitation, fit only for the wild beast,
or obscene bird; — a miserable hiding place, for
which there was no owner; look out from it,

when he would; he was pretty sure to encounter a pair or two of eyes; and hear disagreeable noises, for which he was not wholly prepared, in the dead solitude, which he had chosen, as it were, in derision of the terrible stories that men told of it. The eyes of a she-bear — a fox — or a wild cat, now and then, he could have borne, patiently: Or the crackling of branches overhead — indicating the portentous movement of an old panther, following him, in the tree tops; and waiting her opportunity for a leap, as he wandered in the great wood: Or the sharp rustling of the dry leaves, through which he might be wading, half-leg deep, on a warm day; — causing him to catch his breath, and spring aside; lest he might set his lifted foot, upon the loitering copper-head, or the coiled rattle snake: Or the trooping of wolves — pack after pack — trotting by his very door, in the dead of night; or coursing their prey — silently — through the great wood; like shadows — at full speed — hour after hour: — All these things he might have borne. He was prepared for them; and had — with a plenty of powder and ball, a tomahawk or two; a good rifle, and a woodman's large knife; a stout heart — a strong arm — a quick eye — and a deadly aim, for their comfort, and his own; but he was not prepared for; he never would be prepared for—the indecent, active, annoying, eternal — desperate curiosity of the people about him.

He could bear to hear voices in the wood; shouting for the " spy," or the " squatter ;"— *that* gave him little, or no uneasiness. He could bear to hear a spent ball rattling in the bushes, through which his path lay; for, he knew that no serious mischief was meant; or likely at all to happen : But, he could not bear — he would not — patient, cool, quiet and peaceable, as he was ; he could not bear the savage, brutal, coarse familiarity of the country people; or their continual, persevering, impudent, cruel intrusion — without apology, or pretence — at all hours — day after day — upon the sanctity of his retirement.

So, too; he could bear to lie a-bed, on a warm, quiet, sleepy afternoon; as he frequently did, in the summer time ; after having been kept awake

all the night before, by the wolves — or moschet-
toes; the owls, or the heat; or, after he had
been out all night long; abroad in the great,
magnificent woods — unable to sleep — unable
to write—for the beauty and power; the grandeur
and calm about him :— He could bear, patiently
enough, so to lie, after such a night — half
asleep; and hear the bullets rebounding, one
after another, from the outside of his hut; as the
hunters, on their way home, after a long day's
work — would stop for a moment, as they went
by; and let off their pieces, at a particular part of
the wall, which had been a target for their fathers;
and for all the riflemen of the country, time out
of mind — year after year; they never dreaming that
such a place could be inhabited; or that such walls
of great, solid, heavy timber, could be penetrated :
Nay, more ; he would even sit still, with his
pen up, and his paper before him, while the
marksmen were in low conversation, just outside
of the wall; within a few feet of him, perhaps;
listen to them, without knowing it—lost in thought
— while they were preparing to fire; pacing off
the distance ; or scratching a circle, peradventure,

in a line with his very head; wait patiently, as if
he had no concern, whatever, in their sport, until
some one of the large bullets — missing the round,
heavy timber, and passing through the blue clay,
with which the holes and cavities were filled up —
would glance along, inside of the room, where
he was; enter the opposite wall; bound back,
and roll at his feet; or, striking the chimney,
would fall, entirely flattened, upon the floor; —
when, recollecting himself; and, perhaps, thinking it high time to interfere, he would come out
from the old, overgrown, miserable ruin; appear,
suddenly, before them, without any sign of serious
displeasure in his face; and seem to enjoy their
dismay, and perplexity.   All these things, he
could bear, with a smile; for he knew that neither
mischief, nor evil, was in their hearts toward him;
and that no one of them all, would have hurt a hair
of his head; however much, they might be willing
to frighten him; or, however much, they might
endanger his head, itself, by their careless gun-
nery; but he could not bear, — he would not —
fifty other things, which most people would have
borne, far more quietly.   They spoilt his temper;

— they wore his heart away; — they made his life a burden to him.

He never went abroad, without securing the door; — so far as he could, by the simple contrivances of the time; a wooden bolt, button, or latch. He never came back, without finding it wide open; or, if he had been long absent, — his few books, in disorder; his maps and papers tumbled about; his furniture overthrown; his very drawers wrenched open; his whole house ransacked, and rummaged, with a wicked, ferocious temper, which he would sometimes have given his right arm—perhaps both arms—for an opportunity of punishing. He spoke of it, openly; at a tavern, before a number of wicked fellows, who had lately " come out " of the " New-Hampshire Grants"—where such things were common. They had been " smoking out a squatter; " — *i. e.* a person, who had "squatted" himself down, upon the vacant land, which was then a matter of dispute, between two or three of the northern states. " I would shoot any man —" said Peters, while speaking before them; " I care not who he is; if he were to play such a game with me; and I

will put a ball into the first one, that I see
coming out of my house; — if I find my papers in confusion." This only made matters
worse. The very day after; as he was returning
over the top of a hill, within sight of his rude
home; after a few hour's absence; he saw a smoke
issuing from the trees, near it. He stopped — he
thought of the ruffians, whom he had seen, the
day before — he knew their character well. They
were outlaws; confessing no allegiance — paying
none: — So, looking narrowly to the condition of
his rifle, he set forward, upon a slow trot; resolved,
in his own heart, whatever should come of it, —
life or limb — to keep his vow. A few minutes
after, while crossing a piece of burnt ground —
(rough land, cleared by fire) — he heard a shrill
whoop; afar off — in the skies, he thought;
and, immediately after, coming in sight of his
home — (that other name for a bosom) — he saw
the smoke bursting out of every fissure and
crevice. He stopped — he stood still — his
heart swelled.

People never much like to be burnt out, unexpectedly — whether insured, or not; — however

willing they may be, to burn their neighbours out, in the way of business; or themselves, after due notice. It *was* hard. — No man likes to see that place on fire; though it *be* the den of a wild beast — wherein he lately passed a comfortable night — perhaps the very night, before; that roof tumbling in; though it *be* but a wretched pile of logs — which he has just left: that ship driven ashore, which had given him a shelter, in peril; picked him up at sea; or borne him over the waters — though she were a pirate. For a " ten dollar bill ;" if the hut or lodge had been his property, Peters would have set fire to it, with his own right hand. But, now — unprepared as he was; knowing that he had no right of shelter, there; knowing too, that he had carefully put out every spark of fire, lest an accident of the sort might happen; he could hardly help shedding tears—old as he was — when he came up to it, all out of breath; and saw the smoke bursting through every part of the roof, and sides. He ran to the door. — Great logs of wood; such as would require the strength of three or four men to remove, were piled up, on the step. He looked

about him—listened; held his breath; leaned
upon his rifle; and communed with himself.
Every tree, within reach of the hut — all that he
had spared for their beauty, or grandeur —
was felled; in the hope, undoubtedly, of crushing it.   Only one, however, stood near enough.
A branch of that, in falling, had broken through
a part of the roof.   On further examination, he
found all the windows fastened, as the door was,
inside; a board over the chimney, through
which the ruffian must have crawled, when the
job was over; and a fire made of rotten wood;
the smoke of which was very offensive — loath-
some — and of a nature to make any place unin-
habitable, for a week, or more.

Of course, he understood it all, then, — it was
perfectly clear; — they had been " smoking him
out;" and, of course, he must have been watched;
some of the gang must have been stationed, where
he could he seen, if he should return, while the
others were at work; and, " of course !" — the
rifle shook in his hand, — as he remembered the
cry, that he heard, on his way home.   It was,
undoubtedly, the signal of some one, high up in

the tree tops; watching him, from an elevation, which overlooked all the approaches.

There was no time to lose. He took out his watch — went up, to the door — stove it in; pushed away the rubbish; threw off the board; set open all the windows; and hurried away — leaving the hut, even as he had found it; all open to the four winds of heaven; the fowls of the air; the beast of the field; and every creep- ing reptile of our earth.

" I am afraid, after all," said Abraham Har- wood; taking out his watch, and glancing over to the old-fashioned clock, in the corner.— " It is very late; — I'm afraid, after all, that we shan't see him, to-night."

" He will certainly be here, uncle; —certain- ly;" whispered Edith; — " certainly; if he's alive."

" It wants only a minute or two, of ten, you see."

" Yes, uncle; but — hark !"

They leaned forward, holding their breath; Mr. Harwood and Edith watching the clock ; — Lucy, the door; —and all wondering if Peters would be as punctual, as he had been, hitherto, in· such matters. While they were yet listening; — some, with a serious look; — some, with a droll one — they heard a rifle-shot, very near the house. A loud scream followed, afar off; and, immediately, there was a terrible, fierce barking overhead, in Walter's room. The clock began to strike — the large bell sounding through the whole house, with a startling, strange loudness; — the preacher started up; somebody went hastily by the window; and, before Edith, who sat, counting the hour, as if she felt every blow of the hammer, upon her young heart—before she had numbered half the time, the door opened, without noise; and Peters walked in, with a prodigious rifle resting over his left arm.

"You are welcome, sir; take a chair," said the preacher; in some little perturbation, at his look.

"No. — Answer me one question, first. Have you any traps laid for me, here?"

"Traps! — no. —"

"Do you take me for a spy?"

"A spy!" —

" Yes — a spy.— No shuffling — answer me."

" Certainly not. — Why do you ask ?"

" Because I know you," — sitting down, as he spoke, with his hat on ; — " because I know you; — heart and soul. You are not a man to take a decided part, for the promotion of *any* purpose whatever — good or bad ; you are a —"

" Why!—Mr. Peters!" cried our little heroine ; " why; why! — uncle Harwood; how can you put up with such language ?"

" Peace, Edith Cummin ; peace !" — "High !" — " A word with you, sir ; your loyalty and your patriotism are both alike. You are one of the bats ;—neither bird nor beast, —mayhap, till the war is over. You are doubted of all parties — trusted of none. Be not surprised, if I, whom you call your friend — have some doubt of my safety, even among your household gods. You are playing a deep game — a safe one, perhaps, Abraham Harwood : — nevertheless, be wary. The time of trial ; the day of judgment is near."

" You don't say so ! — " exclaimed a voice. " O Lord ! O Lord ! if I'd a thought o' — "

" Silence: The day of judgment *is* near. All

who resemble you, Abraham Harwood, must abide our condemnation — be they, or be they not, people chosen of the Lord. They who are not for us, are against us. — No neutrals ! The friend of no party is the worst enemy of all parties. — Blockhead !" — Jotham was down upon all-fours, near the rifle ; examining the lock — but, without venturing to touch it — " Blockhead ! — what are you after ? — "

" Nothin', squire !"

" What are you looking at ?"

" Nothin', squire." — " Booby !" — " Same to you, squire." — " Jotham !" — " I tho't I see'd somethin' a crawlin' out o' the touch-hole, daddy." — " Get up, sir ; and come away." — " 'Twas nothin' but a leetle smoke, arter all." — " Get up, I say ! Is the boy a naiteral ideot ?" — " Natural ! — no ; he is making believe. Thrash him well for it, in season ; or you will have another Winslow about you — a lie, all over ; a lie, from the crown of his head, even to the sole of his foot."

" I heard a shot, sir — as you came in, sir — I — I believe, sir," said Edith — very timidly ; without

227777777722722722722777777227227227777722722772277227227227772277

lifting her eyes, or speaking above a whisper. "Where is Walter Harwood?" — "Up stars." — "Stairs, you mean; are you sure, — quite sure?" — "O yes?" — "I heerd Panther jess now"—"Heard—just now. I am glad of it. I was afraid of—"

"I'll call him, sir. — O—h! Watty!"

"No, no; be quiet."

"Afraid! Mr. Peters; afraid of what, sir?" said the preacher, who had been watching the squire; and starting, with a look of deep anxiety, whenever he opened his mouth; "afraid of what, sir?"

"Does he ever go out ' a mohawking' ?"

"Never."

"I am glad of it."

"Why?"

"Does he never go?"

"Never."

"No, no, uncle; he was out once, you know; but, when it was all over, he put his two hands — he did — upon the great Bible; and made a vow, never to go out, again." —

"He's a brave boy. Make him keep his word."

"That he will, sir! — His word—he never broke it, in all his life—let alone a vow."

"Let alone!—pshaw!"

"Ah!" quoth Master Jotty; nodding to Edith; "ah; but he wouldn't cross his fingers, and wish he might die, if he did. —"

"Peace, blockhead. Whatever is worth doing at all, is worth doing openly—bravely. The Indians have enough to answer for, on their own account. It is base, cruel—cowardly, to work mischief, under any other shape, than our own."

Peters alluded, here, to a fashion that began to prevail through the whole country, just before the war broke out. When a "tory" was to be tarred and feathered; or any other mischief done — serious, or profane; the people did it, in the disguise of Indians. It was a party of these counterfeit Mohawks, that boarded the East India ships, in Boston harbour; and emptied every tea-chest, with which they were loaded, into the sea.

"What is the matter, pray?—you are very pale; very."

" We heard a shot in the woods, a minute or two before you came in."

" Very like."

" And I heerd a screech, too, father."

" So did I!" — " And so did I."

" Very like. I fired at something, a little way from your house. It followed me through the bushes; dodging about my path, till I could bear it no longer: — so, I gave it a ball."

" What was it!" — " a Mohawk!" " a cattermount! — or —— " The preacher, and Edith, interchanged a look of alarm. They saw that, in the eyes; they heard that in the voice, of the stranger — that, which made them both afraid. —

" Some wild animal, perhaps; it followed hard upon me; or some lurking Indian; — I heard a little whooping in the wood, this afternoon; or some loitering rascal, who has been out a Mohawking, to-day. However — I care not which. It is high time that your people were a-bed."

The preacher looked, as if he would have given the world for a short reprieve; while this humour was on; — as if he was afraid of being left alone with Peters; yet more afraid of refusing. — " Go

to bed, my dear children," said he, at last ; — "go
to bed." — " Good night, father !" — " Good
night, uncle ! — good night, sir !"

" Compose yourself, Abraham Harwood,"
quoth Peters; after a few minutes. " We are now,
by ourselves.   I understand you ; — compose
yourself.   I have only two or three questions to
ask ; — nay, nay, don't be frightened. I shall ask
none, that you may not safely answer, — to any
body — any where. You have suffered, greatly, I
perceive, since we parted."

" Oh, yes ; unspeakably. More than you
would believe it possible for a man to suffer, in so
short a time.   Spare me, I beseech you : whatever you think ; whatever you may believe ;
spare me !"

" I will.   It is not for me to sit in judgment
— whatever I may imagine, or conjecture —
upon a fellow man."

" I am barely alive, now ; a single word,
sir —."

" Be quiet.   Subdue this dreadful agitation.
Speak in a firmer voice ; I can hardly hear you.
But, above all things, don't betray yourself to

any body. I *know* nothing; remember that;
I wish to know nothing, which it may be proper
for you to conceal."

" Thank you, sir — thank you ;"—a pause.

" You had another son; had you not ?"

" O, yes — yes ! Poor Jasper !"

" How ! — grief — real grief !"

" O, sir ! O, Mr. Peters !—my friend !—my
dear friend ! you little know what you have done.
I haven't heard my poor boy's name for years:
I have never been able to speak it; or hear it;
or to think of his miserable end, without a convulsion, of the heart."

" Indeed ! — is it even so ! Can I have been
so long under such a terrible delusion ! Are
you — you, Abraham Harwood; are you really
weeping for the fate of my — of that poor little
boy ? Was he, in truth, so very dear to you ?
or, do I mistake the natural joy of your heart;
suddenly relieved as it is, from a crushing weight,
for the sorrow of one, that will not be comforted ?"

" Dear to me ! — yes, yes ! — unspeakably
dear. But, how could you put such a ques-

tion? how could you, sir? Dear to *me!* He
was dear to every body. Such a temper, as he
had — so gentle — so affectionate; so ——."

" Your hand, Abraham Harwood! — both
hands — forgive me!".

" Forgive you! — for what?".

" I have wronged you — forgive me. I am
sorry for it — forgive me. God! — our Father,
and our God — have mercy upon you! and comfort you!"

" Forgive you! — *sorry?*"

" Peace — peace — thou poor, heart-broken,
afflicted man! I have been very cruel; very unforgiving — very. But O! our Father! forgive
thou me, in the skies, hereafter, as I now forgive
this, mine enemy; this, my repenting brother
now; this, a man of sorrow, and acquainted with
grief."

" Your enemy! — how so? Who are you,
incomprehensible man? What are you? —
What have I done? I am not your enemy;
I never was; I know not whether I — is it possible! — tears! — I can hardly believe my own

eyes! A man like you;—of your age—of your temper — weeping bitterly!"

" How did Walter bear his death?"

" Badly enough; poor boy! badly enough. He was half dead with grief. He ate nothing for several days; you know his temper — how ungovernable it is. I never saw such a boy; so obstinate: — no power on earth could force him to eat!"

" By and by, that will go by another name. Obstinacy, in the boy, is resolution; steadiness; firmness; courage, in the man. — There is not a ——."

" Do you believe in dreams?"

" In dreams! — No; why do you ask?"

" I had a very strange, clear, terrible one, last night. I have had it, several times before. It was a — but why trouble you with it?" A long pause. The preacher took heart, again. " It was a — a — I saw poor Walter on the scaffold."

" Really!"

" His blood running; his — ah! you look as if you do believe in them."

" Blood ! — Sir ! — then he was beheaded —
hey?   Beheaded; was he? — Beheaded, like a
man.   I give you joy."

" Joy ! — me ! — for what, pray?   I never
saw you so — Lord ! how your face changes !
I should hardly know you.   Why do you give
me joy !   I — I — I don't perceive the —;   a —
a —."

" I give you joy, I tell you — joy — joy !
Don't you know the meaning of the word, sir?
Joy! — If your dream of death have any significa-
tion; it is this.   Your brave boy, come what
may of this rebellion — smothered, or not; stifled,
or not — your brave boy shall die like a man;
a great man — with his head upon the block. He
shall not go off, before a multitude — like a dog
— with a halter about his throat !"

" Man ! man ! — who are you? — what are
you? — I begin to be afraid of you?"

" Afraid ! — afraid of me ! Why so, Abraham Harwood?   What have you done, that
you should be afraid of *me*?"

" I do not know; I am quite unable to say; but
your face; your look — your — gracious God !

who are you? Have I not seen you before? — somewhere — I know not where? — in some other shape? Your voice; your carriage; both are altered, now. They are no longer the same. Stay — stay — I feel dizzy — I can hardly get my breath; stay with me, I entreat you. These are symptoms that never deceive me. Do stay — there, there ! — there ! O, my head ! my head !"

He began to shiver; his voice died away, into a low, dismal whispering noise; and he fell back into a large arm chair.

" Shall I wake the family ?"

" No, no — by no manner of means."

" By no means — dead, or alive."

" How your face alters !"

" Mine ! — you are mistaken. It is yours. Your eye-sight is disturbed; your lips are blue; your hand shakes; your throat is convulsed; your — God help us ! — what a strange malady it is !"

" No, no, no — nothing," said the preacher; " Don't be alarmed ——— Ah !" — His under jaw fell. — Peters, who, stood over him;

holding up his head, and looking him in the
face, uttered a groan — a sharp cry, rather —
and sprang off to the door; believing the
preacher to be a dead man; but, before he could
wrench it open, he heard a noise behind him; a
sort of hoarse breathing. He turned about; and
saw the head of the sufferer in motion; the lips
apart; one of the hands lifted, in prayer; and
his whole body shivering, with a sort of ague.

The fit was already over; the sick man rose
up; and, immediately, the lifted hand fell,
athwart his lap, with a torpid, long shudder; but,
in the pitiable distraction of his mind; or, by the
involuntary motion of his head, for a time, he
had shaken his long hair forward, over his pale,
distorted visage; like the dishevelled hair of a
mad woman; so that his appearance, after the
fit was over; and he sat back in the chair, gasping for breath, was more frightful than ever.
The face was like the face of a corpse; like the
face of one, who, after having been buried alive
— in a trance — had waked, in a convulsion of
terror; and become rigid, once more, while

tearing her black tresses; and screaming for breath, in the darkness of her burial chamber.

And yet; he would have carried off the whole matter, with a smile, when he recovered. — He was afraid of death; afraid of confessing, even to himself, that he was in danger. Nay; — lest he might be undeceived, by their looks, or cries — he would not permit his own children to be near, in the time of his trial. — He was one of those men, who, lacking firmness, to withstand peril, or out-face calamity, go, skulking and cowering, over this brave earth, till there is no help for them: one of those, who never tell the truth, of their own maladies — never; not even to their own hearts — not even to their Maker: one of those, who, if they consult a lawyer, in a case of life and death, are sure to deceive him: one of those, who, if they call a physician, will never confess what they feel, up to the last hour: —people, whose prayer for mercy, put up from their death-bed — if there be any body near — is conditional.

"Go — go — go on with your story," said he; as soon as he could speak.

" With *my* story ? — Yours ; you mean."

" True — true ———— a — a — go on with it."

" You were speaking of a dream."

" Right. I remember it perfectly, now. It made an impression, that nothing will ever destroy. I saw it as plainly, as I now see you." — Articulating with difficulty ; greatly disordered — yet, affecting a pitiable air of unconcern. — " I saw the block — the bright axe — the drapery — the multitude" — nearly shutting his eyes ; like a painter, while he is hunting for beautiful, hidden colour, in the common earth about him — " troop after troop of soldiers ; the fierce and awful array; the headsman ; the —— back ! back ! — what a face ! — what a terrible face ! Away with it !"

" Rouse yourself; recollect where you are. It is only mine, that you see."

" Your's !—your's ! — pho, pho ; it is more like that of the headsman ! I remember it, perfectly. I have seen it, fifty times, before — drive it away ! do, do, drive it away ! — Don't you go, my dear friend, please ;—no, no ; don't leave me. Where are you, now? — speak to me! — O, speak to me. — Where is your hand? — let me feel it — let me hear your voice; do — do — or I shall go distracted. — Ah! — there! — there! — I see the shadow of my dead wife — pale — pale — I have not seen it, for a twelvemonth, before — pale — pale — poor, dear Mary; still and quiet; pale as the dead body, that I left — ah! — who is that!"

"Awake, Abraham Harwood; awake! Let not your blood be upon your own head!" cried Peters — trying to recal him, with his powerful voice.

"Ah — where am I! — who are all these people about me? — Jasper — Mary — Warwick Savage — the dead body. — Men of justice! — I am innocent, I tell you! — innocent, whatever you may think! —— So! — vanished! — altogether alone — so suddenly!"

"Yes — yes — altogether alone. Compose yourself."

"I will — I do. You are frightened, a little, I dare say. Pho, pho — never mind it; never mind it, man. They are only shadows, you know; they can't hurt us. However; I don't

much wonder, at your fright; for you have never
seen them before : I have ; — that makes the difference.   By and by, you'll bear them, as I
do. . Speaking of dreams, however; what is your
idea of — I don't believe in 'em, tho."

"You do believe in them; but, compose yourself. Your mind is troubled. Your health suffers.
Your vision is disordered. Reform. Awake,
Abraham Harwood; awake !—Reform ! repent !
— or your understanding will be disordered."

"Well, well — what say you to the dream ?"

"To the dream — nothing; to the dreamer,
much.   Your sleep is gone — your appetite
— your peace of mind. What wonder, therefore,
if the delicate machinery of sensation; the miraculous intertanglement of nerves, which run over
your whole structure — inside and out — should
have become partially deranged ? Repent; —
reform."

"Yes, yes — but Walter — what am I to
do with him !"

"Give him a good education; a few plain
words of advice; and let him go forth, to seek
his fortune."

" I — I am not entirely myself, yet ; I must keep him at home, awhile."

" You cannot. With, or without your consent, he goes. — If a war should break out — you will find him among the foremost reapers, in the field of death."

" What a temper he has ! "

" True. Beware how you trifle with it. — He begins to feel his own power ; — the young lion of his heart, is already awake. He will be a dangerous man."

" I hope not."

" Hope not ! — why so ? would you have him a blockhead, sir ? The strong ; the wise ; the brave ; — are they not always dangerous ? Be prepared, for what I now say : your boy's head will come to the block yet ; or, he will turn out a great man — perhaps a good one."

" You scare me."

" Nay, — never hide from a voice like mine. Rouse yourself. Be a man. Learn to look Death, in the face, *like* a man. Your boy is adventurous, by nature. You have made him

rebellious. The trial time is near. Awake,
Abraham Harwood; awake!"

"Where am I? what ails me? who are you?
I feel as if I had been asleep; as if I were coming out of a trance; the trance of death." — His
afflicted eyes were shut; — nevertheless, he got
up; and went groping his way by the wall; —
steadying himself, with his two hands, which left
a print all the way, upon it, like a heavy sweat. —
" I feel somehow," continued he; " somehow ;—
as if I were near the Evil One, himself; — the
Tempter! — the — the — give me some water,
Edith. —— I — a — a — I feel giddy and sick;
very faint — *very* — Jotham! Walter! where
are you all? — Speak to me! O speak to me!
— help, there; help!" —

" Help, there; help!" shouted Peters.

" God bless me! who was that?" — a violent
barking was heard in one of the rooms, above:
— "you my friend — was it you? It sounded, like
the voice of a stranger to me; but very loud and
powerful."

He was interrupted by a great noise, overhead; a fierce barking; a scream, or two; fol-

lowed, instantly, by a disturbance at the top of the stairs — or about half way up; and a voice just outside of the door, which was violently shaken; the voice crying out — " Father! father! — what's the matter? — where be you, dear father?"

" Here I am, Walter; — my dear boy," answered his father; speaking, with as much composure, as he could; and making a sign to Peters, that he might not interfere. — " Here I am. What is the matter with *you*?"

" With *me*, father? nothin' at all. Open the door — please; and let me come in; do, father."

" No, my child; no. I am very much engaged: I can't be interrupted, now. Go to bed."

" Father!" — " Well!" — "Who is that, with you? — I hear somebody breathin' — close by the door — a strong man, he is too; I'm sure." —" Go to bed, I say; go to bed; — and leave me in peace."

" That ain't your voice, father!" (*Isn't*, quoth Peters.) " Let me come in; pray do — *do!*" Becoming more and more impatient; shaking the door; and heaving at it, with all his weight;

while Panther kept up a low, steady growl, a few feet off.

" He smells you," said the preacher. " Come away from the door, I beg of you. If it should open — your throat will be torn, before I can aid you."

" I'll risk it."

" I hear somebody whispering, father. Be quiet, sir !—be still pawing, there ! be still, I say ! Father ! — is that 'air fellow gone yet ?"

" No; young man. — That *air* fellow is not gone. What would you have with him? — Speak."

" Open the door; and I'll tell you. Lie still, Panther ! jest open the door; and you'll see."

" Just — if you please."

" Walter Harwood — on your life — "

" Let me come in, father ! do — *do* ! — Let me answer him, face to face ! Only say the word, father — only say the word; and I don't care who's 'tother side; I'll stave the door in, 'afore you can say Jack Robberson."

" Walter Harwood — !"

" Sir, — father — sir."

" I command you to go to bed."

" Very well, father, very well: come along,
Panther — come along; and, as for that air
feller : *He*, a Yankee ! he's a Buckskin, every inch
of him, I know." — The Virginians are called
Buckskins. — " That's what he is : come along, I
say. — We're goin', you see, father ; but mind —
we shan't sleep a wink — shall we, Panther ? —
till that air great wap-sided feller's gone." His
voice died away, after a few broken phrases.;
and all was quiet, again.

" There, sir !" continued Peters; " there goes
the boy, whom you call so disobedient. There
goes the dog, that you coupled with him, in your
scoffing. Both come to your succour; while
your other son is fast asleep — snoring, I dare
say — in his bed. —— Farewell; I have nothing
more to say to you, now. My errand is over.
You are forgiven."

" Stop — I — I — not yet. I am bewildered,
now; I had something to say; but — who are
you — what ? — I still see that awful countenance."

" What countenance? what are you talking
about ?"

" I hardly know. My temples are sore; my limbs, weak — my faculties, confused. I feel some how — I cannot well describe it — somehow, as if I had met with a severe fall. I remember a strange face; a face, of prodigious magnitude; a strange, powerful, sweet language — thunder and smoke — shadows and shapes — one of which threw me into a swoon; or pushed me down a great precipice, with an arm like a giant."

" Pho, pho ! calm yourself."

" I will — I am. We were speaking of poor Walter." — " Yes, — yes — tell me where he goes; night after night. You foretold a death of of terrour, to him; perhaps — perhaps — let me see your face."

" My face — there !"

" Perhaps, you know that he is already in the way of such a death. How ! no alteration : — what are you made of? You talked of treason — of traitors — rebels. Hear me ! you have been a father — have you not ? — Ah ! I thought so; I thought so; your eyes *do* change colour, now ! Tell me, I beseech you, with whom does he confederate ? what are his views ? why is he al-

ways wandering away into the mountains ? Hear
me ! I never saw you so moved, before, as you
have been this night.   We are about parting
— perhaps, for ever."—

" True — true."

" We may never meet again."

" Quite possible."

" Never — never ; until we meet before the
bar of God. Look at me. There is a devouring secret here ; *here* — within my heart ; one,
that will carry me to my grave. I know it —
I am sure of it. You, perhaps, are the only
human creature, that can relieve me. See — see
— look how I am wasted away. But a little
time ago, I was a strong man. See to what I am
reduced ; a skeleton ; a miserable shadow ; and
why? Because I have done evil — because I
have sinned, awfully — so that I cannot sleep."

" Repent, Abraham Harwood ; repent."

" I do — in dust and ashes. But I dare not
fully atone, for my transgression."

" I pity you."

" Every breath — every sob — and every breath
is a sob, with me now—every breath ; every sob is

carrying me on — *on* — for ever on, like a tide, nearer and more near, to the judgment seat. A few more days; — a few more nights; and I shall be on trial, Jonathan Peters, for the soul of that boy; nay, perhaps, for the soul of thousands, hereafter to be born of his blood. Look at me. Think of what may happen to me, through him. Pity me. One wrong principle, instilled into the heart of a child, may spread, like the leprosy; and be perpetuated perhaps, through countless generations. Ah! you are sobbing! — Look at me;—let me pluck away your hands.".

" Be still — Be still — I am not sobbing."

" No matter. Cover your face then, if you will. You are a father — I am sure of it; and I dare not venture upon the awful, pure, deep solitude of your thought."

" Man! man! will you drive me distracted? — will you provoke me to tear you, piecemeal, before we part ?"

" Yea — yea! limb from limb, if you have the courage! I am afraid of death — so afraid of it !—O! there's no language to tell the crushing, miserable apprehension, that I feel, when they speak of death; and yet! I will give up my life —here — here, upon the spot—if I can be assured of one thing !".

.".What is it."

" Only this; that I shall not have to answer for the transgressions of that boy. For the sake of his blessed mother: — Ah! your countenance alters, anew — darkens — withers. What have I said! what have I done! Hear me! hear me! — do not abandon me, yet! I adjure you!—I adjure you!—I beseech you! by all that you have experienced, hitherto, at my hands!"

" Dare you adjure me, by these words! me — me, Abraham Harwood! Have you the tremendous courage, to call upon *me*, by such words of power? — to — "

" Well! why do you stop? Go on, go on; I entreat you! So stern — so resolute —so unforgiving *now*; and, but a moment ago, so kind; so gentle; so benevolent! Dare I! Yes! thou implacable man.—What hast thou ever received, at my hands, but good; and not evil? Yes, yes; I have courage enough to adjure thee, by these —

these words. I dare to cry out; by all that hath been done to thee, or thine — by me, or mine ! — whatever thou art! By all thy own sorrow — untold — unspeakable as it is ! By the transcendant mystery, of thy nature ! By thy power over the hearts of men ! By thy duty, as a believer — by thy hope, as a Christian ! —— By thy — no, no ! thou shalt never pass over my threshold" —putting himself in his way; and clinging to his garments: — "never !—never!—thou proud, unconquerable, bad man, till I know from thee ; for thou knowest — I am sure of it —whither leads the path of the lad ; and what are the perils that beset him !"

" Let me go, Abraham Harwood; let me go, in peace. My work is accomplished."

" Never; never !" — striving with him, all the way to the door. " O, that his mother were here ! the beautiful, dead woman ! the creature, whose awful eyes — and sweet, plaintive, clear voice —"

" Never ! —— We shall see !" cried Peters, tearing himself away from the desperate man setting his foot; and flinging him off. " Never

Were the walls of iron, I would pass through them, now !"

Saying this, he went up to the door, wrenched off the fastenings; tore away the wooden bar; threw them all aside, with a noise, that alarmed Panther, and set him barking; caught up his rifle; uttered a low cry of anguish — of bitter, bitter anguish — like the convulsive moan of a dying man; a cry, which he that heard it, never thought of afterwards, without a shudder; went blindly over the threshold; and staggered away — not in the direction of his home — but in another, which led, first, into the grave yard; then, over the place of murder; and, after a little time, into a wood, so dangerous, that no man of all that country, would have gone there, after night-fall, without a dog, and a loaded gun.

CHAPTER IX.

TRADITIONS. — THE WRESTLING MATCH. — BOB
CARTER. — APPARITION. — BALD EAGLE. —
PANTHER.

NOTHING more was heard of the " unaccountable stranger," as they still continue to call him,
in the neighbourhood, where these transactions
took place; nothing, save a few terrible stories;
for a long time, after he went away, so oddly;
at midnight — in a direction, so unusual — from
the door of the parsonage.

It clouded up, very suddenly, after his departure. The wind arose; a few drops of rain fell;
and a little heavy thunder was heard, in the direction of the burial ground; with sharp cries,
afar off, in the dangerous wood — as everybody
knew; for the preacher spoke of it, in full prayer
meeting, a little time after; echoes and cries;

yet no blood was found there upon the trampled grass; or the large trees, near which the shot had been fired; although many were forth to look for it, on the morning after the disappearance of Peters; while the first, who went by his hut, in the great wilderness, found it all open to the sky; a part of the roof carried away; the rest of it smoking, as if the hot, heavy thunder had fallen there, "by cartloads;" the old furniture broken to pieces; and all the woods to the south, strewed with fragments of torn paper, written all over, with strange words and characters, which no man was ever able to read.

Nay; it soon came to be whispered about, confidentially, in the great chimney corners; among the very old, and very young people, that Peters had been carried off, in a whirlwind; cottage and all; spirited away, in a thunderstorm, such as never was heard of, before—by his Master—the Evil One; or Old One. Aye—and, before another week had gone over, there were those, who knew; and were ready to give a reason for the sudden recall of the stranger, in such a style; at such a time; or, as the lawyers would

say, "to show cause," therefor. — It would seem
that, on the very night before he "cleared out,"
in a hurricane; as the Marble-Head fishermen
do, when they have made a league with Old
Scratch; he shot a young catamount, close
by the preacher's door; that her scream was
heard, a mile or two; that, all the family heard
it; and spoke of it, before the stranger — as being very like the voice of an old Mohawk
woman — a witch, if ever there was one; a witch,
whom they all knew, and were all afraid of;
that Peters had owed her a grudge, for a long
time; that she had never been out of her bed,
since that night; would never say what ailed her;
would not allow the "doctor" to come within
pistol shot of her house; and was perfectly well,
the very day, before, having been met in the
woods, by one that spoke of her wonderful activity. Of course, Mr. Beelzebub was perfectly
in the right. He had no other way, perhaps, to
keep his followers from quarrelling with each
other; to the "ruination" of the good old
cause.

Matters went on, smoothly enough, in this way till a great "raising," which had been long under way, took place in a neighbouring town. The building; a famous one — all size and fashion, for that part of the world—was up: the people were distributed about, in groups, over the grass; under the trees — and among the bushes. The wrestling, which always made a part of the day's amusement, was just ready to begin. The multitude were quiet; and a ring was prepared; when, all at once; nobody ever knew how, or where, the story originated; all at once, it began to be whispered about, on every side, that one of the " bad men" was among them; perhaps, the very one; the " unaccountable;" the " stranger;" who had "appeared," a little time before, to poor " Mr. Parson Harwood, of Ginger Town;" tempted him, because of his miraculous piety, month after month; bewitched his whole family; including a little " Virginny gal," who was " keepin' " there; played a thousand awful pranks, in the woods, meeting-house, and grave-yard, which he haunted with especial perseverance; going off, at last, in a clap of thunder,

while in conversation with Parson Harwood —
face to face — on the step of his own door.

Some inquiries followed; a bustle; a quick
general examination of every face in the crowd,
for a minute or so; and all was quiet again.
The toddy, egg-nog, and switchell (a drink made
of molasses and water—half and half—in use, we
believe, at Bunker's Hill), had gone about rather
freely; so that, a few minutes after the ring was
formed, a few heavy tumbles were given, without
a trip, or a lock.

At last " one Bob Carter" appeared; a sort
of champion for the day. The ring was deserted,
immediately; the people gave way, on every side.
He walked up; and, saying a word or two, by
way of a challenge, threw off his jacket. No
answer. He waited a few minutes; and, finding
nobody disposed for a " tussle," became exces-
sively clamorous, and abusive; cursing every
body about him; " daring out" all the country;
all the state; all America; and all the world.
Nobody replied — nobody — not even, by a laugh.
The corporal was there; but nothing could in-
duce him to understand, or see the saucy looks

of Carter, who went up to him, at last; and bullied him, to his great, good-natured face, till the blood of every body else, near, boiled with indignation.

The corporal did not want courage; or power. He was more than a match for the fellow, in bodily strength; but he knew his quarrelsome temper, and was afraid of it. He knew very well, that, if he "flung" Carter, he would have to fight him, afterwards;—a kind of sport, by the way, that a New-England farmer has no relish for. He never fights; never goes to loggerheads; but with a deadly weapon; a sort of religious bravery; and a feeling of right, on his part, even to the shedding of blood.

Many a stout heart sunk, as Carter went about, hither and thither, among the people; naked, from his waist up; showing a broad, formidable chest; a distorted shoulder; and a crooked arm, (the trophies of many a previous battle); giving out his challenge, on every side, in a loud voice, for " Indian hug ; half hug; arm's length" or " close hug"— to " all creation." Still, nobody answered. For a-while, the larger men

were content with pawing him off; turning the
matter aside, with a laugh; or dodging out of
the way; and stooping, whenever he came nigh:
but, he persevered, until this feeling of good-
humour was entirely done with; and a deep silence
followed, every-where; a profound, sullen, cold,
silence—interrupted, at long intervals, when his
back was turned — by a far-off hoarse murmur-
ing, of hatred, and mortification; — a noise, not
unlike that of the wind rising in the woods; or
the great sea coming in, with a heavy swell. Then
followed a portentous calm. The multitude gave
way, for a moment, or so; then, crowded up to
the ropes — and stood still; their faces like stone,
with a shadow upon every one of them.   Their
manhood was outraged; and, peaceable as they
were, by nature, some were almost ready for a
serious battle, with weapons of death.

Men, who are collected in a crowd; any-
where; at any time; will do that, while there,
which they would never be guilty of, any where
else; or, at any other time. They will break out,
when they are together, into noisy, clamorous,
general approbation of that, which every one of

the whole would be afraid, or ashamed of approving, were it not for the people about him: they are carried away, by each other; transported by sympathy; and will rejoice at any display of personal courage, or bodily strength, or address, at such a time, however brutal it may be; or affronting; or saucy; and, however, the putting up with it, may impeach their own valour. They make a noise, to conceal their fear; break forth, into clamorous outcry, to escape the imputation of cowardice, when they have been bullied with effect. So will the crowd behave, in almost every case; but especially when they are gathered about prize-fighters, or wrestlers; yet here, they were quiet—all quiet—quiet as the grave; mute and immoveable, as if execution were going to be done, straightway, to some individual of their number; all stern, cold, and serious, too; as if each were thoroughly prepared in his own heart, for whatever might happen, either to himself, or to his brother, when the lot should be drawn.

Walter Harwood was there; standing aloof, and apart from the rest. All eyes were upon his haughty, pale face; for the changes thereof were unspeakably sudden — fierce — and violent; growing more and more terrible, at every breath, till Carter, was going round, for the fourth time, " daring out" all the strong men of the country by name; Winslow, among the rest; brandishing his arms; whooping, like a savage; and calling them, all, in so many words, a great " heap o' snarlin', sneakin', braggin', bullyin', cowards."

Walter's head fell upon his bosom, when he heard Carter say this. He turned pale—deadly pale;—and would have tumbled forward, but for one of the bye-standers — a large, powerful man, whom nobody knew. After a short, vehement struggle, with himself—the boy recovered; and, without lifting his eyes, to see who had upheld him, went a few yards further off; and stood awhile, with his back to the rope; his arms folded; his hair flying; his large eyes on the turf, into which he was grinding his heel; as if debating with himself, whether to return, or go away, entirely. After a minute or two, his head sank; he grew very pale; turned away; and hurried off, with a quick step — describing a curve, as he went; like one, who would, but cannot; has no power to withstand, a great attraction; persevered for awhile; stopped; lifted his head; started — on finding himself so near the very spot, from which he had set off; and stood still, there — eying Carter askance; with brows gathered; lips blue; teeth set; his mouth bloody; the veins, all over his white forehead, swollen; the colour coming and going, at every breath, like flashes of inward fire. Again he made the attempt; and again he came back to the very same place.

The stranger followed him—cautiously and afar off — as if he understood all the changes, that he saw; the sharp throes of a fine, brave heart; while cowardice and hatred; fear, and fiery courage — desperation — were all at work within it.

At last, our hero began to hurry in his walk; to breathe, more freely; to tread, more firmly. A moment more; and he threw up his head; came straight forward; and set his foot within the deserted place of contention. Twenty arms were outstretched; but he would not be plucked away. Twenty voices broke out, into anxious, loud whispering, all at once; but he stood still, nevertheless. The stranger saw it; came forward; and, without saying a word, gently drew him away from the prohibited spot, before Carter perceived him. Walter lifted his head; and, when he saw the stranger's face, he leaned away from it; shook violently, as with an ague, all over; and faltered out his name. He knew it — he knew the man : — it was Jonathan Peters, himself; but so unlike what he had been; so altered, by his rude farming dress, of striped woollen cloth; his large hat; and hair, combed smoothly down, over his forehead, even to the eyes; that Walter might have passed him, twenty times, in the crowd, without knowing him.

"Not a word, more—I charge you," said Peters. Walter frowned; shook him off; stepped off a pace or two; the people going away on every side, until there was another vacancy, of which he was the centre; — began a deliberate survey of the tall men, about him—one by one— his large wet eyes full of bitterness and scorn;— called Panther; — gave him two or three farewell caresses; and sent him away, as if determined, whatever might come of the trial, which was near, to have no aid, of man, or beast. Having done this — he tore off his jacket, before any body could prevent him; — went up to Carter; and flung it in his face, without saying a word. His heart was too full; if he had opened his mouth, voice and tears would have come together.

The people were amazed — afraid — when they saw this. They rolled back upon their neighbours; and a general whispering — a few loud words — with one or two broken cries — were heard. Some thought him crazy; — but no! the eyes of a crazy creature never looked like his. They were too mournful; — too dark, with awful resolution; more like those of a religious man, going wilfully — deliberately — to martyrdom. Others thought him in liquor. They were mistaken. He was perfectly sober. Not a drop had passed his lips the whole day through.

Carter smiled, when he saw him approach; called him "gawkey," "lubber," "parson," — all the bad names, that he could "lay his tongue to." But, finding that our boy was not of a temper to be laughed out of countenance; he came up to him —

close up; thrust his head into his face, and told him, that, if he didn't walk off, about his business, he would take him over his knee; slap him soundly—that's what he would — right away; and pack him off to his mammy; putting forth his right arm, while he spoke, to seize him by the collar. The boy anticipated his purpose, in time to avoid the clutch; and, casting another look upon the rabble — it was like the winter lightning; cold, bright, and preternatural — sprang aside. Carter saw the look;—his arm· fell — and he retreated, a step or two, before he recollected himself.

The boy lost no time. He saw him recovering; saw the black blood shadowing his whole face; overspreading his forehead, like a swarthy heat; so — shaking away, his own rich hair; dashing off the sweat, from his· clear temples; he began to feel about, for a good foot-hold, in the turf.

Peters interfered, again; went up to Walter; reasoned with him; expostulated with him; — pointed out, in a few brief words, the rashness, and folly of his intention. Walter made no reply; but, in wrenching away his arm, that which

Peters held, he saw something afar off — stopped
— and followed it, whatever it was, through the
trees, upon the hill side — as if he saw comfort
among them. All eyes were turned in the same
direction. But nothing could be seen; — or
nothing, save a solitary Indian, loitering on the
way toward a group of his people, who were lying about, under the large trees; half awake;
half asleep; smoking their pipes in quiet, while
the rest of the multitude were all in confusion.
It was Bald Eagle; the little Bald Eagle; a small,
active, wily, red man, of whom the white people
were more afraid; peaceable as he was; indolent
as he was; than of Bob Carter, himself.

"Is that Bald Eagle?" said Peters. "Why
do you ask? — yes!" — "Then I need not hope
to prevail!"—"No; leave me. I have nothing to
say to you—leave me!" Walter's face brightened
visibly, when he saw the brave Eagle; but, when
he spoke to Peters — in the same breath — his lips
were white; his large eyes, full; his throat convulsed
with shame—while his deep chest heaved up, and
collapsed, four or five times, very violently. "It
is more than your life is worth, young man;" said

a bye stander. "Dont buckle to the great brute, whatever he may do." "No, my lad — no, no !" cried another. "No, no — for the life o' goodness, *dear* young man !" "Who is he !" "What is he !"—"What's your name?" cried several others. "'Tis the son o' Mr. Harwood." "You don't say so." "Poor feller, poor feller ! — Not Mr. Parson Harrod !" "O, yes !" "God help him, then ! — you may go your way. There is no hope for him."—"What ! — is he the chap that's bewitched ?"—"Oh — yes" —"No !"—"How you talk !"—"O—h yes !"

"Stand back ! — stand back ! — form a ring !" cried Peters. "Form a ring ! form a ring ; — Hourra for you !" shouted all those, who were interfering, before ; "Hourra for you !" Bob Carter was now ready. He leaped, from the outside, into the centre of the ring ; more like a wild beast, raging for blood ; — much more — than like a human creature. The crowd held back ;—motionless and breathless ; — but, on turning their eyes to Walter, who stood bravely up to his adversary, they saw upon his forehead, bright signs of hope for him ; and a wo to the champion.

"God bless you! God bless you!" breathed
out one voice, above all the rest. "Ready, now?"
said Carter.   "Aye, aye; all ready!" answered
our hero. "What play?" — "Arms length."

The people were thunderstruck.   They were
wholly unprepared for such desperate courage,
in a youth. A general rush followed — a general
murmur; a thousand cries and whispers, of disapprobation.

"Back, back," said Peters:—"Back, back;
let him have his own way!"

"His own way! that air boy, there — with Bob
Carter — at arms' length.   Yon are out o' your
head, I guess, whoever you be; — aint ye?"

"Nobody here's able to keep his feet afore
Bob Carter, at arm's length, I tell you," cried
one of the multitude.

"Save an' except our Eagle, if you please,"
added another; "Keep *his* feet, where a cat
could'nt — I know!"

"Arm's length will not be so dangerous for
the boy, though it will give him no chance of
throwing his adversary," said Peters.   "Back,
back; they are all ready, now."

" They began. Walter was very graceful;
quick, sharp, and " soople, as a great snek."
His action was a little tremulous, at first; and,
apparently, weak. It soon became cat-like; a
sort of motion, like that of a young leopard; or a
fine racer, when led out, over the green, cool
turf. Bob Carter depended upon main strength.
His huge muscles wrought, with every motion, all
over his body. He appeared powerful enough
to crush the boy — sinew and bone. At one time,
during the heat, there was a commotion, for half
a minute or more, in his prodigious frame, which
the people spoke of, long after, as really tremendous; altogether beyond any thing, which they
had ever seen, or heard of.

Carter made four desperate efforts, to pluck
the boy down, by mere bodily power and weight;
but Walter, to the amazement of all the crowd,
withstood him, like a steel spring; crouching to
every pressure; and recovering, each time, with
a bound. Once or twice, there was a general
shout of encouragement; which was instantly
quieted, by the older men — lest it might interfere
with his fine playing.

Carter grew more cautious. Finding how easily the boy withstood, or eluded his might, he began to " show foot," for another, and more active demonstration. Walter saw his purpose; heard his breathing — twas like that of a war-horse; kept off; and acted altogether on the defensive; wasting no atom of his wind or power, in retaliation. Both, however, were soon out of breath: wrestling is a grievous occupation, for the lungs. They separated, for a minute or two, by mutual consent. Some of the people shouted for joy: but others, who knew the champion better, shook their heads: and all were afraid, when they saw him girding up his loins, anew; setting his large bare feet, as if they were shod with iron — holding himself away; and scowling at Walter with half shut eyes.

They met again. They played about one another, now, like adroit wrestlers; crouched; leaped; showed foot; and stood on one leg — bending nearly double, in every direction, as they did so.

But Carter was awkward; and, after a few heavy flourishes, he gave up that kind of play, to

his little "spry" — "springy" — antagonist;
nay; contrary to the rule, of generous, bold warfare — stood up, like a pillar of iron, as far off,
as he could — played square — and offered only
an occasional trip, of which nothing could be
made; or a round-about unwieldy lock, which
nobody would venture to take, unless he wanted
a leg or two broken. Walter growing more con-
fident, as Bob grew more cautious; tempted
him at last, in every possible way — in every
kind of posture; so that a byestander, ignorant of
wrestling, would have wondered how he was able
'to keep his feet, for a moment. But Carter
knew well what he was about. He had already
learnt, wary as he was, that our boy's trip was
like a flash of lightning; that, while it was perilous to trip him, there was no way of bringing
him down, by mere force. Nothing remained,
but a "twirl" or a "lock." Both were dangerous.
Walter would not permit a lock, but on his own
terms; and Bob was afraid of trying it; because,
if he failed in throwing his youthful adversary,
nothing could save *him*. So, too, in the twirl;
he knew that a tap, skilfully put in, would bring

a giant upon his back, in the middle of a balancing lock; or a critical sharp "twirl." They drew
up — made play; breathed hard; retreated; showed foot; half locked — sprang, at each other;
and wrenched away, for half a minute, as if their
sinews would snap; cried out; broke their hold;
grappled, anew — blindly and furiously, for a
single moment; passed a trip or two, like a flash
— interchanged a blow — and parted, instantaneously. Away, went Carter, to one side of the
circle, where he staggered upon the ropes; and,
away went our boy to the other — flung off his
feet, with a piece of Carter's waistband clutched
in his " right paw."

"Foul play! foul play!" — shouted a part
of the multitude — as the boy bounded off; and
came erect upon his feet; while Carter fell upon
his knees. "Foul play! foul play! — shame!
shame!"— "He broke his hold!"

"Who broke his hold?" cried "our Bob" hoarse
with passion; "ye're a liar, whoever ye be. Come
out here, if ye're a man; the more, the merrier —
one, two, or a dozen of ye!"

Nobody answered. But, when his back was

turned, a fellow, of much experience in these things, declared, in a whisper, that if Bob had not broken his hold, he'd 'a been flat enough; " like a shad in a platter." — "Aye — that's what he would !" said another; " like a flap jack in a fryin' pan; that's what he would, faith !" Several persons broke into the ring; and went up to Walter, whom they showed great solicitude about; while nobody loitered near Carter — nobody spoke to him — nobody cared for him. He felt it. He was in great pain. His wrath was terrible.

They met once more. Carter's tongue was out: his lips were swollen; his great eyes, fiery; and, about his mouth, was a little white foam, like sea froth. Walter was very pale; his dilated eyes were blood-shot; his hair had broken loose; and his look was that of one, who, come what may of it, never will be subdued. Carter stooped; heaved; gasped for breath; — strained, as if he were heaving at a mountain; uplifted our boy into the air; and attempted, a dozen times running, to throw him upon his back — while his feet were off the ground; but all to no purpose.

The boy came down, every time, like a cat o'·
the mountain. Carter grew desperate; collected all his power; made a tremendous plunge;
caught him up; and swung him, round and
round, all·clean from the turf, till both were gid-·
dy. Walter's feet were in the air, for nearly
half a minute but Carter could not break his
hold, or fling him off— otherwise our hero must
have given over the ring. The grass flew —
·the turf glittered, wherever his feet struck;·
and all the people shouted for joy. At last — all
at once — both of them went reeling away, together. A short struggle ensued; Walter was
upon his knee, for a single moment; and, immediately after — as quick as thought — hurled
five or six yards over the head of his adversary.
He fell outside of the ring.   The people crowded
in to his relief; tearing away the ropes on every
side; and showing their sympathy, by every possible attention.   He was lying afar off— quite
stunned — sick—helpless — with his fine hair all
abroad over the grass. Two of them lifted his
head; another tore open his collar : a fourth
washed his temples with spirit; while Peters kept

aloof, with his eyes upon Carter, who stood all
apart from the rest; gnashing his teeth — bruis-
ing the turf — panting as if his black heart
would explode, upon the spot; his dark, savage
countenance, made fifty times more savage,
by his plentiful, coarse, torn hair; and a smile
of barbarous exultation — cruelty—which brightened his very temples — and rocky, square
forehead — as if the blood of his heart were all
on fire.

Our Eagle, seeing the result, put away his
pipe; leaped upon his feet; and, after looking
about, for a moment or so, called Panther from
the wood, where he was lying ; and came straightway to the place, where Walter sat, with his
head upon the knee of a stranger. The people
went back; and were silent. Carter lowered
his voice: and Eagle, after looking at Walter, for a minute, or more, without any visible
emotion, shook away the blanket from about him ;
and put his hand, quietly, upon the heart of the
dying boy. He was alive. Wherefore, Eagle
stood up; called Panther; and was turning
to go away, when Peters lifted his head : and

their eyes met.   Peters betrayed great concern
— wrath — anxiety — terror, perhaps.   But no
change, or shadow of change, went over the face
of our Eagle.   " You know poor Injunn ? —
you see Ball Eagle, one time?" said he, step‑‑
ping softly before Peters ; and speaking, in a low,
small voice, just audible to those, who stood
within his reach..— " You see Ball Eagle, one
time?" — " Yes." —" Hi ! — You go? You no
go?" — " I shall go, by and by ; not yet." —
" Hi ! hi !"—calling Panther to him ; stooping
down ; whispering in his ear ; and literally giving him charge of Peters. — " Hi ! you no go.
You see him dogue? You go ; him go : You
run much ; him run mucher.   Dogue ; him go
ketch bard marns."

Saying these words, he went off to the same
tree ; replaced his pipe ; fell a smoking, as before ; with eyes upon that part of the ground
where Walter, who had risen up, was preparing anew for the strife.   About Bald Eagle, were
a family of his tribe ; some tearing ash twigs,
for basket work, with fingers of iron — little,
but incredibly strong.   Others, working their

brilliantly coloured porcupine quills, into shot-
pouches, belts, and mocasins; others, polishing
their great bows.   Peters, though prodigiously
troubled by the apparition of the diminutive savage, held his ground; aware that, if he went
off, beyond his ordinary walk, Panther would
fly at his throat, immediately.

The people saw this; and were still as death—
frightfully so.   They withdrew from the stranger, and left him alone; for they saw by the little, bright eyes of the Indian — they were like
those of the rattle-snake — that something was
the matter — something, of no trivial import.
Bald Eagle and Walter Harwood loved one another — most of them knew — with a love, passing that of women.   Eagle hated Carter; and
had told him to his face, not long before, that
he was cruel, and cowardly.   They knew, also,
that if Carter prevailed over the boy, unfairly, it
would be a game of death for him.   But after
all, there was that, in the behaviour of Eagle; and that, in the look of the stranger, (while
the dog sat a little way off; watching him so in-
tently, that, if his body moved or swayed, ever

so little, that of the dog moved and swayed with
it;) a something in the carriage of both, which
none of them all could understand.   They began to think of the mysterious whispering, a little
time before; to examine the faces of one another
anew; to look upon it as a sort of intimation
from above, that something wicked was among
them.   At last, one of their number, after looking earnestly in the face of the stranger, for a
long time, detected some expression, that brought
back to his memory, all at once, the look of the
" unaccountable," who had " appeared," in the
town meeting, a great while before.   He spoke of
it; and Peters, when he looked up, found himself enclosed, on every side — completely surrounded, by a great number of serious, thoughtful, dark-looking men; who, while they stood
afar off, as if they were afraid of him; pressed
upon each other, steadily and firmly, with planted feet, and lowering foreheads; — like men who
are determined, whatever may happen, to prevent some desperate creature from escaping. They
had nearly forgotten poor Walter, for a minute
or two.   All eyes were upon the stranger, whose

right hand was thrust into his bosom, as if to quiet a great commotion there.

He knew not, perhaps, that he, thereby, revealed a sort of military dress, underneath his gabardine, or loose frock; and a something, not very unlike the handle of a weapon; a knife — or the butt end of a pistol, mounted with silver: they saw it; but, instead of retreating, they only pressed the more heartily together, as if willing to abide the lot, which, if they meddled with him, at such a time, was pretty sure to fall on a part of their number. They were all quiet and breathless; but evidently prepared for the worst, whatever it might be; for they stood and looked, as one might suppose the population of a city would, if they had come forth into a large plain, to see a miracle performed; or to wait the second shock of some earthquake, the first of which had overthrown their houses—making the whole country a place of sepulture.

The champion kept his place, near the middle of the enclosure, wholly disregarded; until the boy, having cleared his mouth, from the dust and foam, that were choking him; having washed his

long hair, with spirit; put it away from his face;
and bound it up; recovered his breath, a little;
and got free from those, who supported him,
while they were watching she stranger; started,
suddenly, upon his feet; — shook them all off, —
and precipitated himself, head foremost, like a
young panther, at his adversary. Carter stepped
aside, when he saw him approach. — A moment
of indecision followed. Both stood still; Carter
crouching nearly double; Walter holding his
breath — his knees trembling under him; his
hands clenched; and his large teeth set, with convulsive determination. The people saw his face
— it was no longer human; they trembled, and
were afraid — not for him — but for Carter. It
is an awful thing to see the face of a boy — a
child — a sort of angel, fresh from the moulding,
and impress of the Maker's touch, instantaneously
transformed, by evil passion, to the face of a bad
spirit; an awful thing, to be sure. — At last, both
at once — both, precisely, at the same instant,
leaped forward; each at the other's throat. — A
shriek followed — a fierce gasping — a general
outcry; and all that were near, rushed in, to tear

them apart. Our Eagle, seeing this, got up, again; took out a short rifle, which he carried under his blanket; — called away the dog, lest he might interfere; and gave him in charge to another Indian, who held him, by the large iron collar about his neck; went a little way off, where he could see the stranger; and stood, leaning upon his rifle. " Fair play! fair play!" shouted some one of the multitude " Fair play! fair play!"

" Far play!" screamed our savage, running at full speed into the centre of the circle. — The people gave way, as before; — the combatants, who had been held apart, for breath, grappled anew. The concussion was frightful. They panted, heaved —sprang together, from the ground. For a single moment, Walter's body was bent, as if his back were broken; — the next — his knees were crushed into the chest of Carter. A loud groan followed. — Both fell; struggled — cried out — rolled, over and over, upon the trodden turf — and separated; — no man could see why, or wherefore. The clear blood was running out of Carter's ears. Walter lay, afar off — without life or motion; his head on one side;—and his naked arms thrown out — all abróad — as if his brave heart had burst, in the final stuggle for dominion.

Eagle went up to him. The dog forced his head out of the collar; and came, forward, at full spring;—with his neck bloody, and large ears torn — to protect his brave young master : the multitude, wholly forgetful of Peters, tumbling over one another, in every direction, to avoid the beast.

Eagle saw him afar off; heard his terrible cry; knew it for the signal of death ; and levelled his gun to shoot him; but, finding, after two or three trials, that he could not fire, without endangering other lives, he threw it away; sprang toward Carter; and stood over him, with his tomahawk in the air, just in time to prevent the ferocious dog from tearing his throat, as he lay upon the grass — without life or motion —till they lifted him up. The people screamed with terrour, when they saw the uplifted, bright weapon, the body of Carter, below, and the haughty savage astride of it. — How little they knew the proud Indian. — A tumult ensued; a great uproar.

The boy was borne off, more dead than alive, to his home; Carter was taken to the mill, where he lay for nearly five weeks, in a strange bed, with no creature alive, to wish him out — and all was confusion, till they began to look about for the stranger. —— He was gone.

Eagle was quite angry with himself; his prey had escaped him. He called Panther; and would have put him on the track; but the dog refused; — he would not leave his poor master, whom they were carrying off.

The Indians, who were under the trees, then drew nigh; and one of them, being enquired of, pointed in a direction, which he had seen a person, like the stranger take, while the rest of the crowd were making a noise.

" Bard marns, bard marns," quoth Eagle " very bard mans, Garter Snake. You cotch him."

Off went a young savage, without speaking a word, in pursuit.

" Who is he? who is he?" cried fifty voices, in a breath — " Who is he? a witch or a wizard, or — "

" Stop im talk. Me say 'um good — high! —
noise too much — high !" said Eagle, disen-
gaging his right arm; throwing off his blanket; and keeping his eyes, on the far wood,
where the stranger had vanished. " Noise too
much, now."

" Peace ! peace !" cried a man of authority, in
the crowd. " Peace ! — our Eagle knows him.
Be quiet !" — They grew still.

" Much time ago," continued Eagle; throwing up his head; balancing his body, with a fine,
bold attitude; and preparing for a speech. "High,
then — hi ! — you see; much time ago; wite
mans, he killed. Hi ! Ball Eagle him go out,
ketch beaver; him shoot. Hi ! — one day, im
walk; sun up dere" — pointing to the meridian
— " peoples, him pray — make preach; make
noise — Hi ! Ball Eagle, him see mans — wite
mans — wite, like dead wite mans — walkee,
walkee — fast — much fast. — Ball Eagle, him
say; wite mans— where you go ? Wite mans he
no speak poor Injunn; him no speak; him no
hear. Then Ball Eagle—him go up, so ! — so !"
— shouting " hi ! — wite mans — him jump ! wite

mans — him no see. Ball Eagle — him go so —
hi!" pointing to the left — " wite man's him go so —
hi ! hi !" — pointing to the right. — " Ball Eagle
— him walkee, walkee, much long time. — Hi!
hi!" starting back, as if he saw something terrible, under foot, — " hi ! — Ball Eagle — him
fright ! — wite mans dead — much killed ; odder
wite mans." —

" Lord help us ! how you talk."

" Iss."

" O, ho !" cried out one of the crowd; " O
ho ! I know what he means, very well, now; he
speaks of the murdered stranger."

" Lord help us !—Lord help us."

" Don't you, our Eagle ?

" Iss — Iss."

" Pray then ; if I understand your story, you
mean to say, that, a great while ago, you met this
very man, while you were out, in the woods;
on the Sabbath day ?" " Iss." While the folks were
at meeting ?" " Iss." " That he was white, like a
dead man ?" " Iss." " That you spoke to him ?"
" Iss." " That he did not see you ?" " Iss;"
" Did not hear you ; did not reply ?" " Iss."

" That you hallooed ?" " Iss." That he jumped ?"
" Iss." " That you went off one way; and he
another ?" " Iss, iss." " That, by and by, you
came to a dead body; the body of one, who had
been killed *much*, as you say ; or murdered ?" —
" Iss very much."

" This man, therefore ; is it so, Eagle ? — can it
be ? — was he the murderer ?"

" No, no ; Ball Eagle, him no say too much ;
him no say all dat."

" But why did you not mention it, before ?"
said one of the bye-standers. " The apple-tree
didn't flower for nothin', arter all, neighbour," said
another. " The old scratch ! I never thought
o' that !"

" Why, Ball Eagle no say him 'fore ? Him
feard. Him poor Injunn. Wite mans no love
poor Injunn. Him hang — *hi !* — hang, like
dogue. Ball Eagle — him speak preacher-mans,
much long time ago."

" How ! — what ! — what preacher-mans ?"

" Ball Eagle — him go see white man's make
preach : He speak 'em all. Preacher-man say —
go, go, poor Injunn — go, go — by 'm by — you

you see him, one time.　You speakee me — so you do. — Hi !"

" Follow him ! follow him !" — cried out all the multitude, as with one heart.　" Home to your houses, every man of you ! — To horse ! and away ! — To horse ! To horse ! — Leave the man-slayer no city of refuge !　Away ! away ! ' Whoso sheddeth man's blood — by man shall his blood be shed !' "

The assembly broke up ; and dispersed, in every direction ; scouring the whole country, for the man of blood ; every one believing, more firmly than ever, in the terrible stories that were told of him.

CHAPTER X.

PETERS. — THE MANSLAYER. — WHO ? — THIRD
APPEARANCE. — FRIGHT. — MYSTERY. — OLD
NICK.

THEY heard no more of Peters, for a great
while. The Indian, who tracked him, was baffled;
a dog, that pursued him, was found, with his
throat cut: and, although hundreds were on foot,
or on horseback, after him, scouring all the
woods, and guarding all the ways, they got
no tidings of him; for his garb was that which
every body wore; and his look that of every tenth
man, to be met with.   It would seem, almost, (if
it were not for the great North American wilderness; a wood, where a whole nation might
hide from one another,) as if the story which is
now told, of his final disappearance, were true;
namely — that he vanished, without noise or

motion, from the middle of a great multitude, at
noonday, while their eyes were all upon him;
as if the earth had opened under his feet, and
swallowed him up.

Winter was near. The stranger was already,
as if he never had been; except when some accidental remark brought him to the minds of
people, for a moment or two; causing them to
lower their voices, and look about, on every side,
as if they expected him to appear. Walter had
been grievously ill; but was beginning to go
about, again; with a new and more serious temper. Yielding to the entreaties of Edith, he had
begun a course of severe study, side by side
with her; under the eye of the preacher, who
took to his bed, on receiving the news, about Peters — the "murderer," as they called him; the
manslayer — whom he had eaten with — slept
with — associated with, day after day, without
any suspicion of his true character: and had never left it, until the neighbourhood was all quiet,
again; the chace given up; and all hope of
bringing him to punishment, abandoned. The
autumn went over: the winter — the spring —

and he began to hold up his head, again. War had broken out: blood, the first of rivers, that *were* to flow, had been spilt. Our young hero was all on fire. He was pining away — his own spirit was devouring him. Whatever he did, was done with a sick, impatient, peevish temper — so unlike himself, that his father was alarmed. He was no longer the fine, bold, adventurous boy — going about, with a peremptory air, and a strong tread; a rifle over one shoulder; a hunting net, over the other; a powder horn, here; and a bullet pouch, there; with a large dog at his heels, ready to fly, if his master but whistled for him, at a she-bear's throat; or the cub of a catamount, before the face of its own mother. No — but he would sit by himself, with a book in his lap, hour after hour; without opening his mouth; or turning a leaf; wholly regardless of every thing but his "dear little Edith," who, if she spoke to him, kindly, in these fits of sorrowful abstraction, would bring the tears into his proud, beautiful eyes.

The name of Peters they never mentioned. Walter would not speak it, aloud; and poor Edith

dared not. Nevertheless, there hung upon the
hearts of Abraham Harwood, and of his whole
family, a solemn, sure belief, that, after a time,
they should see the stranger, whatever he was;
man, or devil — homicide, or not — once more.
Once — twice — had he come — twice; and
whatever he might be, they began to give way
to the popular superstition of the age, and believe that he would yet appear for a *third* time.

Every stranger that came nigh them was
watched; particularly, if he wore a large hat.
And, soon after the " raising," two or three men
from " down east," who journied, by accident,
over " Gingertown — (the parson's heritage; a
nominal incorporation of some fifty families or
so — scattered over a township of about five
miles, by eight) — were pursued, for a long time
through the woods, by people on horseback;
chiefly because they, the strangers, wore striped
woollen frocks, over a better dress; large
flapped hats; were shy of questions; or had
something " unaccountable," in their eyes. It
was even said, by certain of the older men, that
a " shape" like that of the Tempter, had " ap-

peared" once or twice in the grave-yard, after
night fall, haunted as it was; and once in the
dangerous wood, since he, the "Tempter,"
had vanished, at neighbour Zekey's Raising. :
Luckily, however, the portentous apple-tree;
though it showed signs of putting forth a few
green leaves, did not flower again, this year;
a forbearance, which went a great way, toward
calming the people, and re-assuring all of them—
in their superstition, " It hadn't flowered, for
nothin', arter all."

Well — Peters *did* come again; but only
once more, for ever; perhaps to confirm the pre-
dictions of the Mohawk woman, witch Hannah,
who had foretold it, years before; perhaps, to
thrill every heart anew, by a *third* visitation; —
as he had, more than once, by " appearing"
suddenly before them, without notice, while the
great, old fashioned clock was tolling the hour —
like the summons to a burial. He was not a
man, for serious, or profane trifling, one would
believe, to look at him; and yet, certain of these
things rather savoured of a disposition to prac-

tise, deliberately, and mischievously, upon the idle fears of children.

One day — it was on a warm Sabbath afternoon — a heavy shower came up, of a sudden, while the family were sitting all about the parlour; being tired by their long walk from " church;" and half asleep, in the damp, sultry, oppressive heat of the weather. The pitch wood was lighted; and set in the fire-place. All was quiet — so quiet, in the deep, awful darkness of the thunder cloud, which overhung the cottage, that even the noise of the flame, which the lighted wood sent up, sounded like a roaring, in the great chimney.

A tremendous clap of thunder broke over the house! — another! — and, while the reverberations were dying away — like the roar of battle afar off, a light, quick tap was heard, on the outer door. The preacher's new help went softly to it, on tip-toe, and let in a stranger, who, requesting her to say that he had come for the preacher, went forward, into the study, as if it were a familiar place to him.

Abraham Harwood was almost asleep; and

sat afar off — so that he could hear nothing of the voice; but a tall shadow shot along the white sanded floor, up to his very feet, as the stranger passed away. It was a terrible apparition; a shadow of death to the preacher. He knew it — he could not be mistaken. His heart sprang to his throat — he felt as if his last hour had come. But he arose, nevertheless, when the girl delivered her message; and walked bravely forth; so that no one, there, suspected aught of the matter; — bravely forth, into the passage, — where he waited, a little time, to recover himself, before he ventured upon the solitude, wherein the stranger — whatever he was — had chosen to conceal himself.

The struggle over — it was a very short and very severe one — the preacher hurried along to the study; set open the door; and, catching his breath, walked into the room. It was even as he feared. A man was there; a tall man — a homicide—if what other men whispered of him were true — standing up to the window, while the prodigious thunder was rolling about him; the great earth trembling under him; the whole fir-

mament — sky and air — alive, with a perpetual
broad glimmer; great shadows — cloudy shapes
going over it; as if the superior angels of God
were afloat, on their unbounded pinions, beneath
a transparent, illuminated sky.

"How is it with you, Abraham Harwood,
how is it, with you?" said the man — "Guilty, or
not guilty?"

"Spare me! spare me!" answered the
preacher; locking his hands; trembling in every
joint; standing in a posture of supplication, before the stranger; and speaking just above his
breath. "Whatever thou art, O, spare me!
Remember, I pray thee, if thou art, as I begin
to believe, the Avenger of blood — O, remember,
that my roof hath been a shelter for thee; my
house, a refuge; that we have eaten, together —
prayed and wept, very bitterly, together. O spare
me! — I have but a little time, now, to live."

"What! — spare you! and go to the gallows
in your stead!—spare the man, who has wronged
me, beyond all other men! — go skulking about,
in woods and caves; burrowing, night after night,
with reptiles, in the holes of the rocks; hunted

of all the earth; a bye-word, and a curse among all my race — month after month — year after year — that my chief enemy — he, to whom I owe all my affliction — all my sorrow — may escape!"

" In the name of God — who are you?"

" Why should I do this?"

" Because you have promised."

" No — never. I promised only to spare you further questioning. I shall keep my word. I have not forgotten, as you say, that we did *weep*, together, once. That has made me endure all this. But how, if, weary of my life — how, if I go this very night; give myself up to justice — and abide my trial? I am tired of living, sir; I am ready to die for *you*, if God will have it so. But, if he will not — if I should be acquitted — if any thing should come out, on the trial — any thing, to turn the people's thought once more to the time, that has gone by — what will become of you?"

Perhaps the colour of the sky; or the pale, quiet, mysterious lightning; or the solemn, strange appearance of the air, contributed somewhat, while he spoke, to the desolate and forlorn

expression of his dark face; but such was that expression, whatever were the cause thereof, when
Peters declared, with a voice of sincerity, that
he was tired of life, and quite ready to die, after
all, for another man; for his chief enemy, too;
that Abraham Harwood forgot his own peril —
forgot his own sorrow — heaved a thick sob, or
two; broke forth into prayer, for him; reeled
away to the wall; and cried, like a child.

" What say you, Abraham Harwood? speak
— will you permit me to surrender myself?"

" Are you not afraid ?—"

" Afraid ? — no ; — not for myself; but I am
for you."

" And I, too; I dare not stand a trial."

" And yet, sir — yet — you would have me
believe you innocent !"

" Yes—for innocent I am; so help me God !
innocent of deliberate, wilful murder; but not so
innocent, I fear, that I may put myself, with
safety, upon trial, before those, who cannot look
into the heart of a man."

" Indeed ! - say you this, in truth ?"

" In truth !—as I hope for mercy !—as I hope for pity, hereafter !"

" Give me your hand. I will go away, for ever. I will bear the opprobrium — for I — *I* have no children, to be crushed by it, when I am dead. Farewell !"

" Nay, nay—whither so fast ! why this bitter — *bitter* agony ! Is there aught, under the sky, that —"

" Man — man ! I wouldn't live another day, as I have now lived, week after week — hunted of the Red Eagle ; no — not for the whole of this great world. I have been afraid, for you. I would have stood my trial, but for you. I would have left my country ; but I could not go, without seeing you, once more ; I could not go away, for ever, without saying farewell to your children. I have been afraid, sir, that, after all, you were not innocent of your brother's blood. I have been ; — but I am so, no longer. But now ! —now, that I am satisfied ; what if we go, together ? Come, sir, come ! God — let us put our faith, in him — God will not suffer the brave, good man, to perish—for want of proof. I would sooner look for a miracle to be wrought, for his preservation. What say you? Rouse yourself. Be a man. Bid your dear family farewell, for a time; and go with me." -

" With you! your manner is wild — your voice, terrible! your — "

" No wonder — I am half crazy, for lack of nourishment."

" I know not whither to fly!—With you! — in such a temper — at such a time!"

" What are you afraid of?"

" Afraid of! I am afraid of *you* — of the sky — of the night — every thing — every body."

" Pho, pho; for shame! pho, pho — give me a mouthful to eat; prepare your family; take my arm; and let us go, to the judge. You may sleep quietly, then; but never, till then."

" O, no — no! — no! — I have no courage for it. I dare not. I should perish, with fear."

" No courage for it!—no confidence, either in yourself, or your cause!—no hope, in your great innocence! after all; no hope, in the mercy — or power — or justice — of Him, that made you! Then will I go, alone!"

" Oh, no! —*no!* How can I ever show that, of which there was no witness? how can I ever ✓ show the true meaning of my own heart? No — *no!* Bear with me but a little time, sir; and you may do this. My day is nearly over, now. I am sure of it—I have not long to live—I shall soon be out of the way."

" And would you be out of the way, thus? Are you cowardly, and wicked enough, Abraham Harwood; are you—to die, and leave the vindication of your character to your children — years and years, after you have destroyed — you, yourself—their only means; their only hope, of doing it ! — *Here ! — here !* — here, to the window. You would have me believe you. Rise up ; and come out of that hollow darkness, if you dare ! Come out! Turn up your face to the Almighty—up—up — if you dare, as I do mine— while the light of his tremendous look is pealing and flashing over your forehead !—Bravely done ! bravely dared ! blasphemer ! You have courage enough. Here — here — give me your two hands. We will abide one trial, together — come what may of it ! Now! every clap of

thunder hath a meaning of its own : remember
that ! Every flash of lightning hath its own particular commission; every bolt, a tree, or a life.
—Remember that; and say to me once more, that
you are not a wilful murderer — that you have
not been. — Say this, if you can.   Say it, if you
dare."

"I can — I will! Hear me ! I am not — I
have not been, a wilful murderer !".

" I believe you.   Farewell, Abraham Harwood ; farewell. · We never meet again — farewell !"

" Farewell ! farewell ! God for ever bless
you !"

" Stay — I must eat a mouthful more, though
I die for it, under your roof.   You have a new
maid here, I perceive.   Send her out of the way ;
prepare the children; spread your table ; and,
after I have broken your bread, I will go, in
peace."

The preacher did so ; and well was it, perhaps ;
for, with all their studied preparation — assured
as they were, beforehand, of his innocence, Edith
screamed ; Jotham tumbled out of the way ;

Panther showed his large teeth; and Walter started upon his feet, when the reputed homicide came, following the preacher, out of the darkness.

"Abraham Harwood, I thank you," said Peters; taking a chair, and "falling to," as if nothing had happened: "Is that female deaf — are you quite sure of it?"

He spoke of Lucy Armstrong, the dumb girl, who sat apart, in the corner, suckling her dark, ✓ strange baby.

Panther lifted his head; and sat listening, as if he heard voices in the low wind. Lucy started, — coloured up to the eyes — caught her brown boy closer to her heart ; and, with a look of unspeakable distress, began to make signs to Edith.

"Yes — perfectly deef; — hears nothin' but her child, I believe. Can she, Edith ?"

"O——h, yes ! — any loud, or near noise will disturb her; but she doesn't hear the words of people in conversation — or distinguish their voices."

"Ah ! what expressive, innocent eyes ! — I never saw any thing so clear, and beautiful. Dumb, too, I suppose ?"

The child, hearing a strange voice, after puffing
and blowing two or three times — turned his head
— smacked his wet lips—cuddled up his fat, red,
lubberly feet — his bright eyes twinkling and
snapping, all the time, as if he had been suckled
with champaigne; took a peep at Peters; kicked
up his heels — put his queer, little, red mouth into
a precious pucker, as usual; and, after a prelimi-
nary sob or two, set up his pipes, like a fine fellow.

"No, not entirely dumb.   She still speaks a
few simple words; and a few common phrases;
but her intonation is frightful."

Lucy began to sooth her baby; lulling him
with a sweet, plaintive, strange melody, like
that of the Indian mother; keeping her eyes
upon the dog, while he was watching the door;
and making swift signs to Edith, until her young
face grew pale.

"The deafness came by lightning," continued
Abraham Harwood; getting quite anxious, in his
turn, as he saw the looks of Edith turned repeatedly upon Peters, while he was devouring
the food, as if he had not eaten a mouthful, for
a week before.

Panther got up, at last; growled; shook himself; and stood, as if ready to leap forward.—
Lucy saw him — started — one or two bright,
large tears fell from her eyes. He sprang to the
door, with a fierce yell; the child began to hold
his breath; and Lucy, seeing the stranger put
his hand quickly upon a large knife, that lay
near — sent forth a sharp, terrible cry. It was
like the brief piteous wailing of a wild woman —
over a torn baby.

"Ah!" said Peters—"Ah;" rising deliberately; throwing off his loose coat; and appearing,
precisely, as when they saw him last; — wearing
the same dress; — the same carriage; the same
look. "I am pursued, sir—hunted —hunted, for
mischief! — that is the Bald Eagle. Send your
women away. I will never be taken alive. —
Walter! — my brave boy; will you stand by me?"

"To be sure, he will", answered Edith, "To
be sure, he will — for my sake!"

"You will?"

"Aye, aye, sir; that's what I will! — aye,
aye, sir; to the last drop of my blood — if you
are not guilty."

" Will you take my simple word? "

" Certainly ! "

" But if I should refuse to give it, sir ?"

" Then I will take you prisoner myself. —"

" You ! " —

" Yes, I ! — or help any body else ; Edith ;
Miriam — Bald Eagle — Father — anybody."

" You are a courageous boy. I like you all the
better for this. *I am not guilty!* "

Walter set his foot ; and prepared for the
worst.

Edith laughed and cried, for joy ; while Panther stretched himself out, once more, by the feet
of Lucy Armstrong, as if the peril, whatever
it was, had gone by.

Peters waited, without moving or speaking,
till the dog was quiet. — " Children," said he,
then, " Dear, *dear* children, I have come to take
leave ; to bid you, farewell ; perhaps, for ever."

" For ever, sir ! — for ever ! " said Edith ; turning away ; hiding her face ; and shaking her loose
hair over it.

" And as for you, sir," — continued Peters ;
addressing himself to Walter, who stood sternly

before him. — "As for you; it is high time that you were at work. You are wanted, sir; your country has need of you. Get your father's blessing: Be awake! be prepared; harness ✓ yourself; and go down to the war."

The boy shook with emotion. "I will," said he, "I will!" — turning about; — glancing at his father; and putting his hand, very gently upon the shoulder of Edith Cummin. — It heaved beneath her bright hair; as if she were sobbing.

"Don't entirely forget me," continued Peters. "You have thought badly of my temper; badly of my disposition; you will not, after I am gone. Had I been less honest, you would have liked me better, for a time; all of you — but I should have been speedily forgotten. — I have no fear of that, now. You will not forget me now; you cannot. I have told you too many disagreeable truths. You have already begun to acknowledge this; — each of you, to his own heart. By and by, you will quote my words to one another, as authority."

"We have driven you away from among us! and I shall never forgive myself."

"No. You are deceived. I am driven out, from among you, to be sure: though not by any of your household. — A Superior Being hath done this; not you, Abraham Harwood."

"You tremble, sir?"

"Yes, young man — yes. For the thought of going out, into the wide world, again, chills and affrights me. I had cast anchor, here, as I thought, once. But I was wrong. — There was no home for me; no fire-side. I could cling to you — to all of you — desperately — if that would be of any avail; but it would not. You have no power to shelter me. I should only bring a swift and sure destruction to your house."

"How? — in what manner?"

"There is no help for me. I knew it — I foresaw it, from the first; but I shut my eyes, wilfully; and here is the reward of my transgression!"

"Your language — I do not well understand you," said Walter; — "If you are not a murderer, what are you?"

"You will never know more than this — if I can help it. I am a bad man; — a wretched,

wronged, sorrowful, injured man ; — a man, who ✓
dares not make a friend of any human creature ;
lest, upon that creature's head, although it were
trebly anointed with holiness, the hot, heavy,
displeasure ; the insupportable wrath of Almighty
God, should fall. — Edith !"

"Sir ! sir ! — do not speak in that voice !
you'll frighten us to death ! you will so ! — you
will, indeed !—see — see ! — poor Lucy, herself,
is afraid."

"Poor child!—poor Lucy !" continued Peters ;
looking at her, as if he saw her not ; and speaking, as if he were altogether alone ; "Poor
child ! — poor Lucy ! what have they to fear?
Who is there, to harm a deaf mother?" She
had sprinkled the face of her baby all over with
large tears — without knowing it ; and appeared
as if she were no longer sensible of her infirmity ;
as if she had forgotten her child, for a time, while
studying the look of Jonathan Peters ; who, after
a long pause, recollected himself, and proceeded.
"Hear me patiently, Edith ; and you, sir ; and
you — and you — all of you," said he ; "It is

the day of my bereavement; a day of ünspeak-
able sorrow — of death." —

"Of what !"

"Be silent. You are a family of peace. Kneel
down, every one of you, after I have passed over
your threshold — kneel — and bless the Maker
of all men, that he would not permit me to abide
with you. Bless Him, that he drove me away
from your hearth-stone, as he did. Pray, all of
you — every one of you — pray that you may never
know who I am. Keep this night, for ever — as
a festival — a thanksgiving. — You know not
how much reason you have — may you never
know ! Had you become aiders and abetters of
my rebellion; had you comforted, or counselled
me."—

"Talk no more of rebellion," said Walter.
"The time has gone by for that word, in
America."

"Silence. You are not able to read my speech,
aright. My rebellion is beyond what you are
thinking of. It is not so much, to one king; as
to the King of kings. Farewell ! — Had you
come to pity me, you, yourselves, had been

sharers, at last, in my lot. Farewell!—I must be gone; or this babbling spirit within, will say that, which may wreck the understanding of one, at least, who now hears me."

" Are you mad, sir ?"

" Even as your father is, young man. A little √ — a very little, perhaps, when my heart is in travail. Edith!—my dear child."

Edith sat, pale and shivering, with her back toward him; her bright hair dishevelled — apart, and away from the rest;—unable to look him in the face — unable to speak; and quaking in every joint.

" A word with *you*, apart, Abraham Harwood; when I have done, here. Walter! — These are my last words for you: we shall never meet, again, I believe. Remember what I say. Do, whatever you do, with power and bravery — with all your heart. Lions are never caught with cobwebs. Edith! — will you not say farewell to me, dear?—will you not give me one farewell kiss?"

" No, sir — no, Mr. Sav — Peters — no !"

" May I not kiss your forehead?"

Edith tried to speak; but she could not articulate a word. Her voice died away, in a convulsive sobbing. Peters bowed over her. She put up her two hands — he took them between both of his; held them to his heart — stooped (while the boy shut his eyes; and leaned his face to the wall, as if he were suddenly overcome with a mortal sickness) yea — set his mouth to her pale forehead, as if he would put a seal there, for ever; and went blindly out of the room, without lifting his head, or speaking another word. He was followed by the preacher, who, when they had got back to the study, began to prattle with him, as if nothing out of the way had occurred. " What's your hurry?" said he; " what's your hurry? won't you take a chair, for a moment; or a bed — or a" —— " What say ?" — " Won't you take a bed with us, to-night?" —" No." — " Hadn't you better ?"—" Pshaw — you wouldn't have me take a bed with you, for your own right hand. Help me on, with my coat."

"You spoke of Jasper, t'other day"— " Well."— " I have thought much of it, since." — " Well." — " And — and — perhaps you knew his mother ?"

" A cowardly way of putting the question, sir." — " Cowardly ! how ?"

" Still, that you may have nothing to charge me with — Gracious God !"

A flash of lightning, followed by a tremendous clap of thunder, that shook the whole house, interrupted the reply of Peters; overpowered him, and literally drove him away from the door, which he stood holding partly open. There was a loud echo to his cry ; a voice, afar off. He was afraid ; and so was the preacher ; for both saw the shadow of a third person — clearly — plainly — palpably — on the lighted floor. They stepped hastily aside, for the intruder to pass ; fully believing that somebody would follow. But no ; nothing but a shadow appeared ; nothing more.

" I know it ! — I know it !" whispered Abraham Harwood ; catching Peters by the arm. " It was he, himself !"

" Who ! — what ?"

" Savage — Warwick Savage."

" What ! *who* !"

" The unhappy wretch, whom — hush — hush — I hear it, again —— hush ! — the

miserable creature, that I slew, in my sudden
wrath! Have mercy upon us! oh, Lord!"
Another awful flash; another explosion of bright,
heavy thunder. The solid earth shook; and,
for a single moment, as the volley rattled off, in
the far wood, like sharp musketry — the stars appeared multiplying, and falling through all the
air.

Peters broke away from the preacher's hold,
as if he were crazed, by the noise and brightness.
The large room was lighted up — the whole sky
— for a second or two. There was the shadow,
still—there—there!—just under his feet. A sudden cry escaped him; but, on seeing the consternation of Abraham Harwood, he recovered himself; walked up — and, as it were, in pity for
him, set his foot upon the shadow. — It vanished;
and he was turning to explain the cause,—when
the door sprung to; the shadow entered, again,—
like a dim cloud — a sort of smoke — through
which the walls and furniture could be seen;
the preacher fell into a chair; — and he, who was
ready to explain the phenomenon, a little time,
before—even he—stood speechless with awe, be-

fore it.   Perhaps, after all, it was only a brief
illusion of the storm ; — perhaps, of the light ; —
perhaps — of a troubled vision : or, peradventure
—his high faculties were disturbed, for a moment.
Still, explain it as you may, the Yankee was
afraid ; — his blood ran cold ; for the shadow was
no longer beneath his feet : — no — it stood out
from the wall — as he thought — face to face ✓
with him, like a spirit.

Many flashes of lightening followed ; many
peals of thunder ; but no shadow darted along
the floor — or walked over it, like a man.   The
preacher had fallen over the table. — Peters waited a moment ; — reasoned with himself ; —spoke
aloud ; went up to him. — " Abraham Harwood ;
awake !" said he.   " Awake ! and let me understand why it is, that you call him — the dead
man — the stranger, whom you destroyed, by the
name of one, who is yet alive ! — why by the
name of Warwick Savage ? — awake !"

The preacher was quite cold ; — he neither
moved nor spoke.   " Perhaps," thought Peters,
who had grown bewildered ; " Perhaps, the man
is dead — absolutely dead ; killed, before my

face, by a thunderbolt; or turned suddenly to
stone, by the eyes of a spirit. And, if so — *perhaps*, — who should gainsay it? — *perhaps* — the
shadow that I saw, was the disembodied soul;
for a single moment visible, to a creature of
earth, before it went up, to the Father of souls,
for ever."

" Help there !—help !" cried he; half distracted
with terror; rushing out, into the dark passage,
and calling, as if he would wake the dead.

" Help there — help !" screamed a sharp, clear
voice, behind him, he thought — close at his
elbow. It made his ears ring — it was like the
war-whoop of a young savage. Panther yelled,
in reply: shrieks and cries, of " help, there !
help !" were heard — strange voices, too ; — and
all the family came running through the blind
passage, —tumbling over each other, in the dark ;
— and repeating the cry of " help, there ! help !"

They met a person, hurrying swiftly forward ;
overturning every body in his way. — They knew
him — it was Jonathan Peters. He went by
them — as if he were pursued, by something. —
Walter, who was behind — having bethought

himself, on his way, and gone back for a torch —
caught a glimpse of him, as he went by, with his
large hands up; arms out; and face averted—a
glimpse only; nothing more — for the pitch
knot, as it streamed backward, in the current of
air — high up, over his head — with a fierce,
dazzling, noisy splendour, gave little or no light
forward; so that, before he was able to speak;
or get his breath, or call out for aid — Peters, who
neither heard, nor saw them, was gone for ever.
Forth went he; forth — he, whom nothing but ✓
shadows could frighten—forth—into the storm,
and heavy darkness; the big, lighted thunder-
bolts falling on every side of him; at every step;
firing, tree after tree, within sight of the house;
—forth —as if he were better able to outface the
skies — any thing — every thing,—above, or below — the savage, or the wild beast — weary and
sick as he was; desolate and frightful, as it was
abroad; hunted, as he was — than to abide, for
another short hour, in a place of refuge, where
the dust, which came out, in a cloud, from the
shaking walls; agitated —loosened —as they were,
by a thunder storm, like an earthquake — would

not settle, again; but immediately, in the disorder of his afflicted senses; the confusion of his
proud faculties — affrighted as they were; the
trouble, heat, and hurry of his blood — became
like a great multitude of apparitions; crowding
upon him, in the exhausted atmosphere, till he
was nearly suffocated; stunning him with cries;
and pursuing him with voices.

The preacher came slowly to his recollection.
But he, and all his family, during the time,
were silent, pale—afraid; looking about, upon
each other, as if they had been shipwrecked,
in their sleep. Walter stood sullenly apart; —
with a more than usual seriousness, about his
forehead; a more than usual haughtiness, about
his mouth; and a mischievous, bad light in his
large eyes. — The women were all together, just
inside of the door; Lucy and Edith watching it,
as if they expected something to appear; Abraham Harwood, as he came gradually to himself,
surveying the room, on every side, as if he were
not fully awake; and all the faces there, as if
some were missing. Jotham was torch-bearer. —
He would not venture within the study; but

stood in the door-way — lifting the pitch wood
up, as high as he could reach ; — overshadowing
his dilated eyes, with his large hand ; peering
about him, as if ready to jump, at every breath ;
staring at his father ; and crying out, every minute
or two, with a look of stupid — ludicrous — yet,
affecting astonishment — " Oh, Lord — O, my !"

The atmosphere was full of smoke ; a sort of
bluish flare ; a mist, like a sea-fog — through
which, the noisy flashing of the lighted wood, as
it gushed forth, into the room, appeared like that
of a beacon-fire, over the waters.

" Oh, Lord ! Oh my !" whispered Jotham ;
" Oh Lord ! oh my ! Look 'o there, now !"
pointing to a prodigious book, which lay on the
floor, wide open, just under the feet of Abraham
Harwood.   " I say ! you — our Watty !" —
" Well ; what now ?" — " That air's our great
Bible ; aint it ?" — " Where ?" — " Why, there ;
what if you pick it up, now? You aint afeard
o' nothin', our Watty ; be you? which I stump
you, therefore, to pick up that are Bible — if
you dare." — " Ah !" said Walter ; taking it up
reverentially : — " Ah ! I told you so, father ; I

knew it. I knew the lightning had struck, somewhere. See!"—" Well, well; what now?" said
his father; trying to recollect where he was.
" Why; the great silver clasp is turned quite
purple, sir." — " By gosh then, smell o' that,
brother Watty; smell o' that, if you dare."

" The leaves too, sir; the beautiful parchment
kiver— why; they look as if they'd been scorched and shrivelled, with fire." " By snum! our
Watty!" — " Pho! pho; speak louder; what
are you afraid of?"

" Afeard! who's afeard; if I didn't see it, I'm
up a tree, our Watty; that's all."

" See it! — See what? — where? — when?"

" Why; here! jess now; the great fiery dra-
goon; — oh Lord! oh my!" — "No! — old Nick,
brother?" — " Yes."— " Hush, Jotty; hush—do
make him hush, Walter; do." — " High! hush
yourself, then, our Eady: who cares for you, I
s'pose. I shant hush for you; nor nobody else.
But I seed him, tho'; arter all."

" How did he look, brother?"

" What say?"

" How did he look? — how was he clothed?"

" As 'much like a Mohawk, as ever you
seed."

" What !" said Walter ; glancing at Lucy ;
" what ! — is it even so ! Has *he* appeared again,
to-night ?—where's the dog ?"

" Yes — yes — dear Walter ; it has appeared
again to-night ; I saw it myself, once ; I do believe.
Don't be cross, now ; don't. Poor Lucy," — crying—" why ; she couldn't help it ; and, as for
Panther, he is gone off, on the trail of the shape."

" Shape !—shape !" said our afflicted preacher ;
turning away from the face of piteous, foolish
wonder before him ; and speaking just above his
breath. " What shape was it, my son ?"

Edith started up. " Oh ! Walter ! Walter !"
cried she—convulsively clasping her pretty hands.
" O Walter — think of poor Lucy !"

" Nothing, sir" — said Walter — making no
reply to Edith ; not even looking at her. " Nothing
at all sir, but — a — a — I cannot say what,
sir."

" Have you ever seen it, before ?"

" Yes — often. Out in the dim wood ; sitting
by the water-fall ; crouching in the tree-tops ;

aye, aye — shouting to the Eagle of the waters;
aye, aye; chasing the wild cat — running down
the deer; in short, sir, it is the shadow of one,
that goes where he will — *when* he will.   It was
that crazy fool, Copperhead, I dare say; or, the
ghost of our Great Bald Eagle — or the little
Bald Eagle himself."   Saying these words, he
flung out of the room.

CHAPTER XI.

SOLILOQUY. — SINCERE, BOYISH LOVE. — SOR-
ROW. — JEALOUSY. — ADVENTURE. — " FRESH-
ET." — INUNDATION. — ESCAPE. — YOUNG,
PURE, INNOCENT LOVE. — GIRLISH PRIDE.

Two, or three hours after this; while the rest of
the family were asleep, or abed; our young hero
found himself — he was never able to say, wherefore — lying out, with his dog, in the open air;
under the broad blue sky; over which the mighty
storm had passed like a shadow.

Above him, were great rocks; while, about
him, on every side, were huge fragments, which
had given way, year after year, to the rain,
or the frost. On almost every one, rude ini-
tials were to be found; or letters, which he
had written, at the hazard of his neck, upon the
steep side of the mountain, far — far above, where
any other boy was courageous enough to climb.

He lay, musing about Edith — Peters — Bald
Eagle — his father — and Lucy Armstrong. His
heart was heavy. He thought over the whole
business of the whole night; how, all of a sudden,
the voice and look of Peters had become very
gentle, and affectionate ; how he leaned over Edith,
and put his mouth to her holy, smooth, clear
forehead; how, it seemed as if her little hands
had found his, of their own accord — while her
eyes were looking another way; how they dwelt
within his — palpitating like hunted birds, in their
natural home; how her beautiful hair was disordered and wet; how her youthful, dear face
burnt, as he spoke to her, so tenderly; how her
naked arms blushed, up to the shoulder; how
he held her two hands, with great energy to his
heart, until he had showered his large tears into
her face; and put a seal, upon her young brow,
for ever.

The boy was unhappy, while he thought of
this; wretched — sick — and weary. A fierce
waterfall shot forth, above his head, as if it were
issuing out of the sky; and, after a plunge or
two, came rattling over the large rocks, which

trembled under the continual discharge, in a profusion of petty cascades; leaping forth, here,
from all the veins and fissures of the quivering,
dull granite, with a sparkling, brisk, incessant
activity; oozing through the rich moss, there —
drop after drop, like tears; and bubbling, out
of the solid rock, a little further off, with a
dazzling brightness.

He lay with his young, pale face, turned up to
the sky — the superb, awful sky; but he saw it
not. By his very ear, went a great volume of
water; plunging into the solemn abyss, with a
continual roar. Yet he heard it not. Nor, did
he feel the shuddering of the mountain; the
delicate shower, that fell about him, like a fine
small rain, from the water, that struck, and ex-
ploded in mist, below him. No; nor the heavy,
large dew, which the dark fir-trees, and white,
slender birches, above — as they trembled; or
quivered; or tilted, in the night-wind — shook
into his brave bosom — over his very heart — as
he lay.

The waters accumulated in the hills. It had
been raining, steadily, for twenty-four hours be-

fore, in the high lands. The lakes, and reservoirs of the upper country were beginning to overflow. The noise grew louder and louder. The great, loose rocks trembled, more and more violently, as the volume of waters augmented. The shower fell thicker and faster, from the overhanging foliage. The dog rose up; shook himself; and stood, eying the dark branches above, while they quivered and sparkled in the starlight, as if they were alive. But our young hero was in a fearful revery. He heeded neither his dog; nor the trees; the sound of mustering waters, afar off; nor the throes of the earth about him.

Walter Harwood was no stranger to the meaning of these admonitory symptoms. He knew very well, what it portended, when the trees of the mountain shook; the caverns roared; and all the air was full of a strange noise. He had seen the waterfall become a torrent, while he was loitering near it; the small brook, a river — loaded with spoil; the wreck of mills — farm-houses — trees, and shrieking animals—tumbling forward, like a deluge, and filling the whole sky, in a calm, beautiful day, with smoke and uproar.

He had seen, over and over again, the great rivers of North America, in the spring of the year; when the snows melted, or the rains fell, breaking up, all at once—like the foundations of the earth — in thunder and earthquake; the black, swollen waters — black as midnight — encumbered with ice and ruin — cattle and plunging timber — pouring through the valleys, and over the precipices; tearing up the earth, and crushing the very wilderness, on their way to the ocean.

He had seen a little riband of water, while it was flashing to the sunshine, over the side of a hill; or wandering away, like a large, bright, lazy reptile, through the long rich grass of the valley; many a time had he seen it grow in a single hour, to a turbulent, impassable stream; a white, formidable cascade; a torrent, which, after a few hours, would vanish—leaving the earth ploughed up; the rocks and shrubbery spoiled of their verdure; the long, smooth, beautiful grass of the great meadow drowned.

He knew all this; had seen all this; and yet, lying out as he was, in the very pathway of the waters, he never thought of them, till he was ready to fall asleep in the noise of their approach.

He had slept in the same place, before. He took a pleasure in the sprinkling of the tall trees overhead, when the low summer wind shook them—beneath a clear blue sky—at midnight; a pleasure, in watching the spray, as it gathered anew on the brave green foliage, that over-shadowed him; and fell through the moonlight, with every change of the breeze — drop after drop—coloured, heavy and bright, like the large dew of the grape; a sweet strange pleasure, in giving himself up, as it were, body and soul, to the spirit of the place.

It was a most beautiful night; calm over all the skies, calm over all the earth; so calm, that, but for his dog, Walter would have slept more sweetly than he had, for a long time; while the green, soft, bunchy moss, upon which his head lay, gave out, with every sob of his heart, and every turn of his body, a profusion of little rain-drops; like spattered quicksilver — a fine sweat

—showing thereby, that, like every thing else about him, it was completely saturated; over-charged with moisture.

A most beautiful night, in truth : and yet, he lay out, under the great sky, face to face with it ; contemplating the beauty and brightness, thereof; without any sort of emotion ;—the movement of God's blue empire — at midnight — in full swing —the revolution of prodigious worlds—over him, and about him — hour after hour — without one cry of transport.

" The stars— be quiet, our Panther," said he ; " be quiet; will you ?—The stars have a strange, queer, dizzy appearance to-night;" lifting his head, and putting out his leg, as if it were asleep. " How they tremble !"

No, no—he was wrong. The rock, upon which he lay, trembled—it was that, which had grown dizzy; not the stars.

" They don't appear nait'ral, some how. I never saw them so unsteady, before — in all *my* life; I never did, I declare; nor so bright; nor so plenti— that's a tear, faith !—nor so plentiful; nor so — Lord ! how large they are, now ! Be

quiet, sir—and as for—will you be quiet, sir?—
how blue it is, over head! how very blue! It's
the rain, I dare say; or the wind; or the—lie
down, sir—how it washes the sky. I've seen it
afore now; on a sharp, clear night, in cold
weather; I've seen it look, as if—as if—as if,
somehow, the stars were alive; and—by gosh!
if I ain't a cryin'!—bigger fool than our Jotty—
poor Jotty; and as for that 'air outrageous feller,
to come here, jest when he likes—that 'air
Peters; and—O Edith! Edith—lay down, sir;
lay down! What ails ye, now?"

Panther was very troublesome. He had been
growing worse and worse, every moment, for
the last hour; but now, he set up a loud baying,
with a voice that brought a shower of rain-drops
from the foliage over him. He was immediately
answered by echoes, on every side; above and
below.

One particular tree; a thin, delicate mountain
ash, the roots of which were more in the way of
the torrent, perhaps, quivered and shook, with a
great noise. Panther saw it; and, setting his
two fore feet, barked more furiously than ever.

"It is gettin' plaguy uncomfortable, here," said Walter, in a peevish, low tone; "very cold and wet. I shall never like it agin, *I* know; — my pleasure in't, is all gone. The stars have lost all their beauty — they have; the trees are uglier than ever — they be; the waters, too; the —— but she shall never come here agin, with me, while I draw the breath o' life — tell me on't, if she does; tell me on't — say I've broken my word; no, no — and I'll never come here agin, with *her* — never, never; only to think, when she sot up there; on that 'air very rock — Panther, I say! — be done, will ye? — why, what's the matter with ye, now; — devil?"

Panther stood, as if just ready to leap into the shadow.

"Do ye see any thing, fool! There's nothin' up there — its only the wind. Be quiet, sir, be quiet; or I'll ——."

A star shot over his head. He followed it, with a hushed heart, and a steady eye; till it vanished; leaving a thread of light, on the wonderful, dark blue, over which it passed.

"Ah, ah — how beautiful! How swift and

beautiful !" cried, he; catching his breath; and lifting himself up, from the dangerous and foolish posture, in which he had been lying, with his feet close to the verge of the precipice. — " I have been very wicked — very; there *is* a beauty in the stars after all; there is, indeed.   I am sorry for what I said — a — a — goodness! how stiff and sore, I feel; and weak as a child.   Here, Panther — here, here — poor feller — poo — oo — oor feller — *you* won't leave me, will ye, my boy? Let him go — what do we care?   I don't much like Bald Eagle's flummery, though; and if he goes there, agin, father shall know of it. I'll not have him skeered, over and over agin, for nothin'; — poor Lucy! what *will* become of her, though, if he cuts her adrift? Ah ! — what's that ?' I never heard a cannon, or a batterin' ram; or a — what a rumblin' it makes, though ! and what a strange noise, too, in the air !   I shouldn't care much, arter all, if the story was true, about archers, and armies, and horsemen; with ships and great flags — and all that — coming up, out of the sea; and fightin' away, like fury, overhead — I don't believe a word of it — faith !"

He had partly risen; but, overcome with drowsiness, after a while, he caught by a loose fragment of the rock; and stood, looking up — giddy and sick — through a sort of under firmament; a broad canopy of green leaves, tilting away in the night air; upon their innumerable, thin, delicate pillars; up — up — to a dark blue, sky over it — all in confusion — as he thought.

" No, no" — said he; beginning to lose himself; " no, no, I never *did* see the stars look so awful, before; and if I wasn't abroad, in the open air, I should believe I was dreamin'. Perhaps I be — who knows? — who can tell? O, yes — yes — yes; I do love the night wind; so cool and comfortable, as it is, when my forehead is hot. Yes; yes; but I can't bear the look o' the night, or the darkness, now, as I could, once. They make me feel afraid as death; and very unhappy, now I've done sleepin'. Oh — if I could sleep, now, as I did once! — before that wicked, vile, mischievous —— Lord! if the whole sky aint a fallin'! — stars an' all!"

He lifted himself up; and caught by the projecting roots of a large tree.   It was a strange

delusion. "I really thought 'um fallin'," said our
hero; beginning to recover a little — and wiping his bewildered eyes. — " They shook in their
places, I thought; and appeared, more as if they
were under the sky, than a part of it : — as if
they were between me, and all that blue air,
away up, yonder. — What if they *should* be inhabited ! — Wise men have thought so — and
it's in our geography ; — I should like to know
sartain : — what a strange population they must
be — women, with wings, I dare say — men, with
armour — and lions, with——O !"—throwing up
his arms, with a cry of giddy rapture ; — "O! if I
was a little higher up — I'd gather 'em, into my
bosom !"

Panther yelled again, as he lay, crouching
close to the rock ; and Walter, having withdrawn
his hands from the root — after balancing a moment or two — gave way ; and slid along to the
slippery edge of the precipice, over which the
waters were now running.

The courageous dog would not leave him ;
but crawled nigher ; and lay between him and the
edge ; — eying it with a look of terrour the while ;

moaning piteously; and pawing the wet moss. The boy understood him; and crept away from the brink; over which the dark, muddy waters, augmented, of a sudden, by the yielding of some barrier, perhaps, in the higher parts of the mountain, rushed and roared, with frightful impetuosity.

" I can't keep my feet," said Walter; groping his way along the side of the cavity, half way down which, he had been asleep. — " How feeble I am; — I can't see my hand afore me; — I feel jest as if I was goin' too, all the time — *poor* Panther! poor doggy! — that's you! — keep close to me, as you can. May be, it's the apperplexy. When my poor mother had it — poor, dear, *dear* mother! — may be, I've got it, now? or may be, 'tis like father's! — I hope not. — Ah! — death, beast! — what a mood you are in, to be sure! — Do you see anything, or not? — Makin' sich a plaguy fuss about nothin' at all: — I'm quite ashamed of you; that's what I am: — would you bring the wolves about us, agin? — I hope 'tis the apperplexy — I *do* so — can't be more 'an three o' them fits; and this'll

go for one, I guess.   Only two more, and I shall
be dead. I wish I was dead, now !   No, I don't,
faith ! sorry for that speech: rather awful, I'm
a thinkin', to die; however, we may talk, in a
huff. To die so young, too; afore anybody
knows me; afore I know myself—afore I've
done a job, to be remembered by; O, it is very
hard — very — very.   Who knows what I may
do, if they'll give me fair play, among 'em. Be
quiet, will ye?   I *should* like to know the plain
truth !   If 'tis the apperplexy, I'd like to know
it; for I'd like to give Edith Cummin a bit o' my
mind, afore I go; that's what I should, faith;
and I will, too — if I don't go plaguy soon.
To fall away as I did, jest now; sich a ringin'
too, in the sky; all so dark about me; sich a
heavy, crushin' weight, in the dark air; jess the
same dull, ponderous atmosphere, as my poor
mother called it, when she spoke to me, on her
death-bed, about my temper — *my* temper ! —
she'd better speak to Edith Cummin, about her'n,
I guess; and yit — O, if I could only see her
once more — dead, or alive — my poor, dear,
mother ! dead or alive."

The dog stopped; whimpered; looked him up in the face; and wagged his tail, as if he understood him.

"Get away!—ye poor silly beast. Ye'll never see her again, ye fool; — never, never. — She's gone up, there; up, into the sky; so, push along, faster; don't keep under my feet, all the time — ye'll trip me up, if ye do. — That air Jonathan Peters — he'll be the death o' me, yit; — I wish Eagle would ketch him, whether or no."—He stopped; and stood, looking down; — regardless of Panther's loud, continual barking; — regardless, too, of the stones, that, loosened above, and about him, were tumbling, at every step — into the abyss of rocks, and water-falls, under his very feet. While he was there, in a perilous revery; all of a sudden, the noise increased, on every side of him; the great rock underneath his feet, shook violently; — a loud crashing followed, above; a sort of explosion, below; — a tremendous uproar, like the discharges of subterranean heavy ordnance—growing louder and louder, every moment.

Walter caught by a branch, that was near;

while the brave dog, starting off, with a loud yell,
sprang, head foremost, into the abyss.   The
whole earth shook — the large trees — the rocks
— the very sky — and lo ! .the stars rushed all
together, for a moment. A great noise followed ;
a faint echo — and a sharp . scream, afar off.
The boy turned away. from the gulph — without
knowing where he was — till he heard Panther.
below, a few feet off, he thought — when he
called out for him, with a passionate, powerful
cry.   The dog answered ; his bold breath, coming up through the darkness and smoke, that
concealed him, as if he were very near, though
invisible.   There was no time to be lost.   Our
hero knew that his dog waited for him ; so, calling out once more, he plunged into the cavern,
after him, through the mist and spray. — Panther
heard him ; saw him ; saw that his feet were
upon the solid earth : and set off, again, with a
similar noise.   Walter waited, until he could
perceive the dog — a few feet lower down ; where
it was much higher — crouching close to the
rock. — He followed him — the dog repeating
his cry, and, immediately bounding off, as before.

Walter began to lose himself, at last, in the tremendous tumult about him : — He could neither see, nor hear; — a thousand voices were calling to him — wolves and catamounts, he thought — as he stood, upon a slippery projection; holding his breath; and clinging with frantic, desperate power, to a few bushes; from the roots of which, it seemed as if the soil had been completely washed away, by the torrent. He had still sense enough to watch the motion of his dog — his last earthly hope — though he could not hear him now, for the roaring of the waters, above and below him. The creature lay close up to the steep wall; watching a part of the rock overhead — as if he saw a spirit. — Our hero would have called him away; but he could not; he had no voice — no breath; he felt as if the naked, frail root, by which he was clinging, would give way, if he spoke another loud word. —

Anon, the prodigious rock above, began to shudder, anew. — He looked about, in despair — he was ready to let go his hold of the root, and perish; for there was no refuge; no safety —

look where he would ; — above, or below — to the
right hand, or to the left. — His bodily power
was gone — his hearing — his eye-sight — he
had no hope. —— A loud explosion followed ;
— a tearing away of roots, and earth ; — a noise,
like the powerful breaking up of a great river,
under the ice : — it balanced — quivered —
groaned — a death-like stillness followed, as if
the torrent were gathering all its power, for a
final effort ; a few pebbles — a very few — one
by one — rattled by the poor boy; and, after a
moment or two, rang pleasantly, in the waters
underneath his feet : while the roots, by which
he was upheld, began to give way, inch by inch.
— He caught his breath, and shut his eyes. —
A quantity of loose earth tumbled from the great
rock — it swung — tilted up — turned, as if
invisible giants were heaving it over. The dog
saw it rise ; and screamed, louder than ever ; —
echoes, with voices like wolves — answered him,
on every side ; — and, immediately, the smoke
rolled out ; and over, went the deluge ; over,
into the great abyss, with a noise like heavy
thunder,—cartloads of crumbling stones —crush-

ed earth — and old, broken, dislocated roots, —
the dust of which, notwithstanding the spray of
the waters, which darkened all the place, for a
minute or two, arose in a cloud over the deep
gulph. —— Then ! — then ! — while the boy was
deafened with noise — and suffocated with dust
— and gasping with terror — down came the
great, everlasting rock, itself — down — down —
as if the very foundations of the earth were giving way. — Walter shrieked for mercy; and
crept into the loose rubbish about him — assured,
in his own soul, as he felt our earth sliding
away under his feet; and heard — above and
below — the tremendous commotion ; — assured,
in his own soul, that a great part of the mountain
had fallen — the stars — and, peradventure, the
skies.

He lay still ; without venturing to look up ; —
waiting the awful issue; wondering, that he was
yet alive — and able to draw his breath.   Panther saw him ; and gave a loud, joyful cry of
recognition. — That was the happiest moment
of Walter Harwood's life.   He felt as if — and
he was ready to scream for joy — as if, whatever

had become of the skies, or the world, he was not
altogether alone. — He roused himself; gathered
up all his proud energies; — caught by another
small tree branch, that overhung the last inter-
vening space; and swung himself courageously
over it; hurried away; — found a passage; — a
sort of path — which the torrent had spared;
and, after a few minutes, felt himself once more
upon the level earth — unable to remember
where he was — or what had happened — or how
he had escaped.

The air blew colder and colder. The inundation roared behind him. He knew the meaning of the noises; — they were like the rumbling
of continual thunder. He knew that, long before
day-break, the beautiful green valley; the valley
of peace below him — would be all under water;
he knew that his home, with all that he cared for,
was in peril; and yet, he knew not whither he
was going; nor what he was trying to do. He
was bewildered — exhausted —and, after a while,
he threw himself down upon a wet bank. — " I
know not where I am — " said he.   " Every
thing about me looks wild and queer. — *Why*,

Panther ! — how you behave ! — poor feller — poor feller ! — sich a to-do ! I never saw you lost, afore. — "

The dog behaved, as if he were lost, indeed. His courage was gone; — his brave temper was completely subdued — completely.   Instead of dashing, straight forward, as usual: instead of exploring his route, like a blood-hound, after his prey, without hesitation, or doubt; he loitered near the feet of his afflicted master, till both were tired; shivering with cold, and weak with ter- ror — his long wet ears dabbling, at every step, in the meadow soil.

"It may be," continued Walter; beginning to feel, as if the hand of death were nigh — " It may be, that I am never to see her agin ; — that I am to die here — here — away from all human hope; away from all human succour — for my disobedience, perhaps; or my — God be mer- ciful to me ! I can't get up, out o' the grass; I can't go another step ! very well — I see how it is, now — here, boy, here ! — how sleepy I feel — here, boy, here ! — poor feller, poor fel- ler ! — good bye to you, good bye, Panther ;

farewell ! — I am 'a goin' — farewell. You have
been a true friend o' mine; that's what you have ;
— poor Panther — good bye :" — His rich voice
dying away; large tears running down, to his
mouth ; and his weary eyes gradually closing, in
the sleep of death ; or, in that, which appeared
like it, as he continued —— " Ah, Panther, Panther ! if you could only speak, now, what a message I'd give her ! — a leetle — teeny, mischievous, good for nothin', abomi — a — abomi — God
bless her, tho' ! — I can't bear to call her names,
arter all : and yet, if 'twasn't a shame, I'd crawl
back ; and jump into the very place, where the
mountain fell.   If I could have my way, now, —
she'd not see my face agin — I guess, in a hurry;
no, faith ! and if I could help it, she'd never know
where to look for my bones ;—a proud, ungrateful — a — a — ."   The sentence died away, upon
his lips. — *   *   *   *   *
*   *   *   *   *   *

About an hour before day, while the cold, far
light of the eastern sky, was coming up, like a
thin vapour out of the sea — Edith Cummin sat
leaning out of her little chamber window, half

asleep; her heavy eyes, throbbing temples, and parched lips bearing witness to the state of her mind : — her pale, sweet mouth brimful of anxiety and grief; her dishevelled hair blowing about her face; and her night-gown falling away from her white shoulders.

In the bed behind her, lay the deaf woman — poor Lucy — one beautiful arm about her brown boy; the other abroad, upon the pillow : — the mother and child both asleep. Edith saw it, and wept for half an hour, without knowing why.

She had not been able to close her aching eyes, for more than a minute or two, at a time, the whole night through. She was unhappy. Something—she knew not what—a new sorrow at her heart — a sweet, mournful presage — kept her awake, while the baby lay breathing gently, in the bosom of its own dear mother. She grew weary, at last ; — faint, wretched, and weary : so — slipping out of bed ; stifling a sob or two ; — and huddling up her night-gown, about her bosom — she went softly to the window — threw it up — and sat, looking out, while the stars were fading away, one by one ; — the great, pale moon

going out — and all the eastern sky preparing
for a transformation.

She had listened, while she lay in bed, hour
after hour, to the heavy sound, afar off; but had
no suspicion of the cause. — Having never been
kept awake, before, in all her happy life, the
poor child mistook the loud, strange noise, that
she heard, for the natural roar of midnight; —
as if the darkness had a voice, like the great
ocean.

But, after a time, it grew louder; — more alarming — more like the sea, coming heavily in,
before a storm. She began to be afraid — anxious — to look out over the sky; — as if she were
expecting those apparitions to appear; — those
armies, that men talked of. Her heart misgave
her, at length; — for, the winds—waters—mountains — woods — altogether, she thought, were
not able to make such a noise — even though
they had all the sky to themselves; — in the dead,
awful, overpowering stillness of night.

But no; — there was nothing to be seen, overhead; — no broad banners flaunting away, in the
blue zenith, like a thin vapour; no dazzling

phenomena to fright, or perplex the nations of our earth; no indistinct commotion to be interpreted of the dreamers, and prophets, and soothsayers of —— New England.

Still, however, she had well nigh fallen asleep, in the bluish atmosphere, and cool, soft river breeze, in spite of her anxiety; and would, perhaps, but for the flowers on a shelf near the window, while she was leaning out, watching the sky; holding her breath; and listening with all her heart, and soul. — They caught her attention. — They were faded — rumpled — miserably torn; as if a heavy shower had fallen, during the night. She was grieved; and her clear eyes ran over — they had been waiting, a good while, for an excuse — ran over, instantly, with tears, like large flower dew; while she leaned further out; and — letting her loose hair go — her night gown —every thing — began to put them in order, with a childish eagerness; — pausing, every minute or two; and, losing herself in a revery; as if some sweet, strange, melancholy thought were unfolding itself, within her own heart —

leaf by leaf, all the time,—like a pale, pure blossom.

She was really grieved. One would have thought, perchance, to hear the poor thing sigh, and see her tears, that she was half an idiot; or that, peradventure, the cruel storm had been spoil-ing bright birds of their plumage—instead of the red poppy, and blue corn flower: — But, while she was weeping over these frail blossoms, which had only blown, to be rifled—her shining, soft hair had interwoven itself with nearly all that were left; — a smile of gentle and affectionate resignation had begun to appear about her pale, patient, beautiful mouth; — and her clear, pleas-ant eyes, refreshed by their own sorrow, were moving about, over the sublime, quiet beauty of the landscape; — reposing now, for a long time, steadily, upon some part of the far, coloured sky, like those of a young devotee, awaiting a miracle; now, upon the wretched flowers, below — as if they were more precious to her, fifty times over, than either skies or miracles; her hands employed, the while, in gently detaching her tresses from the green tendrils, and brilliant blossoms. While she was thus occupied — all of a sudden — the earth shook — the house — the trees — and, out poured a prodigious volume of white smoke, from the near mountain — rolling forth, upon the transparent air, like a sea fog, till it met the river breeze, on its way through the great pass of the mountains.   It stopped — heaved — pitched forward, a little way — stopped, once more — and rolled up, cloud over cloud, until it had overcome its adversary; when it shot forth, in every direction, over the calm, blue skies.

Edith was terrified; breathless — half crazy with fright — speechless — and yet, she cared little for the smoke, or the noise; or the fire and earthquake — if earthquake, it was.   Her whole attention was occupied with a shape — hardly human — which appeared coming out of the mist and shadow.   She started up — tearing away the flowers, with which her fine, bright hair was interwoven; strove to call out; strove mightily — but no sound issued from her faded lips — while her eyes grew very dim; — reeled away — covered her face — and fell over the bed, just as Panther was heard below.

Lucy awoke, with a loud scream; caught her boy to her heart; saw Edith rushing out, as if she were crazy; and pursued her; while a great voice came up, from below — calling, as it were, to the four corners of the house; and a powerful hand, laid hold of the outer door, and shook it, so that all the windows rattled. "Awake! awake! awake!" cried the voice — it was like the voice of a trumpet.

Lucy pursued her, until she saw what appeared like a dead body, lying out, under the shadow of a tree — half naked — bare footed — bare headed — with a profusion of wet hair, spread out over the green turf — like the hair of a drowned, pale woman. By the body was a large dog; a little way off, a shape, that she knew. In the terror, — in the transport of her poor smitten heart — she screamed, with such violence, that her ears were partially unstopped; so that, feeling the change — forgetful of every thing else; — and holding her breath, she stood still: — The earth, air and sky were full of melodious noises; brimful of miraculous harmony, to the newly restored sense. The shape—it was that

of Bald Eagle — vanished away, at her scream,
while her arms were outstretched for it; and
she, half delirious with joy, and surprise. At last,
however, she recollected herself, and went up to
the body. It was that of poor Walter Harwood.
He lay near the door, under a large tree; with his
cold face turned up to the sky; frightfully rigid
— motionless — quiet, as the grave. A female sat
by him, on the wet earth; wrapped in a bed-gown;
pale as if she too, were of the dead; with just life
enough in her, to allow of her sitting upright,
while she supported herself, with her two hands
outspread on the turf; her head on her half
uncovered breast; her torn, tangled hair, encumbered with gorgeous flowers, and miserable
weeds. — It was Edith Cummin. She knew the
body afar off, and fell upon it, with a faint cry,
as if her heart had broken, for ever, on the spot;
— and lay there, until she heard Lucy; when
she awoke, white with unspeakable dismay; —
covered with confusion; — lifted herself up;
— and would have torn herself away from
Walter; but she could not — she had no heart,
no power to leave him — alive, or dead: — So,

she sat still — choking with shame and grief; —
ready, but for a bashfulness, that was new to
her; ready, to throw herself upon the body,
once more; and yield up her young spirit there;
yield it up, for ever, though all the women of all
the earth, were standing about.

Lucy Armstrong was afraid of her. She
hardly knew the innocent, poor child; she saw
only a mad creature — a tawdry phantom — her
torn tresses braided with strange flowers, glitter-
ing and flaunting about her distracted eyes —
cold, white forehead — and half naked bosom;
sitting on the grass, and watching the body, with
a look of the most pitiable, and affecting de-
rangement.

But, in the meantime, every body, within the
old house, having heard the call, was now running to the spot. One had been dreaming of the
Indians; another of war — of murder — of the Tories — another of judgment, earthquake, and fire.

The father stood speechless, and sorrow-strick-
en, over the afflicted boy; believing, that he had
been beset by the wolves, again; — or drowned —
or that, perhaps, the heavy thunder had struck

him; and Jotty was quite foolish with terror.
But, while they stood sobbing over the body; no
one thought of removing it — so little hope, or
sign of life was there — till the stony, blue hand,
stirred a little; that which Edith was holding to ✓
her naked bosom, with all her might.   She started — shrieked — coloured all over; and would
have let it fall, in the transport of her shame; but
for another glimpse of the dead boy's awful,
quiet visage.   It was a reproach to her — the
flush went off — and a death-like paleness returned.   She burst into tears, caught up the hand,
more tenderly than ever; not, as before, into her
naked bosom; but, in both of hers, to her mouth,
where, for a single moment, all the warmth and
vitality of her whole body were concentrated —
while she wept upon it — breathed into it —
kissed it, until the muscles relaxed; and lo! it
slowly opened, of itself.

The father saw it; and fell upon his knees.
Edith's joy was of another kind — fervid —
breathless — mute.   She lifted up the boy's
head, while they were preparing to carry him off;
— kissed his cold wet eyes; no longer sensible to

the reproving presence of the people about; leaned
over him, with her tears dropping into his face
— until his chest heaved; and his lips trembled,
with inarticulate sound.

"Dear, dear Walter," said she; kissing his
mouth, anew — " *dear* .Watty; you are not a-
goin' to die — be you, Watty; — there's a good
boy ?"

He was hardly awake, or alive; but the sound
of her sweet voice affected him; so that he opened and shut his large, dull eyes, three or four
times, with a look of joy; whispered her name,
while their cheeks were nigh together; turned
away from the lighted horizon, as if he were
afflicted by the growing splendour; and sobbed
himself to sleep, without knowing where he was,
in the lap of Edith Cummin.

At last, a bed was prepared, and every thing
was ready for his removal; so, they took him up,
and were carrying him off, when he awoke;
lifted his head — articulated a cry, for Edith;
while a brief expression of strong inward con-
flict went over his whole face, with a shadow,
like that of the apoplexy — and clung to her so,

that she forgot herself, again; caught his weary head into her young, pure bosom; gathered up her loose flannel robe, or night gown, over it, in a paroxysm of deep tenderness; called him her dear, *dear* Watty; and wept over him, as if her heart were breaking.

He knew the voice; and starting up, he tore away the clothes; pushed aside her abundant rich hair; and met her eyes; but, instead of returning the caress; instead of replying to it, with a smile or a touch of gentle endearment, he strove to break away from her, entirely; and raising himself, with a sorrowful, stern, carriage, he looked at the superb flowers, of scarlet and blue — they were like gems in her magnificent hair—at her dress; at her pale, sweet countenance; at her disordered eyes; and spoke to her. " Edith; Edith," said he; " I know you, now, dear; I know you, well enough. He has bewitched you, too, I see : poor thing ! poor thing ! — we are all crazy; father and I, and ——"

Edith caught once more at his hand; forgetting and forgiving all, in her deep thankfulness for his restoration; but he withdrew it,

haughtily; turned away; shook his head; and
gave himself up to Jotham, as if he had no other
hope. That was enough. She arose, and stood
up; faint, very faint; with unspeakable anguish
in her eyes; and a convulsion of shame at her
heart; seeing, for the first time, the nakedness
of her little feet; strangers about her, wondering
at her beauty; and women, with eyes full of sorrow and amazement, looking at her, on every
side. Walter was borne off, like a dead body;
with his dog following hard after it. ·A word—
a look — or a whisper — and she would have
taken the dear head, into her bosom again, before
all the women of all the earth, whatever they might
say of her; whatever they might believe. But
no — neither word, nor sign, would he vouchsafe,
the proud boy; neither look, nor whisper, though
his mournful eyes were turned upon her, with a
calm, reproachful steadiness, to the last. Her
heart swelled — a flush of resentment — a shade
of pale and swift sorrow, went over her face.
The pride of a wronged woman arose; the passion of slighted power: the gushes and spasms
of outraged affection followed; a tear or two — a

thick sob — and she darted away, from the place of humiliation; the very nature of her heart altered — for ever — and ever — within a little moment, or two.

Having run up to her quiet room, she fell upon her knees; prayed fervently — wept — and arose, with a shade in her eyes, that never left them afterwards. From that hour, Edith Cummin was no longer the same creature. Her look of ✓ childish love went away. Her simple and affectionate behaviour gave place, gradually, to the high and haughty bearing of womanhood; ✓ peaceable as the grave — solemn as death, when seriously affronted; so that, after a little time, nothing was left of what she had been, but her sincerity — and her innocence.

CHAPTER XII.

APPEARANCES, AFTER THE " FRESHET." — MI-
RACLES. — CHARACTER. — DISCOVERY. — IDIOM.
— WALTER HARWOOD GETS LEAVE TO SEEK
HIS FORTUNE.

THIS prayer — the brief aspiration of a wounded spirit, over, Edith Cummin arose, full of
serious determination; wiped her eyes; put up
her disordered hair; kissed poor Lucy, with
more than usual affection; dressed; and, without
any more ado, went with her, to see Walter
Harwood, who was already in a comfortable
sweet sleep. She sat by him, till he awoke.
" How do you feel, now, cousin ?" said she, with
a mild, firm, unusual voice; on seeing him
throw his arm, pettishly, over the pillow —
" You have slept a long time — very quietly."

He lay, as if he heard her not. He neither
moved, nor spoke.

The pale, proud girl was not prepared for this. Her mouth trembled; her eyes filled; and she turned away her head, quite unable to pursue the inquiry.

" The wolves have been out, I guess; huntin' the cattle," said the preacher. " The dog is cruelly torn; hardly able to drag one leg, after the other. The cows are all in a sweat — poor little browney is gone off — and — "

" Poor browney !" murmured the boy.

" Hush, uncle, hush ! he's droppin' asleep, you see, now."

" Poor boy ! poor boy !" — continued the preacher; stooping forward; feeling his pulse; and speaking with a whisper, hardly above his breath : — " poor boy; they have run him hard; he was covered with meadow soil; his clothes were full of grass and wet leaves : when we un-buttoned his jacket, a heap of rubbish fell out. But you will suffer yet, in your turn : what could possess you, to run out, into the wet grass, bare-footed — enough to get your death a-cold — "

" Was he hurt, uncle Harwood ?"

" What-say ?"

" Is poor Watty much hurt?"

" You don't hear a word."

" O yes — but I do, though."

" You haven't heard a syllable of what I've been saying, for the last half hour."

" The last half hour! — I! — you! — not a syllable! — yes, but I have, though!"

" Well, then — what was it?"

" Why; you said a plenty, that I don't remember, at all: but you said how the wolves had been after him; how he was cruelly torn; how he couldn't drag one leg after the other; and how they beset him, in the cave, where he will go, for ever, in spite of all we can say; and how — and how — and how —"

" Fiddle-de-dee! no such a thing. But how came you in such a pickle? barefooted — your clothes falling off; and hair flying about — your — "

" As if I could stop to do up my hair at such a time; or pull on my shoes and stockin's, while the roof was tumbling about my ears; and poor Watty a comin' up, out o' the fog — lookin' as if he was bewitched, runnin' all round an' round, with a — ah! what's that 'ere noise, uncle Har'ood ?"

" Sure enough ! — ah !"

" Don't be scared, sir; pray don't — I — I — I've heard it, all night long—I have; or — or — or maybe 'twas all a dream; or a —— "

" Lord have mercy upon us !" cried he; throwing both his arms up, with a look of dismay, as he caught a view of the window; " Lord have mercy upon us !"

The whole earth, as far as the eye could reach, was covered with a heavy white fog; above which, nothing could be seen but a few green branches, of the great wood, rejoicing bravely, in the hot sunshine.

By and by, the smoke began to tremble; to separate into large masses; and, after a little time, to roll up, as before a strong sea breeze — toward the chief hollow of the mountains.

The waters were then visible. The low lands, with all the meadows, which, the night before, were as green, fresh and beautiful, as the warm soft summer showers could make them — were now, completely covered with a dark, turbid, and apparently deep sea : And who should say how deep it was ? who should say, while gazing upon the rough, noisy waters — loaded as they were, with ruin—that, in the night season, their original dominion over the dry land, had *not* been recovered by them, for aye ?

The danger was already over; the work of desolation, complete. The roaring, which they still heard, was only that of the subsiding deluge, quietly finding its way, through a number of old forgotten passages, to the sea; subterranean passages, which had been wrought; or paths, which had been ploughed up, in the early ages of the world, by the spring freshets.

In America—North America — these inundations are frequent. The rivers of New England rarely fail to overflow the " intervale," or low lands, through which they run, two or three times a year; once, when they break up, in the spring, with a tremendous uproar — discharging their waters, like a torrent, along their course; and piling up the ice, on either side, from ten to thirty feet high; and, always, when there have been very heavy rains, or a sudden melting of the snows, up the mountains, or in the " back parts" of the country.

In the southern states, rivers have risen so suddenly, as to prevent the passage of a troop of horse, in full pursuit of their beaten adversary, who had passed a few minutes before, without hazard, or difficulty.

One or two of these " deliverances," which occurred rather seasonably, for the Americans, during the revolutionary war, were entered up among the " miracles" of the day. But — after a while, one of them having been wrought for the British, *all* were posted, in silence, to another account.

In the south, too, the waters generally subside, as unexpectedly, as they rise. While you are loitering through the pine woods—under a clear blue sky—without a shape, or a sign of darkness to alarm you—along by the side of a rivulet, per- haps, the source of which is in some neighbour- ing elevation — a roaring will be heard; a sort of rushing noise; the waters will darken, tumble — rise up — and pursue you, with surprising velocity. Wait an hour, or two, and you will see the same rivulet, winding its way, as before — a little deeper only—a little darker—but as quiet, after all, as if nothing had happened.

It was a whole month before Walter Harwood was able to sit up. " I am quite well, now, father," said he, one morning, as he awoke, from a long revery; " quite well, I declare. So — if you please, I've made up my mind — if you please, father — to go and seek my fortune — *if* you please."

" If I please; to be sure ! — a creature like you — a spectre — with hardly flesh enough to cover your bones; — *you*, to talk about seeking your fortune !"

" Yes, father — if *you* please, father; it's no use, my stayin' here, you see.   And so, if you've no objection, I'll pack up my duds, and push off."

" But what can you possibly hope to do, for yourself, in such a world, as this ?   What are you good for ?   Who will employ you ?   How will you earn your bread ?—going out alone, at your age, into the great crowded world."

"Alone, sir! — O, no; I shan't be alone, sir. We are goin' together."

"Together! — We! — who — what! You have'nt been a filling your brother's head with any o' these foolish notions; have you?"

"O—h, no; father!"

"Look me in the face. I hope, sir — you puzzle me, more an' more, every day. Surely; you don't mean your cousin, Edith; do you?"

"Father!"—

"Well, then; who was it? Edith; or Jotty, or —— you don't persuade yourself, I hope, that I would be childish enough to go with you — at my time of life — much as I love you."

"Much as you love me, father!"

"Yes; what's the matter with yer? what ails yer?"

"Nothin' father; nothin' at all, if you *do* love me."

"If I *do* love you, my boy! Have you any doubt of my love?"

"Yes, father — if you please."

"But why — wherefore?"

"Because, in the first place, ye didn't say so,

jess now, as if it came out o' your heart — plump.
It was only an arter thought, I guess, to keep a
feller quiet. And, because — you never speak
to me — you never did — you never will — as you
do, to Jotty."

"Well; but I treat you with more respect."

"O, father! father! I can't bear that!"

"Poor Jotty! you know, he's rather under
par; and you — O, you are quite a wonderful
boy, if you would only make a better use of your
faculties."

"Under par! He's a nait'ral fool, parson
Har —— gulp — father — and you know it.
But I wish I was one, too. You'd like me all
the better for it, I dare say.

"Walter Harwood! 'He that calleth his
brother or sister a' —— "

"No, sir, if you please. 'He that calleth
his brother, a fool' — there's no sister in it — 'he
is in danger of hell fire.' And what if he is!
Everybody's in *danger* of hell fire, I 'spose —
hey?"

"Silence!"

"Yes, father; but I'm right, arter all. That's

the first bit o' the Bible, you ever larnt me; and I shan't soon forget it, I guess; nor the lickin' I gut with it, jess for tellin' the truth."

" How ! — have I not always treated you with great consideration, for your age ?"

" That's what you have, sir ! And its that very thing, sir — that alone, sir — that's breakin' my heart, sir."

·" I was too familiar with you, for many years, till — till — our ——"

" Don't speak his name, father ! I can't bear it; I hate him; he's gone, I hope now, for good an' all."

" Till he taught me better. I had mistaken your disposition, I saw. Ever since I knew him, I have treated you more like a man."

" Yes, father; and I wish the dev —— ugh !"

" Walter !"

" Sir !"

" Never let me hear such a word, again, out of your mouth. I shall continue to treat you, as you, yourself, desire — *like a man.*"

" Very well, father — very well; an' the sooner I go, the better, that's all."

"But who is going with you?"

"Only Panther, sir."

"My poor boy! — what *will* become of you! To think of making your way, in the wide world, with no other friend or companion, at your age, than a great wolf dog! Your simplicity amuses me, while it brings the water into my eyes. What shall I say to you? This comes of your reading, for ever and ever — poring over story books; night after night; month after month."

"No, sir; no, father — you are mistaken, if you please. It comes of my not being able to get any thing to read; of my being out all night long, without any book at all, to employ me — nobody to talk with; nothin' to do."

"Well, well — time enough yet. Push on with your studies: and hereafter" — "Hereafter!" — "One o' these days, when you are fit for the business, I'll see what Quaker Ashley can do for you."

"Yes, father; but —"

"But what! — I've no patience with you, Walter Harwood."

"But, father! —"

" There it is, again ! there you go, head over
heels ! You'd like to be off, to-night, I dare
say."

" Yes, father."

" For shame. Wait a little. When you are
strong and hearty, it will be time enough, then,
for you to leave my roof; high time, for such
a ———"

" Father !"

" Well; what now ?"

" I shall never be hearty; never be strong,
sir, if I stay here. I shall die very soon, if
you don't let me go. I tell you so, now — I shall
die — certainly."

" Walter ! Walter ! — my dear boy !" cried
the preacher, struck to the heart with instanta-
neous conviction : — " Walter, my dear boy !
Don't give way to any such fear ! never talk of
dying, after all that we have suffered, on your account."

" I can't help it, father — I can't, indeed. It
is all very true; and you'll find it so, if you don't
let me go. I am persuaded of it—I shall die, sir;
— I know it; and it's my duty to tell you so,

that you may have nothin' to charge *me* with, when it comes to pass. — O, father ! — father ! — Why not let me go, at once ?"

"Because you are sick. — Our Doctor Emory says, if we're not very careful — you may have a relapse." — " Pho ! — Doctor Emory's a fool, father." — " How !" — " That's what he is ! he told me 'tother day, when I was half sweltered to death, under a great pile o' blankets ; — the winders all down — a great roarin' fire made — a —"

" You had a fever, my child. — "

" You'd have a fever, too, I guess, if he'd a sarved you, in the same way."

" Pho, pho. — "

" — I don't believe in him, at all — father. — He told me, if I drink't any cold water, 'twould kill me. — So I tried it."

" No !" —

" Yes, but I did, though ; right away. Up I gut ; and off I went, in such a sweat ! while neighbour Winny was layin' over the foot o' the bed, fast asleep ; off, into the milk-house, on all-fours :—an' if I didn't have a capital time of it !"

— " Possible — as much as your life was worth."
— " So they told me." — " You didn't drink
much o' the milk; did you ?"

" Milk ! no; not a drop ! — no, indeed —
but I swallered pooty nigh a gallon o' ryley
water, I guess — right out o' the spring; I did
so."

" You frighten me; it was enough to kill a
dozen people."

" It cured me, though. I begun to git well,
that very night. Everybody said so."

" What a temper you have — how ungovernable it is !"

" No, father, if you please; no, no — there
you're out, agin. I know how to govern my
temper, whenever I like."

" You deceive yourself."

" Darn me, if I do, father ! — I've tried it, out
an' out."

" How ?"

" You know Billy Gibbs; don't you ?" — " To
be sure." — " Well; one day, up to Mr. Colo-
nel Chowderhead's tavern, somebody told me,
that he was a-goin' to gi' me the lie, wherever he

met me. — So — I went over — sayin' to myself,
that I wouldn't be mad with him, whatever he
might say, or do."

" Well—did you keep your word ?"

" Yes."

" *Did* he give you the lie ?"

" Yes, indeed; afore twenty people."

" And what did you say ?"

" Nothin', father—not a word."

" Is it possible ! — I never could believe it !
—not a single word!—you *are* a brave boy ;
but — "

" Well !"

" What did he do, after that ?"

" He gut up."

" *Up !*" — " Yes." — " Up ! — how.?"

" I'd knocked him over."

" O — ah ! — I understand you, now. You
said nothing ;—not a word ?"

" No."

" You only knocked him over ?"

" Yes, father. "

" Are you serious ?"

" To be sure."

" This, then, is what you call governing your temper ?"

" Yes; — I did my duty, like a judge."

" How so ?"

" Why; you see, father. I weighed his offence — I found him guilty — I passed a sort of judgment upon him, you see — cool as a cowcumber, all the time; and as I knew nobody else *would* punish him, for his abominable sarse; why, I *did* — I let him have it."

" But you should return good for evil, you know."

" Always, father ?"

" Certainly."

" I don't believe that, father."

" Walter Harwood !"

" No, father; because, if we do, folks 'll treat ✓ us badly, to git the reward, yer see. The worst men 'll be the best off, yer see. Nobody 'll be punished ; and, 'stead o' hangin' a feller for murder, we'll set him up in business — Lord ! how pale you be !"

" Have done, sir; have done ! The scriptures

are not for argument, or levity — but for obedience."

" Not blind obedience, father. We are not a — a — I mean — the Great Being above dooz'n't look for slavish obedience, agin' our sense o' right — I hope, father — dooze he ?"

" Hold your tongue, sir ! " — " Father !"

" Be quiet, for the present. Give up all idee of goin' away, now ; — and, a few years hence, if we can bring the matter about, — I'll —"

" A few years ! — Father ! father ! don't *you* deceive yourself. What I say is true. We shall be in our graves, long afore that, if you don't let us go."

" We ? — *us* ? "

" Panther an' me, sir. — His brave heart is railly set upon goin' away; I can see it, plainly. He dooz'n't look as he used to — his courage is all gone."

" Upon my word ! I've no patience with you."

" You never had, father."

" Are your wits turning ? or is all this pitiable simplicity put on ?"

" I don't understand you, sir. The dog, as
you know, goes mopin' about, from mornin' till
night — *you* know whether it's true, or not. — He
wun't eat; and, when I saw him yesterday, he
was as thin as a lath, poor feller !"

" That's because he won't go out o' the house,
while you are sick; and because, they won't let
him stay with you."

" O — ho ! — that's it, is it? why not let him
stay with me? — why not? — he's always jest outside o' the door. I can hear him whimperin'
there, all night long — poor feller !"

" Would you have him sleep with you ?"

" *To* be sure !"

" In the same bed, I dare say ?"

" *To* be sure ! — why not ? — He's cleaner 'an
our Jotty."

" A great nasty whelp !" whispered Miriam,
who had come back, for the winter. " I hate
all sich cattle, as I do, p'iz'n."

" I tell ye, what 'tis, aunty ; — I've seen you,
afore to-day ; — you needn't turn up *your* nose —
I've seen you a-bundlin', head over heels, with a
great nasty, as much dirtier than he is —

Very well!—there you go! clear out, if ye like!—I won't have poor Panther abused, by any body. He's the only frind I've gut left."

Away bounced Miriam; banging all the doors to, after her—bang—bang—bang—all the way.

"No more o' these jokes, on our help: you driv her away, once. If she should git another miff, we'd never be able to appease her."

"Yes, father;—an' she knows it: she *will* have her own way; an' so she shall, if you like, with every body, but me.—You don't hear me, sir."

"No—I'm a-thinkin' of your plan.—Let me see you set still, for five minutes—if such a thing be possible."—

"Yes—father—yes:—wait a minute, or so. Let me git fixt.—Ah!—there goes the clock!—Hourra! hourra!—now I shall see Panther, agin!—I thought so; I knew 'twas pretty near the time, by his confounded scratchin'—now, father—now!—open the door; please."

The preacher pulled open the door. Panther came bounding in, with a loud cry; and leaped upon the bed.

" Now father, if you please — poor Panther."

" Have done playing with your dog, if *you* please; and hear me."

" Yes, father: be quiet — be quiet! poor feller !"

" Look me in the face. Tell me how you feel, when you think of going abroad, into the world — at your age — *alone;* a boy, like you."

" Not alone, you know, father."

" Nonsense. I do not speak of your dog. Answer my question. How do you feel, at such a time ?"

" *Feel,* father ! O, I never *can* tell yer! it's impossible; it is, indeed. I feel as if my heart was all afire—as if—as if—somehow or 'nother, mighty flood-gates were openin', somewhere, inside o' me; lettin' a deluge in, at every breath : *Feel,* sir ! O I feel, as if I would give the whole tote o' this world, I vow, only to sleep like brother Jotty."

" And why do you not sleep ?"

" I don't know—I can't tell—I try hard enough, the Lord knows—beg pardon, father : — I used, a little time ago, to creep out, and lay down by

myself, on the new hay — in the moonlight — in
every beautiful—every silent place—where others
fall asleep, afore they know it; an' yit I've
never been able to get a wink.   I wonder how
they do it—I could sleep, any where else, better, if
I wasn't afraid o' sleepin'."

" Afraid—how ?"

" I — I — I don't know, father.   Men have
done dreadful things, afore now, in their sleep,
I expect.   And if I *should* happen to walk in my
sleep; and if I *should* happen to come across
that 'air— you know who— some dark night —
I might do him a mischief, afore I knew it.
Besides, all that — I'm sure I've gut a divil."

" A what !"

" I'm possessed, father ; believe it, or not. — I
am so.   There's an evil sperit comes up to me, every
night; an' makes faces at me — an' tears me,
while I'm dead asleep, with strange, black dreamin'.
O, I'm half afraid now, to shet my eyes, any
where ; especially at night.   I never do, till I
forgit where I am.   How do I feel, sir—when
I think o' goin' abroad !   Why, the fact is; I
feel as if—as if — oh, father ! father ! I've jest

gut it ! I feel as if—did ye never hear the wind a-bellowin' over the mountains — the crashin' o' trees—the pealin' o' thunder — the yellin' o' the wolves — and a noise, like fifty rivers, all about yer ? That's the way, I feel !"

" My poor boy ! thou art indeed, possessed."

" I told you so : I knew it. By an evil sperit, father ? "

"Yea ; by the prince of Evil Spirits—the chief."

" So much the better—who is it ?"

" The spirit of Ambition : the most unappeas- ✓ able, and wasting of all." The preacher covered his face, and wept.

" What's the matter, now, sir ?"

" O, my son ! my son !" Our hero put his large arms about his father's neck.

" Ah, my boy ! my dear, dear boy ! would you go away from your poor old father, and leave him to die, alone ?"

Walter was mute. His father kissed his clear, white, ample forehead. " I am growing old, apace," he added ; " feeble and weary : I shan't live long."

" Father."

" What now ?"

" I *will* stay, if you desire it."

" Will you, my brave boy! will you promise to live to home? will you, indeed?"

" No, sir—no, my dear father. I can't promise to *live*, to home; but I am ready to die, to home; or any where else you like."

" Oh! if you would consent! why not stay here, and be happy?"

" Stay here; and be happy !"

" How! I see a strange levity in your eyes. What is the meaning of it? what are you laughing at?"

" Only at Panther, sir; he looked up so funny, at me, when you talked about our bein' happy — here — poor doggy! he knows better, himself."

" Have done playing with him, sir; and hold up your head. Are you ashamed, already, of the sorrow and contrition, which you expressed, only 'tother day, for your undutiful behaviour."

" No, sir! no! — all 't I said, I'll stan' to."

" Till you get well, I suppose."

" Ay — father."

" Only till then ?"

" How do I know? we are all good enough, while we're sick. There's no tellin' how I may alter, when I git well—though I don't mean to, if I can help it — there — there! that'll do, beast !"

" Make him be quiet."

" Be quiet, Panther — be quiet, I say — be done lickin' my foot. Lay down, as father says, and be —— gulp — to you." The dog obeyed.

" Alas, alas !—I did hope to see you more of a man !"

" Of a man, father ! did you say man ?"

" Yes — that I might make you more asham- ed of yourself."

" Was that all ?"

" No—for you air a man, already, in stature and faculties; and will be, in age, before long."

" I thank you, father; I thank you ! God bless you for that !"

" Are you crazy ?"

" Don't be scared, sir ! I've been waiting for this. I am satisfied, now; and you shall know the truth. I *am*, what you have declared me to be—a *man*. Wo to him, that shall venture, ·

from this day forth, to question the title that you
have bestowed upon me !"

"You terrify me ! your language—your look
— your voice."

"True. My language, hitherto, has been that
of a boy. Why? Because I, myself, was only a
boy. I should have become ridiculous, had I
spoken to those, who thought me a boy, as I
now do, to you — my father — you ! that have
called me a man, to my teeth."

"I can't believe my own ears. Why have I
never heard you speak, in this way, before ?"

"Because, my dear father" — his large eyes
filled — "because, the bad man, who was one of
us, for such a time, was eternally plaguing me,
with his corrections. I wrote every one of them
down — I studied every one of them — I prac-
tised, whenever I met with a stranger: But, I
have continued still to speak my mother tongue,
at home — because I love it; and was afraid of
mortifying you, and poor Edith; for even *you*
do not speak so correctly, as I *can* speak. I was
too proud, sir, to own myself in the wrong; or,
that bad man, right; or, under any circumstances,

to imitate him.   Yes, father, yes — I *am* altered:
— a single year has done it, sir — altered, I am
sure, heart and soul."

" Altered, for the better, I hope."

" I'm afraid not, sir.   Then, I was willing to
die; now, I am not.   Before I began to study,
I didn't wish to see another sun rise.   Now, my
only fear is, that our allotted life—the natural
age of man, will be too short for me.   Then,
I was afraid of living; now, I begin to be afraid
of dying; yes — and what is more than all, father, I was only a boy, 'tother day.   *You* called
me a boy — you, yourself.   But now — now,
father; I'm all a man.   *You* have owned it — I am
satisfied :—it shall be my business, now, to make
others acknowledge it."

" How ?"

" Wo to him, that shall treat me like a boy,
now !   Before I fell sick, father, I was disobedient;
unruly.   I shall never be so, again.   I was ready
to go, abroad, any how, then; with, or without
your blessing.   Now, I am resolved, never to go,
but with your leave, and your blessing, into the
bargain.   Say the word, father ! only say the

word, sir—and I'll make battle with a giant for you !"

Up sprang the dog, at the sound of his master's clear, strong voice; up—with a cry, as if he were baying the wild beast, in her cavern; his terrific teeth—white as ivory; and blood-red gorge—all in sight.

" Then, sir," continued Walter; " then, sir; I felt a yearning after adventure. I was weary of your authority — it was more that, I dare say, than a serious desire of employment. Now, it is quite another thing. Shall I speak plainly, father ?"

" Yes — yes — by all means."

" You look disturbed."

" I feel so. I am struck with absolute awe. The calm, simple dignity of your way — I never saw any thing like it. Go on — go on — I am proud of you. But still, I do not well understand how you have been able to keep the secret, so long. I have overheard you, talking to yourself. I've seen you carried away, by passion; — talking with Edith — entirely off your guard, as I thought; and speaking a language, absolutely childish, in comparison with what you are now speaking."

" True, sir, true — I have well nigh betrayed myself, many a time, by overdoing the matter — by talking broad Yankee, rather too broadly; and fifty times, I dare say, by talking as I do, now, for a minute or two — till I recollected myself — when I was warm, or taken by surprise. You have observed it, repeatedly; and spoken of it — so as to put me on my guard."

" You talk better, when you are heated."

" So do you, father; so does Edith; so did *he* — so does every body, I believe — use better language, I mean."

" But, why talk to *yourself*, in this every-day dialect? — why, when you are altogether alone."

" Because I love it, sir — it's more natural to me — not so tiresome. Besides, father, I found, after I had been practising, by myself, in the woods, a great while — saying over, what I had learnt of Mister —— you know — I found that I had been overheard; and so, partly out of shame — partly, to keep my own secret better; and partly, because I do love my mother tongue, as

Edith calls it, I have kept on, using it every
where — with her — and while I was quite alone.
She's a little consated — conceited, I mean — for,
being a favourite with — hang the fellow — I
never think of his name, but I begin to talk, as if
he overheard me."

"Well — and what if he did."

"What if he did! I would'nt have *him* know
it, for this right hand, father; — no — nor cousin
Edith, who thinks him such a wonder: — They'd
say that I have left off my way of talking, for his.
No! — I'd rather sing through my nose, all my
life long — never sound another *g*, while I have
breath in me."

"But, after all; my brave, strange boy;
— after all — what could put it into your head?
why was it — when?"

"I'll tell you, father. Don't you remember
the night — about a twelvemonth ago — when I
tried, for half an hour, to make myself understood — while I was upon my feet? — Well; that
very night, I took a solemn oath, after the fashion
o' the Bible. I put my hand, by stealth, under
Jotty's thigh; and swore to overcome the silly

shame, that made my tongue cleave to the roof
o' my mouth — whenever people were silent,
about me. I have kept my vow. I can speak
now, standing or sitting — any where — before
any body ?"

" But how have you learnt? — where ?"

" Why; there's a college-man over at Mr. Co-
lonel Chowder-head's tavern, you see; and I've
been talking with him, two or three times a-week;
half the night through, ever since. They think
I go there, to play checkers with him."

" Possible ! — what may we not hope, from
such a manly temper; such unconquerable determination; such power over yourself, in keeping
a secret !"

" Why, sir, I'd been reading the story of one
Telly Machus. They'd praised him so, for keeping a secret, about his mother Pennylope — as if
it were any such great matter, for a boy to hold
his tongue; they'd praised him so, that I determined, if I ever had a chance, to try it, myself.
Besides, father; I was working, all the time, to
get ahead of Edith — she's eternally making fun
of my Yankee; as you know; and I mean to take

over and over again; — you loved her, and
yet—"

"Yes, Walter, yes — I *did* love her — as no
man ever loved woman."

"I don't believe that, father. — How can *you*
say what other folks do? Was'nt I *her* child
— her *only* child? How could you love her,
as you say, when you took delight in beating her
own flesh and blood, as you did me? I know
better. I'll tell you what, father – I don't like
to see you cry — but, whether I go into my
grave, or out into the world — and one, or the
other, I shall do, before long, I know — I don't
care which — you shall hear the plain truth, once
for all; come what may of it. — For my own
part, I do believe — whatever you may pretend,
sir " — choking with grief, and quivering with
passion—" I do believe, that you never loved her,
nor me — half so much, as you did Jotham's
mother, and her fat-headed booby."—

"Boy! — boy! — I will not bear this language."

"Why not? — he cuts thick enough, on the
skull; don't he?" — " Peace." — "I have done,
father — I have done — forgive me — I shall

never do so, again . — I have said it, because I
had a call — if ever any body had a call, on
our earth. — My heart is easy, now — unloaded;
—my poor dead mother 'll be quiet, I hope; and
I may be able to sleep, now."—

"Young man—"

"Father ! — father ! — don't look at me, so —
as if I were no longer your own child ! — Beat
me, sir — beat me, if you like !   I can bear that.
I — I — I — don't look at me, so ! don't call me
'young man,' if you wouldn't break my heart."

"Be still.   Hear me — I begin to perceive
the truth. — It is even as you suppose — you
have had a call — a revelation — you are *not* a —"

"Father — father ! — you'll drive me crazy."

"Your Father, my poor boy; — your true
Father — your Father, above ; hath revealed a
mystery to you.   He hath given a watchword —
a sign — I submit.   He hath put a mark upon
your forehead —. He hath given you in charge to
one — with whom I dare not wrestle, another
day." —

"Who is it, father ?"

"Even the Angel of the Lord, young man. —

I give you up to him.   This cannot be a lying spirit — Go then, go ! — Go forth ! in the great name of our Father, above !   He will prosper you, among the nations !"

Walter's heart gave way, in a transport of gratitude.   His long, long prayer was granted. He was to go abroad into the brave world, and seek his fortune !   He had nothing more to ask. He was happy.

with all the mysteries thereof — as they would, a strange country — on their guard, at every step — armed for whatever may happen. They explore every thing, even as they do their own woods — thoroughly, as the wind — but as invisibly — and with more caution; for they are not even *heard.* A Great Spirit is their God; yea, their only God. ·

"You look unhappy, my dear father."

" I'm watching you. There is a warlike, bad lustre, in your eyes; they make me sorrowful. I — I — it is no light confidence, that I am showing."

"Yes, father —"

" Committing the custody of his own soul, to a mere boy."

" In years, father; not a boy, though, in that experience, which comes of deep thought."

" I love your intrepid carriage, my son ; although it makes me afraid for you."

" How, father — why ?" — " It will drive you into peril."

" I hope so. It is only in peril, that great actions are ever done."

" Moreover, I know that God holds me answerable for your safety. He will require *your* blood, also, at my hands."

" *Also* — mine — also !"

" And yet, I have a strange, perhaps, a presumptuous confidence, after all, in his particular guardianship over you, my boy. You will prevail, to the last, I believe, as you always have prevailed hitherto — always — with a certainty, in proportion to the danger of every undertaking. I have misunderstood your character. I see it, plainly, now: it is too late for me to go back; but I have courage enough, to stop, where I am."

" You have been very severe, with me — very."

" Yes; to counteract your mother's partiality."

" Father — father ! don't speak so, of her. I can't bear that. If she was alive, you'd have no trouble with me."

" I have tried many experiments with your temper; most of which have had a bad result. I have no leisure for trying more. Our time is too precious, now.   We are both growing old. But I do hope that I shall be forgiven. — Walter Harwood !"

" Sir !"

" Can't you let Panther alone ?"

" I was only shifting the collar, sir.   It galls the poor dog; see ! — see ! We'll have him sent over to the blacksmith's.   Lay hold, father, lay hold — perhaps we can get out the kink."

" I've no patience with you.   Let him go — leave the collar as it is — he'll do well enough. He's worn it so, ever sence the freshet —— you don't hear me, sir."

" Yes, father — every word.   Poor Panther — poor doggy — so ! all this time, you've been suffering, in this way — nobody to straighten your collar; nobody to knock you in the head; nobody to put you out o' your misery.   Poor fellow ! I see why you didn't eat, now."

" Aint you ashamed of yourself?   A great boy like you — a man, almost — crying about a dog."

" Ashamed of myself ! No, sir ! no. — I am *not !*   Maryam ! — aunt Maryam, I say ! — Jo-

tham ! — Will nobody hear me ! Will nobody
answer me ! — Jotham, I say !"

"What ails the boy ! — are you mad? Where
are you going, sir, with your clothes falling off
your back ?"

" Up garret, sir."

" For what ?"

" For a crow-bar, sir — anything. Devil ! — it's
enough to make a fellow swear his eyes out. All
this time, in such misery —— see, father, see !
I wonder he didn't go mad; or make a die of it.
Poor Panther ! poor fellow ! so patient all the
time, too — so thin — dying by inches — moaning
all night long — pawing at his own throat. It's
a wicked shame" — tugging, till he was dark in
the face ; but unable to flatten the collar — "and
so, as I can't help you; and they won't; why,
to bed I'll go, once more, and see who'll stuff it
out, longest."

" Walter ——"

" Sir — father ! I'm very sick — please to have
the collar taken off — I won't eat a mouthful, I
swear, till you do." He fell back, overpowered, and gasping for breath. —— His dog was

immediately set free; angry as the preacher was; for he knew that his unreasonable boy would keep the promise."

"How are you to get along without him?" said his father; while the dog was tumbling over the boy's feet, in a sort of extacy, for his deliverance. "How will you bear him out of your sight — by and by?"

"Panther, sir!—out o' *my* sight—poor fellow!"

"You are not foolish enough still, to think of taking him with you, I hope."

"Yes; but I am, though. We've fixed all that business, father. He's agreed to go with me!"

"Agreed! — is the boy a fool!"

"I shan't stir a step without him, if — if — "

"What am I to think of you?"

"Whatever you please."

"Walter!"

"Father!"

"You are a problem—a puzzle. One moment, you astonish me, by your noble, strong, brave language; the next, by some action, so insup-

portably childish, that — pray, my dear boy —
do pray, be·more of a man."

"Sir—sir—father! your kindness will make a
babe of me. I was wrong—I am sorry—I—"

"Ah, Walter—that you should ever think of
such a troublesome, poor companion—at your
age."

"Say no more about it, father. Poor fellow—
poor fellow! The idea of parting with him, was
like a thunderclap. It had never entered my
head, before: I had come to think of it, as a
settled matter, that he was to go with me: every
plan of my future life was connected with him,
in some way or other; and *is*, yet—poor fellow!
how happy he looks—I believe, in my heart,
he understands me—don't you, Panther?—see!
see!"

The dog shook his large ears, joyfully; and
wagged his tail.

"Wait a minute, sir. Let me think of it:
perhaps after all—*perhaps*, you are right: perhaps the poor creature and I must part—and
—and if so—why; the sooner I make up my
mind to it, the better."

The boy was totally silent, for a few minutes; leaning on his elbows, with his face buried in his hands. When he lifted his head, both palms were wet; he trembled, and his fine voice quavered. He called Panther to him. The animal stood up, on his hind legs; and put his two fore paws, upon the bed, where Walter was lying, half undressed; wearied and worn out, with a short ramble. Panther stared; but, when his master leaned out of bed; flung both arms round his neck; and hugged him, three or four times, convulsively — he looked him up, in the face, with an expression of absolute amazement — of real anxiety — in his large, flaming eyes.

A small chain, with a light collar, had been put round his neck, instead of that, which was knocked off. Our hero took hold of the chain, with a steady countenance; called his father; and gave it into his hand; looking another way, as he did so.

Not a word was uttered — not, one. But the preacher's eyes were full. The noble brute leaned away, at first, as if he comprehended the effect of the ceremony; moved about, for a mo-

ment, or so; and, then, rearing himself up, stoutly,
to his full stature — he stood, and looked our
boy, in the face.

"Take him away, father! take him away! I
can't bear that. Let me never see him, again!
I have passed him over, like a slave, to you —
and he knows it. Poor fellow! You may as
well cut his throat, father. You may, at once.
He'll never get over it. He won't stay with you
—I see that, clearly."

Saying these words, our hero took hold of the
chain; tore it away — cut off the collar—and set
him free. The dog stood still—still, as death—
resting his head, upon Walter's knee, with
his eyes, quietly fixed upon his—till his trappings
fell upon the floor. Then, he sunk down,
gradually, from his proud port — shivering —
weak — lower and lower — till his long ears, and
heavy coat swept over the sand. Walter, forgetting himself, in his pity for the creature,
leaned forward, as if he were going to caress
him — saw the look of his father — stopped—and
forebore. The dog observed it; and settling
down, flat upon the boards — crept along upon

his belly, till he was able to reach one of the boy's feet, which hung over the bed; when, he lifted himself up a little, and began to lick it — so humbly—so abjectly—so unlike himself, that Walter cried out, with shame and sorrow. " Take him away, father !" said he; — " take him away ! I'm sick as death — I — I — he is no longer the same beast. I don't know what you have done to him — not I. But when I was out in the woods, with him, last — he wouldn't have licked the paws of a she catamount—or crouched before her; no—no ! he'd 'a torn her throat for her, first—with all her young about her. Take him away, sir ! — do — *do !* — I can't bear it."

The preacher led away the dog; returned, with tears in his eyes, and fell upon the neck of his boy. " My son ! my son !" said he ; " I augur well of your course, from this manly behaviour. Make yourself easy. Your dog shall be taken care of; but— but I have something to tell you — a matter of great importance — very great. I have been desirous, for a long time, of — "

" You'll have his neck rubbed with ointment, father ?"

" Hear me, if you please.   You are about going abroad — "

" Certainly, father — I'll show you how to make it; a little hog's lard — a little bees' wax — a — poor fellow! he must have been cruelly treated — beaten — starved — kept, I am sure, without sleep ;—or—bees' wax and fresh butter."

" Walter Harwood !"

" Yes, father — crouching upon his belly — crawling over the floor ! only think o' that, father ! think o' that! crawling — *our* Panther ! after tearing a she-bear — fighting wolves, and wild cats every night a' most, of his life — crawling, with fear !"

" Be still !"

" Yes, father."

" Be still, I say ! sit up, and hear my last words."

" With all my heart, father."

" You are about beginning a new course of life, my friends — ugh — a new course of life, my boy! Think; O, think, therefore, when powerful temptation, or strange allurement.—

" Yes, father. Burn the rascals — to serve him so."

" Hold your tongue."

" Yes, father — don't be fractious."

" Think, O think, when powerful temptation, or" — " Or strange allurement, father — I know the whole o' that, by heart, I've heerd it fifty times over — I ——"

" Be still, I say. Think, O, think; when powerful temptation shall hereafter beset you, my ——"

" My friends — father."

" My dear boy! I conjure you to hear me. I'm not going to say over my charge." Walter was instantly mute. A word of kindness did more than a blow, with him.

" At such a time; that is to say, when the Tempter shall wait for you, at every turn, my dear child; besetting you, on every side, with beauty and brightness — flavour and sweet sound ; the fascination of strange women ; the harlotry of our lewd affections; the mischievous longing of the old Adam — the — the ——"

" Yes, father."

" Of the — of the old Adam — the —"

" The world, the flesh, and the devil — father "

" Peace"—growing more natural. " Father !"

" Peace, my beloved boy. O, think, while you are away from us, and altogether alone; with no friend, or father, to counsel you ; no dear mother to cling to you."

The boy lifted his head. " Go on, father," said he ; " go on, if you please. I could listen to you, for ever, now — that's all new to me."

" With no human being to care for you. —O, think — when you are so beset, by the Evil One ; or his angels — the painted women; O, think, that your old father is before you, ready to go down upon his knees to you !"

" I will, father — upon my word, I will !"

" And O, my child ! — when the Bad Power shall tug mightily at your heart; and you are on the brink of sensual gratification — " " Yes." — " When there is no eye to see you — no ear to hear you — no ——."

" Yes, father — push on." ——

" Peace, I tell you — don't interrupt me.
No tongue to tell the story of your shame ; — "
growing impressive — " remember thou, then,
this hour ! — think of me, thy father, as I stand
here, now ! ready to fall upon my face, before
thee" — tears coming up into his eyes — growing
more and more natural, at every breath :—" Imagine, thou, then, O, my child ! — imagine thou,
then, I say, that the soul of thy father is a host-
age for the safety of thine ! — that *he* will have to
answer — he ! — I ! — I, myself — in a measure,
for thy transgressions !"

Our hero's blood ran cold, prepared as he was,
in some degree for the exhortation of his father.
He had never heard any thing so awful — or
solemn — or sincere — as the sound of his voice,
— when he concluded ; came up to the lad ; put
his two trembling hands upon his head — wept
upon it — and blessed him.

The boy started—cowered—looked about him,
in trouble. His heart misgave him, for a single
moment ; he was ready to question the haughty
spirit within him. But he was weary — faint —

sick; and fell asleep, immediately, where he sat.

He awoke, for a little time, toward night; but soon dropped away, into a sort of trance — a long, drowsy, solemn revery. The pillow was again wet with tears; — the small pure sweat stood upon his clear temples; there was no quiet for him, till near day-light, when, all at once, he found the very place in the bed, which he had been after all night long, as he tumbled about, in the fever of his thought; sank, all over, into it, with a quiet murmur of thankfulness — fell asleep, in truth; and slept like a little child, in the bosom of its own dear mother.

He had begun to dream pleasantly, when something warmer than the early breeze, and more fragrant, by far — breathed upon his eye-lids.

He awoke. It was a woman. It was Edith. He uttered a faint cry; put up his arms, before he knew what he was about; pulled her down to his bosom — and kissed her, till the young eyes of both ran over, with innocent, childish joy.

" How pale you are, dear Edith !" said he ; catching his breath, and pushing aside her loose hair, with both hands, while he lay wondering at her beautiful eyes. " How very pale ! I'm so glad you've come back, tho'. Have *you* been sick, too ?"

" Yes — like you have — I'm right well, now, tho'."

" You watched by me, they say, dear, *dear* Edith ; night after night."

" Hush, then ; will you ?"

" Ah ! it · was very ungrateful of me, Edith. I was foolish and wicked ; I'm very sorry."

" So am I — that's enough."

" When did you come down ?"

" Jest come ; — I've been a-settin' here ; waitin' for you to open your eyes."

" Ah, cousin."

" Well ! — what now ?"

" Why did you ever leave me ?"

" There you go, again ! I told you so — we'd better say no more about it."

" Do let us know — do — *do* — there's a good creature."

"Why; because you turned away your face; and wouldn't see me, or speak to me, for a whole day, together. So — I went away, I did; jest in time to save my life, they say. High! — how happy your eyes look, now!"

"Do they! I *feel* happy, Edith; so happy, that — here Panther, here! — O — I forgot — I thought he was here."

"Well; so he is! — here, Panther, here!" opening the door, and calling — "I met him in the woods on my way. He didn't know me, at first; but, when he did, he turned round with me, and came back."

"Poor fellow! — he was going home, to the Mohawks, I dare say. How glad he is to see me! that's the way, cousin; we never love a body half enough, till — poor puppy — poor. pup — till we've been separated."

"That's for you, Panther."

"No, Edith — no — I spoke to you: upon my soul, I did. Panther,—pshaw!—as if I thought of him, while you were by. See — see — Edith; see! how contented, he looks!"

"Panther,—pshaw!"—mimicking—"Panther,

to be sure ! as if I cared a fig about him, while
you are here.   Look ! look ! — see, see ! — now,
he's waggin' his tail — there ; — now, he's lookin'
at his paws — there ! there ! now he's rollin'
his big eyes, about !"

"Hush, then."

"Hush, yourself.   You'd like another quarrel,
may be."

"No, Edith, no — we've had enough o' that;
we'll never quarrel again."

"Do you know, cousin Watty, how I've been
laying a plan, all the time I've been sick, to keep
the peace between us ?" — "Have you really ?"
"I reckon." — "Well — what is it ?" — "You'll
go off in a pucker ?" — "Try me." — "You're
so unreasonable, you know ?" — "*Yes.*" —
"Hot and peevish, too ?" — "Yes." — "And *so*
silly ! — O, lud — O, lud ! there's no telling how
silly you are, sometimes !" — "True." —
"True ! *true !* — do you say that ?" — "Yes."—
"Then your name is not Walter Harwood; —
that's all !" — "I've been very foolish — cousin
— very — very bad — I own it."   "You do ! —
you very foolish — *you* very bad ! — no such a

thing. — It was that other Watty — one — high!
what am I about;" — clapping both hands over her
mouth. — "Let *me* try, Edith — your two hands'll
never keep your mouth quiet."— " Bossy!" —
" There, now!"—" Leave me be, I tell you! leave
me be!—let go my hand!" — " How altered you
are; what spirits you are in!" — " But I aint half
done with you, yet. — You know — up with your
head now, like a man — you know you've a
thousand saucy, sulky, sullen, impudent — not im-
perdent, as *you* say, here — impudent ways, with
you : And so — if you'll break yourself o' them
— I'll break myself o' mine — of my —of my
— you know what I mean."

" Perfectly — of your caprice — your vanity
— not varnity, as you say, *there*; and forty more
o' your Virginny capers." — " High! Virginia
capers, indeed! — better 'an Yankee tricks,
tho'." — " There it is, again!" — " There you
go!" — " It's your fault." — " My. fault! yours,
more like!" — " Your southern blood is too hot,
Edith Cummin!" — " Your northern blood is too
cold, Watty Harwood!" — " It's pure, though."
— " Pure indeed, such as 'tis! nasty, sloppy

stuff — I wish there wasn't a drop of it, in your
veins — I do so." — " I'm proud of it, our Edith."
— " Proud of it, cousin !" — " Aye; there's no nigger blood, in *us* — no Injunn blood, in *us* — no
foreign blood — *our* fathers never wore hand-
cuffs ! " — " Nor ours." — " But some o' them
did." — " No!" — " Yes!" — " No!" — " Yes!" —
" No!" — " Yes ! " — " No, no, no — no — o —
o — no — *no !* " — " Yes — ss — ss — ss — ss —
yes ! " — Both burst out a-laughing, together.

" I'm a full blooded Yankee, cousin."

" I'd never mention it, if I were you, — *cousin.*"

" I'm not ashamed of it."

" But I am — I could cry my eyes out, whenever I think of it. I'd love you fifty times as bad,
I would so ! if you were any thing else but a
great he-Yankee. — You love candour, you say."

" Yes — and I'd love *you* fifty times more —
that's what I would — if you were any thing else,
but a little she-Buckskin. — You love candour — you say. — "

" I never said any sich a thing; — I don't love
it a bit — nor you, niether — if you tell the truth,

I reckon. — But never you mind — " pettishly —
" I'll not be cotch again, by your tricks."

" Cotch ! — I reckon ! — clear nigger that, I
guess. Might as well say fotch, or holp — or
tote. — "

" Clear nigger ! " — half sobbing — half smiling — " clear nigger's better 'an clear Yankee —
any day."

" Edith !" — " Watty !" — " We are two fools."
— " Yes." — " Let us be wiser !" — " Yes." — " I
am ashamed of myself." — " So am I." — " Very
sorry." — " So am I." — " I'll tell you what, Edith."
" Well." — " What say?" — " How ?" — " *How!* —
I do wish you'd say *what* — I'd understand you,
then." — " Paws off, Panther ! paws off— that's one
of your pretty master's tricks—a kind word or two
— and snap he goes at your hand." — " Edith ! — "
" Watty ! " — " If you'll behave like a woman
— I'll behave like a man." — " High ! the boy's
cracked !" — " I am perfectly serious." —
" With all my heart." — " No more quarrelling." — " No more baby talk — no more pulling
hair — no more pouting — no more making up
— no more — "

" Stop — I can't agree to that — "

" You're a pretty fellow ! — "

" You flatter me — "

" Well — there's my hand! We *will* be wiser."

Our boy was delighted by the sincere, and beautiful expression of her eyes. " O Edith ! " said he; — taking both of her hands; holding them to his heart; — and speaking just loud enough to be heard; — " O Edith! how I *do* love you !"

" *Do* you !"

" Yes, Edith, yes — after all — more than every thing else, in the world; more and more, every day of my life — every hour. O Edith ! my whole happiness will depend—here, and hereafter — I am afraid — upon you. — "

" So will mine, Watty;" half pouting — half crying: " So will mine, Watty, — *after all — I am afraid — upon you.*"

She had never said so much, before. There was but one reply — but one — for such an avowal — so innocent — so ingenuous. He drew her, with a feeling of tenderness— awful as death — up to his very heart; — murmured a prayer upon her mouth; — a very short one; their foreheads quaking with a new intelligence — their eyes, brimful of generous light — and both trembling with sincerity.

"And so; you are going away from us; are you?" said she; gently releasing herself; and speaking in a low, tremulous whisper; "really going away?"

"Yes — "

"I am glad of it; very glad. But what are your plans? Do you mean to join the army? I would, if I were you. — Don't stare; — I know more of what you've been about, perhaps, than you are apprised of. I have heard of your trainings, up in the wood; — of your Indian wrestling-matches — of your midnight meetings — of your.—"

"Edith! — Edith!"

"Walter Harwood! — hear me; once for all. I look upon myself now, as your wife; I look upon you, as my husband. I would have you betray no secret for me; — but — but—I do not want courage. Try me. — Put faith in me; —

deal very plainly with me — children though we be — and I'll go to the scaffold with you."

"How very pale you are ! — How altered ! — But a moment ago, you were a child — a trifler. You are now, a woman ; — a creature, with such intrepid, bright eyes, that mine will not endure their look. Another change ! — what are you thinking of, now ?"

Edith shook her head sorrowfully.

"I am satisfied — I know, very well."

"You do ! — what was it ?"

"Of Jonathan Peters ! — "

"Have a care, Walter Harwood — have a care ! — He — *he*" — fixing her eyes upon his, with a look of alarm — " *he* knew me better than you. *He* trusted me. But — have a care ! — you are brewing that for us, now ; — *that*, which, if we are not wary, will destroy us both, at last. — Don't look at me, so — you frighten me. — If you have any question to ask — out with it, like a man. — Your doubt — any doubt of yours — I will not endure. Out with it."

"I have no question to ask — I am satisfied."

" No; — you deceive yourself, I am afraid. You are unreasonable — you *are* so. — "

And you, dear Edith; — *you* are — a — a — you are, indeed."

" Very serious — I know it. You never saw me in this temper, before. It is time to be serious — you will make me unhappy, — and yourself, too. Let us understand each other; once for all, about Jonathan Peters. You wouldn't have me betray the confidence of any body?"

" By no means; — but — "

" You would scorn me, I hope, if I could not keep a secret."

" Certainly — but ___ "

" But you are haunted by a perpetual desire to know that, which I cannot inform you of, without making myself appear unworthy. Oh —for shame, Walter Harwood — for shame! — "

" No, no, Edith — no, no — you wrong me."

" I have already told you, perhaps, all that I ever *can* tell you; all, I *believe*, that I shall ever be at liberty, under any circumstances, to tell you. —Think of this — weigh it, while you may: — "

" You are right. — What is past, cannot be

helped.   But our new relationship requires a
new rule. We must have no half confidence,
hereafter."

"Agreed."

"I don't promise to tell you every thing,
though."

"Nor I, you."

"But, whatever may happen, I shall reserve to
myself the *power* of telling you whatever I please.
I will never, from this day forward, become the
willing depository of a secret, which I may not,
if I think proper—at any time — under any circumstances — make you acquainted with."

"Manfully said —"

"In short — if we.mean to be happy, dear
Edith, — let us do, as we would be done by. —"

"Agreed."

"Give me a kiss —*therefore*."

"Nonsense. — I don't like it." — "Yes, you
do." — "No, no — no lip service for me." —
"But kissing is heart service." — "Pho !—fudge !
— kissing, indeed — slobbering.——Hands off,
Walter, hands off ! — you would not, surely —
surely — you would never rob one of a kiss ?" —

' No — I would have it *given*." — " You, that; as the story goes — but I don't believe a word of it — you that, when you caught me asleep in the mow, wouldn't steal a kiss." — " No — I chose to wake you, first; — I would have the pleasure mutual — I would share it, with you."

" Pleasure! faugh — pleasure, in putting our two noses, together."

" That's affectation, Edith."

" So it is, Watty; and we'll have no more of it." — " No more of what?" — " No more kissing, Watty. It is a bad practice. It gets people into a habit of toying — I'm sure it's mischievous, Watty, because — because — be — be — "

" Because, you love it."

" Yes — dearly — and *so;* — and so; — we'll have no more kissing, but on particular occasions; after a quarrel — or a long separation — or a — or a — till we are a — a — gulp! — "

" Married! — that's what you were going to say; weren't ye, Edith?"

" Married, forsooth! — nonsense! Two such children as we are, married. A pretty notion to be sure. —— Ah! somebody's coming!" —

" Thank ye — I take the hint — now, or never."

" No — "

" *No !* " —

" Well then, yes ; — *there !* now, — I hope you'll be easy."

" Ay, ay — till I get another. —'

" Good by'e."

" Good by'e. — Don't break your neck."

Away she went, like a bird—leaving our hero to ruminate over the transformations which he had been a witness of, within a single hour.

END OF THE FIRST VOLUME.

Londoꟷ:
Printed by A. & R. Spottiswoode,
New-Street-Square.

Milton Keynes UK
Ingram Content Group UK Ltd.
UKHW020827180224
437992UK00005B/253